Jeremy Guscott was born in Bath and has played for Bath since the age of seven up to his retirement at 36 in 2001. With all-conquering Bath he won seven knockout cups, six Division One league titles and the Heineken European Cup.

He made his England debut in April 1989 in Romania, scoring a hat-trick of tries, and was a virtual ever-present selection until his enforced retirement through injury during the 1999 World Cup. He won 65 caps for England, three Grand Slams and scored 30 tries. He also took part in three British Lions tours: to Australia in 1989, New Zealand four years later and South Africa in 1997, his dramatic drop goal in Durban clinching that series, his second Lions triumph in the southern hemisphere. He was awarded the MBE in 2000. He lives in Bath and has three children.

Mick Cleary, who worked with Jeremy Guscott on the writing of this book, has been rugby correspondent of the *Daily Telegraph* since 1997. For ten years before that he was rugby correspondent and feature writer for the *Observer*, covering all major sports and events. He was editor of *Rothmans Rugby Union Yearbook* for five years and has written several books on rugby, including the official publication for the last two British Lions tours. He is married with four children and lives in Brighton.

JEREMY GUSCOTT

The Autobiography

headline

First published in 2001
by HEADLINE BOOK PUBLISHING

First published in paperback in 2002
by HEADLINE BOOK PUBLISHING

10 9 8 7 6 5 4 3 2 1

ISBN 0 7472 6473 2

Typeset by Palimpsest Book Production Limited,
Polmont, Stirlingshire

Printed and bound in Great Britain by
Mackays of Chatham plc, Chatham, Kent

HEADLINE BOOK PUBLISHING
A division of the Hodder Headline Group
338 Euston Road
London NW1 3BH

www.headline.co.uk
www.hodderheadline.com

contents

acknowledgements

I am grateful to Mick Cleary for his help in bringing this book together; to Maria Pedro and Ali Gunn for their constant encouragement; to Amy Cracknell for her valiant transcribing, and to all at Headline.

'you're under arrest'

Prison. Ten years. Ten long years. It didn't bear thinking about. The trouble was, it was all I could think about. Prison. How could I have come to be in this position? Jeremy Guscott – jailbird. I didn't like the sound of that one little bit. Life was good, my family was healthy, my rugby was going well, the World Cup was on the horizon and my off-field commercial activities were in decent order.

And then, one seemingly innocuous afternoon on Wednesday, 25 March 1999 in Bath's Paragon, it all went horribly wrong. A set of traffic lights, a hot-headed pedestrian, a scuffle – it was over in five seconds. It had seemed so surreal and yet, twenty-four hours later, my solicitor Peter McKnight was with me in the interview room of a Bath police station, outlining what could happen to me. Of course, I knew it was the most pessimistic view but there was little comfort to be had in that. How I didn't break down in tears I don't know. I was shattered and my only thought was what was going to happen to Jayne and the kids.

Midnight Express, Shawshank Redemption – all the prison movies I had seen, complete with horror scenes of abuse, sordidness and utter loneliness, flashed through my mind. Yes, I know, it all sounds daft and melodramatic now, but it was anything but that at the time. A few hours earlier two policemen had come to my home in Bath and arrested me. I later learned that they could have simply phoned to invite me to the station to answer some questions. But no, I got the full treatment: a firm knock at the door, a pair of serious-looking policemen, a formal declaration of intent, a hurried call to my solicitor and off I went into the panda car and down to the cells.

There I was. Jeremy Guscott – of Bath, British Lions and England, a certain bit of fame, TV and radio appearances – in a prison cell and wondering what the hell was going on. I knew one thing, I did not want to be in there for keeps.

It had been a very weird twenty-four hours, and it wasn't going to get any better. The previous day had been like so many others. Up with the kids, the usual bedlam in the kitchen as my three daughters Imogen, Holly and Saskia got ready for school or nursery, and then I headed off to training at the Recreation Ground, no more than a ten-minute drive away. We were in the middle of the Five Nations so the club season was very dislocated; one week with England, the next back with Bath Rugby Club.

Training was routine, finished on time and I headed back home. My wife Jayne and I had lunch and then she mentioned that she was heading into town to buy some new trousers. Now, trawling round stores looking at women's clothes is not normally my scene, but off we went in separate cars – I knew I wouldn't last the course. I played my part as the trusted advisor who proceeded to criticise all the trousers Jayne showed me. Finally, enough was enough, so Jayne and I parted company and I headed off in my Mercedes.

I'm used to killing time in Bath. The routine of a professional sportsman means that you find yourself with a few hours to spare when everyone else is at work. I might do some commercial work, extra training, pick up the kids, have talks with my advisors, head for the golf course or just chew the fat with a friend. It was chew the fat time, so I popped in for a coffee and a chat with an old pal, John White, who has a restoration business in Manvers Street, opposite the police station of all places. After coffee and conversation I left.

It was just after three o'clock. As I set off on the ten-minute walk back to the Rec to pick up my car, I was in a good mood. It had been a very unstressful sort of day, no hassles, no training injuries, no bad news on the horizon. Or so I thought.

On my way to the car I spotted Andy Robinson and Nigel 'Ollie' Redman chatting at the rear steps to the clubhouse, just beside the President's Hut. I had played with them for many years and drunk with them round the world, and they are two of my oldest friends. Normally I would have stopped and joined in but it looked as if they were in serious conversation. I left them to it and walked on. If only I hadn't.

I climbed into my car and headed for home. It was close to four o'clock and the evening traffic was starting to build. I had two choices: did I turn left out of the ground and along Pulteney Road or turn right and go a longer way but one that might be less busy?

I am familiar with the twists and turns of Bath city centre. How to cut a corner, the back-doubles to avoid the traffic – I know them all. Perhaps I knew them too well and maybe I should have taken the straightforward route home. Perhaps. You can drive yourself mad going over what you might have done.

I was in no great hurry but I don't like traffic jams. Earlier in the day I had driven round Widcombe and seen that the traffic was heavy, so I turned left across Cleveland Bridge. The traffic lights were causing a hold-up, so I had another decision to make. Should I turn right, towards town or pursue the back route via Lansdown Road? I carried on, through the mini-roundabout at the top of Walcot Street and down towards the Paragon.

The Paragon, which is lined with tall buildings, rather like the Royal Crescent, seemed relatively free of traffic so I pressed on until my luck ran out towards the end of the road. There was a queue of cars ahead at the busy four-way junction.

Okay, right into Lansdown it was. There were about ten to fifteen cars ahead with their orange indicators flashing to turn right at the traffic lights at the far end of the road. Left it was then, and the lane was free. I indicated left and headed down the left-hand lane. I would soon be home; George Street, Queen Square and away we go.

Something caught my eye. Standing by the lights was a pedestrian. His name was Ken Jones and little did I know how that name was to haunt me. What was he going to do? Was he going to cross? You can tell a fair bit by a person's body language – a hunch of the shoulders, a slight tilt of the upper frame, a twitch of the thigh. You have to weigh all these things up in a split second on the rugby field and you get a feel for what someone might be about to do. You're not always right but it does mean that you prepare yourself for most possibilities. I couldn't believe that this guy was actually going to cross the road. The lights were green in my favour and I had a clear road. I don't know whether he saw me or not. As I drew close to him I looked up and saw that the lights were green just going to amber. I was on the junction so I was clear to cross.

Christ! What was he doing? The idiot had tried to get across in front of me. I missed him by a whisker. Oh God, what was that? A thud on the window. I must have nicked him as I went by. I'd gone through a light that I was perfectly entitled to do and this guy had risked his life by stepping out in front of me.

I stopped the car about twenty feet past the junction. I know, I know. Never stop the car, never get involved. Sensible advice with hindsight, but there I was, merely getting out of the car to tell him that there had been no need to act that way. I saw that he was heading towards me with something in his hand. A rock? I couldn't tell. There were no slow-motion replays here, no TV producer to rustle up fifteen different camera angles. This was the real world, a man was coming at me and it seemed to me that either I stood there and got hit or I looked after myself. I could have struck him there and then in self-defence but that wasn't really on my mind.

Decision time. How often had I been in a tight corner on a rugby field, an opponent closing in, not much space and no support? There, a little shake of the hips might be enough to get you out of trouble, but not in this situation. I took the initiative, grabbing him by the shoulders and pushing him back across the road.

I was pretty much in control. True, I was shouting at him. True, too, that my language was colourful – industrial, you might say. 'Who the fuck do you think you are, taking liberties like that? What the fuck are you doing, risking your life for something so trivial?'

It doesn't sound very good in print, and nor did it when witnesses later recalled it in court. But come on, blokes often use language like that. It's not normally in my nature to let rip at people. I'm quite fond of the one-liner to take the mickey out of mates if only the one-liner would come to mind, but really losing my temper and lashing? It hasn't happened in over ten years of top-class rugby and it wasn't happening then.

Of course I was het up, but I hadn't lost my head. I had simply intended to have a word with this guy but then, as far as I could see, I had to take evasive action. I don't think I was reading too much into his actions. Even if what I thought might have been a rock turned out to be a ball of string, I believe my instincts were right.

I pushed him back towards the pavement, up the curb and into a doorway. As we collided with it I was shouting at him and he suddenly said: 'I've broken my ankle.' Events were taking a strange turn. It can't have been any more than a few seconds from my getting out of the car to Jones making that comment. I was nonplussed. I took a look and said: 'Mate, that's not broken. It looks dislocated.'

A touch unemotional, you might think. Not really

– it was an instinctive reaction. I've seen some pretty horrific injuries on a rugby field in my time – broken legs, busted noses, twisted knees – I was just giving a simple opinion as if I were looking down over a referee's shoulder at someone stretched out on the turf.

'It's just dislocated.' The concern for my own safety had gone and I could see that he was very worked up. He was screaming that his ankle was broken and I just wanted to pacify him. I couldn't quite work out how we'd got to this. I was driving home, for goodness' sake, back to the kids, a bit of tea and television. Normal, everyday routine. Boring even. So what was this chap doing lying at my feet yelling about a broken ankle?

Even at that stage I wasn't particularly worried. Jones was slumped on the floor and it seemed to me that the sensible thing to do was to get the phone from the car and call for an ambulance. I was aware that there was a bit of a scene but it still did not occur to me that there was any real trouble brewing.

Jones by now was rattling the security grille of the shop where he had fallen. It was his shop, in fact, an antiques shop. He was calling out a woman's name and the next thing I know she was beside me, shouting: 'Hey! Where do you think you're going? I want your name and address.' She thought I was trying to drive away in my car. I told her that I was just trying to phone an ambulance for her friend. In all the commotion I never did get to make that phone call, although an ambulance did arrive.

She asked again for my name and address. Or, rather, shouted again. It was then that I realised how serious it might be. Okay, then I wanted his name and address as well. I entered the shop, got a pen and wrote down the details. GBH? Assault? What on earth was she talking about?

Outside in the road my car was causing an obstruction. A lorry trying to get by hooted so I went out to move it. Everything appeared normal but, of course, it wasn't – events were careering out of control. In the few minutes before the police arrived I found myself sitting on a stool outside Jones's shop having a perfectly ordinary conversation with him. 'What on earth have we just done?' I asked.

'It was a red light and you had no right to go through it,' he said.

'It wasn't red, mate, it was green going to amber and you had no right to risk your life. How the hell did you dislocate your ankle, anyway?'

'No idea,' he replied.

There we sat, for no more than thirty seconds, trying to piece together what had happened.

Within a couple of minutes an ambulance and two police cars had arrived. It was a fairly busy part of town and someone must have called them. There was one white and one black policeman. They questioned me but I got the impression that it was a fairly routine matter.

They asked me for my version of events. I don't actually remember giving a statement of any description but obviously I must have done. Name, address, phone number, the bare essentials. That was all I could remember later. It was beginning to dawn on me that this whole affair was becoming serious. As I watched Jones being taken into the ambulance on a stretcher by the paramedics, I felt sorry for him, he looked down in the dumps. And then something occurred to me:

might he be off work while his ankle was sorted out? Should I offer some sort of help? I made to approach him but the two policemen didn't think this was a good idea. I said it to them. 'Look, I realise all this might cause him problems in terms of work and if there is any way I can help, then I will.'

There. A simple offer, made in good faith and without any premeditation. In court, it was alleged that I had purposefully caused damage, that I now recognised my guilt and wanted to offer compensation. Nonsense. I should have realised the implications of what I had said, but I didn't and I don't think many people would have done.

You never know how you will react to a situation until it happens. You always hope you will handle it brilliantly, or that you will never get into a scrape in the first place. If you knock into someone in the street, your first instinct is to apologise, even though it may not have been your fault. That's human nature. Or, at least, it's my nature. That was the case here, Jones was in pain and I felt sorry for him.

I'm not a bad bloke at heart. I had a few bust-ups in my schooldays but that was simply a question of age. I'd never been in trouble on the rugby field, nor away from it for that matter. And here I was, driving home and wondering what on earth had just happened.

I still wasn't worried about the possibility of bad publicity or anything like that. It didn't occur to me that it would ever blow up into anything that big. No, my thoughts were about Jayne and how she would react. When I left her the day had been very, very ordinary. Suddenly, it was anything but.

Within a few minutes I was home, but Jayne wasn't

there. I phoned Dave Powell, a solicitor in Bristol whom I've known for a long time. Dave worked for Alsters at the time, although he's now moved on to Clarke Willmott & Clarke. He has done a lot of work over the years with the England rugby squad and is a good solicitor. He understood straightaway the potential seriousness of the episode and told me he was sending over one of his staff, Peter McKnight.

Dave's concern was to be borne out. I'd only been at home for about ten minutes during which time I'd tried to phone Jayne and had a second conversation with Dave. No sooner had I finished the call than my mobile phone rang and there was a message on my voice mail from the *Daily Mail* asking if I had just been involved in an incident. How the hell had they got hold of the story? Didn't take them long, that's for sure.

By now, the penny had well and truly dropped. This was serious. It was time to get a few things in order. I rang Maria Pedro, who has been my agent since 1991. Maria knows the business well and she and I have worked on many projects together.

There might be bigger agents than Maria, who now runs her own company, but I trust her and she trusts me. It's a good arrangement. She knows her stuff and she knows how the media works. This was a story that could quickly get out of hand. I asked her to get in touch with my major sponsors, Adidas and South West Electricity Board, to brief them on my version of events so that it wouldn't come as a shock when they opened the newspaper the next morning.

Shelly, our nanny, was in the house at the time looking after our youngest daughter, Saskia, who was 18 months old. Jayne got back home just after 5.30 p.m. Her sympathetic reaction was: 'You daft bugger. Why did you get out of the car?' The same thoughts were going through my head. If only I'd got out of bed a bit later, if only I'd stayed longer with Jayne, if only I'd stopped to talk to Robbo and Ollie Redman. On and on running through endless what ifs and maybes.

Finally, I thought: 'It's happened so I'd better get on with it.' And that's what I did. By the time Peter McKnight arrived I'd decided to concentrate on what was immediately before me and let all the other stuff, the bad publicity, the legal implications and so on, arrive in their own time. Peter and I went upstairs to my study – 'the den', as it's known – and he came straight to the point. 'As far as I'm concerned, you are innocent,' he said. 'You have done nothing wrong. Tell me the truth and we will go from there.'

And so I told my story, as you have read it here. No more, no less. Then we agreed a statement that would be presented to the media. The story was already out there so it was important to prepare some sort of reaction. I've always tried to face up to press inquiries. As long as people are straight with me, respectful and courteous, then I will be the same with them. Of course, some matters are confidential but most in the media recognise that. With an event of this kind there is no point in simply running for cover and hoping that it will go away. You have to say something, so you may as well say it on your own terms.

It wasn't an easy night but I was determined to carry on with my normal routine and the next day I went training as usual. There were lenses trained on my every move and journalists demanding interviews.

None of them got a word. The matter would soon be sub judice so the advice was to say nothing. There was some mickey-taking from the boys at first but when they realised that it was actually quite serious they went quiet. It was then that I knew things were bad – the Bath dressing-room is usually a merciless place with no subject too delicate for us not to have a dig at someone about.

I'd briefed Bath's director of rugby Andy Robinson to let him know exactly what had gone on and had also spoken to England manager Clive Woodward. Peter had warned me that I would probably be questioned further and he wasn't wrong on that count. Knock, knock. Who's there? Two of Bath's finest to arrest me.

Yes, it was a shock. I'd have been happy to have gone voluntarily to the police station with my solicitor and answered whatever questions they put to me. But PC 996 Ian Audus and PC 2268 Brian Brady arrived just after 2.30 on Thursday afternoon. I asked them if I could make a phone call, they said I could and then followed me upstairs. I phoned Peter and they took notes – all very formal, all very by the book and all rather unsettling. What did they think I was going to do, flee the country?

I'd been fully cooperative from the outset, although I was going to fight this thing. But they adopted a tough, no nonsense, no leeway approach. I've got a few friends in the Bath police force and they kept me informed of the general mood at the station. There was a feeling that I was guilty, shades of 'too big for his boots'.

There was no small talk in the police car. I wasn't too

pleased about being arrested at my house so I wasn't in the mood anyway, and I told them I wouldn't be saying anything further until my solicitor was present.

By now it was early evening and at the station the duty sergeant checked me in, took all my personal belongings and sent me on my way to the cells. I paced the cell as one does, measuring the width, the length, counting the number of doodles on the wall, deciphering the graffiti – anything to take my mind off the implications of what was happening.

A policeman friend came by to say how sorry he was to hear about it. It took a while for Peter and his colleague Amba Chawla to arrive. I'd been there almost two hours and wasn't in the best frame of mind. My mood didn't improve when she gave me the low-down.

The three of us had gone from the cell into an interviewing room. Amba was very calm and straight-forward.

'Right, this is the situation,' she said. 'You have been accused of GBH, Section 20.'

I was adamant that I had done nothing wrong. I had not attacked him, and his ankle had been broken by accident. I was beginning to know this story by heart. The truth, the whole truth . . .

Then came the bombshell when I asked her to tell me what was the worst that could happen. Ten years! No way. I can just about smile about it now but there was not a flicker on my face then. I don't know how I managed not to cry. I never do but that was as close as it gets.

I burbled on. 'There is no way I am going to do time. No way. I've got three kids who need me. Jesus Christ, you can't do this to me. There is simply no way this is going to happen. No way. Do you understand?'

It wasn't the most coherent speech I've ever made but it was one of the more heartfelt. Amba tried to calm me down, saying that she was obliged just to advise me of the worst, that if things didn't go my way and the judge gave me the heaviest sentence allowed for grievous bodily harm, then I was looking at a prison term.

Her words were to haunt me for many weeks. I tried hard to shrug them off and to focus on what would probably happen, but the chilling thought that I might be imprisoned never left me. How could it? It is such an horrific prospect that you would have to be a cold, clinical sort not to let it get to you.

I was barely listening to the procedure being outlined. 'The two police officers will be coming in here to ask you some questions,' said Amba. 'You can answer the questions or you can prepare a statement that you can read out or that we can read out. The police will listen to that statement but I guarantee that they will ask further questions. You can reply that you have given a statement and that is all you wish to say at this point.'

I knew what the truth was. Why wasn't that good enough? Statements, questions – the whole episode was taking on a life of its own. Get with it, Jeremy, or get blown away by it. The old sporting instincts kicked in, as they were to do many times over the next few months. I may not look that competitive on the surface, may appear at times that it's all very easy, but I can tell you that deep down I am as hell-bent on winning as the next man. I don't like to be beaten. And

I don't like being wronged, either. If there was to be a fight for the truth, then fight it was.

Peter wrote down my statement. I was very shaken at this stage and did not want my voice, trembling and uncertain, to be on the tape. Peter was to read it. The police officers came into the interviewing room, sat down, switched on the tape and said: 'This is PC Brady and PC Audus. The time is 6.34 p.m. . . .'

And so we began. My statement, their interrogation. The routine was the same on every question: they probed, I dead-batted.

'I have made my statement and I don't wish to say anything else at this stage.'

They asked eight or nine questions and on each occasion I looked across at my solicitors, who merely nodded as a sign that I should just trot out the same noncommital reply. The interview stopped after a while and the two policemen left the room at 6.51 p.m. Amba said that we would let them ask a couple more questions when they returned before we asked whether the interview could go in another direction. I had no idea what direction that might be but as the whole scene seemed so surreal my confusion was no surprise to me.

They came back at 7.03 p.m. On went the tape and out came another couple of questions. By now I was word perfect and soon they had had enough. At 7.17 p.m. the interview was concluded when they informed me that I was to be arrested. So, it was finally for real.

I felt helpless at this point as procedure took over. Fingerprints, photograph and – this bit almost freaked me out – a DNA swab from my mouth. It was small consolation to be told that it would be destroyed if I was found innocent. Then, at 8.12 p.m., came the formal charge. I won't forget that time check in a hurry.

'Do you realise that you have been charged with GBH, Section 20?' asked the duty sergeant.

Well, I certainly wasn't there for my own amusement. Now was not the time for a tart one-liner. I was too numb to say anything apart from the standard 'Yes, sir, no sir' routine. A form which contained the date of the appearance at the magistrate's court was handed to me. I gave it to Peter and Amba and we left.

Ten years. Ten flaming years. There were a few coppers about, all saying that they were sorry that it had come to this and that they were just doing their job. I'm sure they were, but movie clichés about just doing their job, guv did not cut much ice with me at the time. In fact, I barely heard what they were saying. My head was elsewhere.

I'd been at the station for about four or five hours. When I arrived home Jayne was livid. She was furious not only that they had kept me so long but that they had taken me there in the first place. She felt it could have been handled in a more sympathetic way. Her face drained as I told her that I had been charged with grievous bodily harm.

That evening was not easy. I was nervous, scared, angry and worried. Not just for myself but for Jayne and the children. I'd never known a feeling like it. I'd been up before my dad Henry often enough in my youthful, wayward days but the feeling of apprehension as I stood before him explaining my latest run-in at school was as nothing compared to this.

Jayne quickly got a grip on matters, as she always does. 'Let's get this straight, Jeremy,' she said. 'We will get through this. You are not going to prison. It will all work out.'

We had decided that we were going to confront the situation. No wavering and no getting weak-kneed. I'm sure that she was just as petrified as I was but she never showed it for the simple reason that she knew that we might both cave in.

We also had to be strong for the children. They didn't know anything at this stage. They were so young – Imogen was six, Holly was five and Saskia was not yet two years old – although it's doubtful whether we'd have involved them even if they had been six or seven years older. No, this was to be Jayne, me and my parents Henry and Sue against the prosecution. I was to have great support too from my legal team, Maria Pedro and a close circle of mates.

I was to need that support. I didn't like what I was reading in the newspapers. The story had made a big splash and it was so one-sided. I normally get on pretty well with the press. I've been accused of being distant and off-hand on occasions but that complaint usually comes from journalists who chat to me for twenty minutes or so and then feel qualified to write the definitive two thousand word character appraisal. I've never been too worked up about criticism of my performances on the field. It's a point of view and the writer is entitled to express it. I may have strong words to say the next time I see him ... no, I'm joking. I take all that on the chin. I also like to think that I understand the workings of the media. After all, I've had ten years in the spotlight and have worked on a variety of media projects myself. I think I know the score.

Anyway, there it was in the following day's newspapers: a full, balanced, objective, both sides of the story report of the incident in the Paragon, Bath. Or not. I was the villain of the piece. 'Rugger rage,' said the *Mirror*. 'Guscott road rage "put pedestrian in hospital",' read the story in the *Independent*. There were quotes from witnesses, who spoke of my bad language and the shock at seeing one of their sporting idols behave in such a way.

It didn't look too good and, if I had been outside looking in, I wouldn't have looked too favourably on me. I tried to put it to the back of my mind. I knew that newspapers have to give a slant to a story, have to make the direction clear and the presentation sharp. The headline sells the piece. I was a celebrity target and there was no point in their eyes in soft pedalling and giving anybody the benefit of the doubt. Nor is there profit in painting the full character of Jeremy Guscott. It was all there in the cuttings: my suspensions and eventual expulsion from Ralph Allen Comprehensive, the teenage rebellion, the adult maturity and unblemished record on the rugby field. But they weren't interested. That was tomorrow's story.

I was in turmoil throughout that first week. There were times when I was fine. I would be confident, clear-headed and calm. At other times I was a wreck, torn apart with anxiety and anger. My emotions stabilised. There were countless messages of support, cards, phone calls and letters, many from people I'd never heard of before. They were all a great source of comfort and inspiration. Standing by your mates is a real virtue in my eyes. Mine stood by me.

My father Henry couldn't believe that it was happening. He felt as though we were trapped in a bad dream. The trouble was we weren't, as my mother Sue wasn't slow to point out. Mum just got on with it. That was the deal. Let's sort it out. So we set about sorting it out.

I felt better once we had drawn up my full statement. My legal team decided on London barrister Sally Bennett-Jenkins to represent me in court. I didn't bother asking about her credentials. I'd long since learned to trust the judgement of those whose work you have already been impressed with. Peter fitted into that category. 'Look, mate,' I said. 'You're the professional and if you think she is the person for the job, then she is the person for the job.'

It was a good choice. My first impression of Sally stayed with me throughout the next few months. You get a feel for people who know their stuff and those who are making it up as they go along. Sally knew her stuff and her presence made me feel one hell of a lot better. In rugby terms, we had Jonah Lomu on our team – a true heavyweight. The gloves were well and truly off.

in the dock

There I stood in court. I was in the zone. That was the term Linford Christie used to describe the way he blocked out all distractions just before the gun went for the start of a major championship 100-metre sprint. Nothing existed but him and the finishing line.

There was nothing now but me and the foreman of the jury at Bristol Crown Court. Christie had managed to train himself into such a focused state. I was helpless. Fear had put me in such a frame of mind that it was almost an out of body experience. I felt as though I was off to one side, staring down at myself in the dock, with Jayne, Mum, Dad and Maria waiting for this chap to deliver his verdict. The whole of the gallery was staring at me, the press bench too. It was as though I was an ant under a magnifying glass.

The only other time I have ever experienced this feeling was when I scored a try for the British Lions in the second Test against Australia in Brisbane in 1989. Different time, vastly different circumstances. I was the new kid on the block, I'd only won my first cap for England a couple of months before and here

I was scoring a cheeky try for the Lions, one that was to turn the series on its head. That glorious moment encapsulated all my childhood dreams rolled into one. For a second then time had seemed to stand still. It was standing still again as I held my breath and waited for the foreman's words. I'd given it my best shot. Would it be good enough?

It had been eight months between the incident and the case coming to court by which time the charge had been reduced to actual bodily harm. We'd twice postponed so as to give me an uninterrupted run at the World Cup. This wasn't a deliberate tactic to put me in a good light as Guscott, England's conquering hero of the World Cup. Just as well. Given the way that tournament panned out I might have lost more votes than I won. No, it was just common sense to delay until November given the demands on my time and the disruption caused by my spells away from home.

I didn't let my mind dwell too much on the case during those months away. Obviously, it was there, a nagging reminder that there was nasty business to attend to, but I put it to one side. I had quite enough on my hands making sure that I was in good shape for the World Cup.

It was a great comfort to know that my defence was in the very capable hands of Sally Bennett-Jenkins. David Powell joined another company during the summer so we had to find a new solicitor, Tim Hayden. We decided on three character witnesses: Phil de Glanville, Nigel 'Ollie' Redman and Barry Frayling, a police sergeant I'd known for many years. We all go back a long way and they are good men, honest and straight.

I also had someone else working for me. Let's just

call him the Man Called Horse. He approached Andy Robinson a couple of weeks after the incident. His line of work was surveillance and he offered his services for the simple reason that he wanted to help. He thought that we'd heard only one side of the story from the newspaper coverage and he believed that there was more to it than that. He worked independently and without pay. My instinct was to trust him, I couldn't see what harm it could do.

He intended to check out a few possible witnesses. He went to the scene, took some photographs, called at a few shops nearby and chatted to people. As far as I was concerned we had to cover every possible angle. It was no different to being on a sports field. Either we sat back and let the opposition take the initiative or we got out there and got stuck in. The Man Called Horse joined us at an early stage, checking reports of other potential witnesses and giving advice as to what I might expect to happen in court. His was a useful voice.

We'd done our homework, there was no doubt of that. I was confident that I would be acquitted, but not because of any innate arrogance or sense that Jeremy Guscott was too big a star to be dragged down by some unknown guy in Bath. I'm not like that. Nor was it merely that I knew my side of the story and felt convinced of my innocence. In fact, my confidence had everything to do with my legal team. Sally was thorough, precise and had seen the right way to proceed right from the outset.

That's not so say that there weren't any nerves, because there were. Plenty of them. You never know which way a jury is going to go or quite what the prosecution might come up with. The law is rarely a cut and dried affair. The trial itself was also going to be emotionally tough. I may well have looked self-assured and impassive, but I was churning on the inside. Sally had briefed me on how to behave, how to look, how to respond to questions and how to deal with the media. It was good advice.

The morning of the trial was a difficult time. I was more worried about everyone else than myself. I could handle what was coming my way, difficult as that was going to be, but for the others – Jayne, my parents, close friends – it was going to be a gruelling few days.

Part of me was hoping that I wouldn't even have to go to court. I was half expecting a call from Sally to say that the case had been dropped. So sure was I that our defence would win the day, I would not have been surprised if there had been talk behind the scenes about doing a deal. In fact, there was talk and I don't know why they pressed ahead knowing what we had up our sleeve. Was it a desire to nail a high-profile figure? I'm not sure how I would have reacted if there had been some sort of deal offered. If the charges had been dropped, then how would the public have reacted? They would probably have been suspicious, imagining that I had friends in high places who had pulled some strings.

Nothing could have been further from the truth, but I didn't want that doubt hanging over me. I was more inclined to stand up and let the evidence speak for itself. So, in a curious way, I was glad we were headed to court.

We'd hired a Mercedes people carrier for the week, so that we could all travel together and give each other support. Bristol Crown Court was about half an hour's drive from home. We parked round the corner, got out and turned left towards the court building. Nothing could have prepared us for the mass of camera crews awaiting us, all wanting a slice of the action. And if *I* felt that, someone who'd spent most of his career surrounded by the media, Lord knows how the rest of the party felt. But, as Sally had told me, it was absolutely vital to make the right impression. So, head down it was, through the throng and into the court.

It would have been good to get straight into it there and then, but there was a delay. Sally had been stuck in a tailback on the M4 caused by a traffic accident. There was nothing for it but to sit around and make small talk, so we headed to the cafeteria, where there were several journalists I recognised. I concentrated on giving nothing away. Does that sound a touch paranoid? Not really. How many reports have you read saying that 'so-and-so was seen laughing and joking around even though some serious charge or other was hanging over them'. No, not paranoid, just sensible.

It was two or three hours before Sally made it to Bristol. I kissed Jayne and Mom and went off to a small room with Sally. Once again she outlined what was going to happen: the arrival in court, who would be seated where, the entrance of the judge, the swearing in of the jury and the opening of the case. Forewarned is forearmed.

I entered the courtroom. To the left and the right were the public galleries. The family were to one side, the press to the other. It was crowded. I looked straight ahead, went through a little swing door and sat down on a large bench. A court official offered me a drink and I thanked him and told him that I was fine. As if.

Judge Simon Darwall-Smith came in and greeted everyone. There was barely a soul in court he didn't seem to know. He turned to the jury and offered them the usual opt-out clause. If any one of them felt unable to give an unbiased view because they knew me from rugby, or supported Bath, then they were to say so. One guy took up the offer and headed out through the door. Lucky swine.

The jury was sworn in – nine women and three men. That made me feel uneasy. Nearly every bloke I'd come across in the preceding months seemed to understand the situation I'd found myself in. That's not to say that they necessarily sided with me totally, but at least they empathised with me. Do you know of any women involved in road-rage incidents?

My discomfort was to increase. The prosecution had the first crack and their barrister, Susan Evans, outlined Ken Jones's case. Of course it seemed one-sided. Of course it was meant to be unfavourable to me. I knew that it would be. I was the big, beefy rugby guy (I wish) picking on the small fellow. Emotional, simplistic stuff, the sort of material that makes for big headlines. It sure as hell wasn't easy for me to sit there and listen.

And so it went on through the day, a one-way traffic of accusation. I felt that I was getting slaughtered. I had arrived ninety-nine per cent certain that I would be acquitted but, by the end of the session, even I felt that I was ninety per cent guilty and ten per cent innocent.

Sue Evans made reference to my fame and my rugby background.

'I expect you have all heard of Mr Guscott. You probably know something of his achievements. You probably know that he represented his country at the highest level in rugby. I am sure that it won't give anyone any pleasure to convict Mr Guscott of this offence but you have to put aside any emotions you may have.'

Fair enough. We argued that I was acting in self-defence. They were having none of it.

'The prosecution say that this was not self-defence at all. Mr Jones did not represent a threat to Mr Guscott. Mr Guscott was angry that Mr Jones had the audacity to step out in front of his car and knock on the window. He was effectively teaching Mr Jones a lesson.'

The detailed evidence seemed shaped to fit that line. Here is how Sue Evans portrayed it in court.

'On a Wednesday afternoon last March, a pedestrian was about to cross the road at a crossing in Bath. There was a car approaching, but the pedestrian stepped out because the light was against the car. Instead of stopping, the car continued, passing very close by the pedestrian. Mr Jones was pretty shaken. He was going to remonstrate and he knocked on the window with the hand in which he was holding a ball of string.'

Ball of string or lump of rock? At the time I thought the latter but at this stage had no opportunity to say so. I felt that he was going to damage either me or my car, and so, in my own words to the police, I felt that I had to 'take charge of the situation by walking Jones to the shop doorway'. That wasn't quite how Jones saw it.

'I got about halfway across the crossing when I felt this car just go flying by behind me,' Jones said in court. 'It seemed to screech to a halt. I went over to slap on the window of the driver's side. I said "Oi", and that was as far as I got. I intended to say that "You went through a red light" but I do not remember whether I said it or not as the next thing I knew I was bundled back on to the pavement and then banged up and down on the floor. Then he started swearing and shouting. I looked down and I said to him: "You've broken my leg." He was saying: "Don't take fucking liberties with me." And I said: "But you went through a red light." He kept saying: "Don't take fucking liberties with me. Never walk out in front of my car like that. You are lucky that I didn't punch your lights out."

'He was very angry.'

Well, he wasn't wrong there.

Jones then outlined the injury to his ankle, with me saying that I thought that it was only dislocated. I was wrong, as it turned out. So much for my medical insight. Mind you, I genuinely thought that it was only dislocated for the simple reason I couldn't understand what might have happened to cause a fracture. It transpired that there were three or four broken bones in his ankle and he was kept in hospital for eleven days.

It was hard to listen to all this without interrupting. But rules were rules and so I sat there expressionless, even though my innards were in a turmoil.

Jones went on: 'I think he [Mr Guscott] realised that he had injured my ankle. He walked away and I thought he was going to get into his car and drive off. I thought it was a hit and run. I started banging on the railings of my shop and shouting inside to say that I'd been attacked and to take the car number.'

At one point the jury was shown CCTV footage of the incident.

Over to Sue Evans: 'The Crown suggests that you can see and hear the aggression that Mr Guscott is employing as he deals with Mr Jones. It's a very fast incident – seconds rather than minutes – and Mr Jones is grabbed very quickly.'

The trump card had been played. Not for the prosecution but for the defence. Of course, the prosecution didn't realise it at the time. To them, the video illustrated that an altercation had taken place and that I was the aggressor. However, we knew differently. We had seen the tape because all prosecution evidence has to be handed over to the defence in advance of the hearing. They were delighted to have such hard evidence, the good fortune to have had a CCTV camera nearby. Little did they know that the same tape would help defeat their whole case. As I said earlier, Sally Bennett-Jenkins had done her homework.

I knew that Sally would pick holes in all this when she had her say, but for the time being we had to take it on the chin. I was being hammered and, even though I was determined not to show it, I was anxious.

The prosecution's final twist of the knife went in.

'Police spoke to Mr Guscott at the time,' said Sue Evans. 'For a man who claims he had acted in self-defence, Mr Guscott wanted to talk to Mr Jones and said that he was willing to pay him compensation.'

And so day one drew to a close.

Jayne was upset. She knew that it was going to be tough but she hadn't really appreciated that it might all seem to be stacked against me. I told her that we could do nothing but trust in Sally. We would get our turn. Sally was very matter-of-fact, just giving us a quick debrief of the day and reiterating that I needed to remain calm and composed.

It was just as well because there was another damning account to sit through the next day. This particular witness was a sixteen-year-old boy who could not be named in court for legal reasons. He was backed up by his fourteen-year-old brother. The only moment of light relief in all those days in that courtroom came when the two lads admitted that they had gone straight home after witnessing the incident and sold the story to the newspapers. The laughter came when the older brother said they'd received £600 from the *Mirror* but just £50 from the *Sun*. I could have told them that.

I'd already read their version in the press the day after the incident itself. They hadn't been backward at coming forward then and we got more of the same here.

'Guscott was basically pushing him with such force that the man didn't seem to be able to put up any resistance,' said the older boy. 'It was the kind of force a rugby player would use. The guy could not have stopped it anyway. He was being pushed back helplessly. For some reason I thought Jeremy Guscott was stopping someone doing a crime, like running away with someone's handbag or something. Guscott was very angry. He was saying: "You can't take fucking liberties like that." Jones then basically slid down the wall to the floor and Guscott let go of him. The man was saying: "Look at my leg." But Guscott said: "It's only a dislocation," and implied that it was not that bad. Hitting on someone's car with a ball of twine does not justify that. I saw no provocation. He was acting like a bully.'

The newspaper reports had me as 'sitting impassively in court wearing grey suit, lilac shirt and patterned tie'. They were right about the clothes but while my face may have shown no emotion it was all bottled up inside. I'd long before learned never to give anything away. Never let an opponent see that he's got one up on you. You'd never be able to take the field against Jonah Lomu if you did.

The lad continued: 'I could hear, perhaps, his head hitting the grille on the shop window. I didn't do anything because I was scared. Mr Guscott was angry. If I had tried to stop what I saw I was worried what would happen to me.'

No one had seen the beginning of the incident, all they had seen were the consequences. But, up to now, that had not been pointed out. I wasn't annoyed about the boys' tale at all. In fact, I felt sorry for them being under the spotlight like this. It must have all started out as one big adventure for them: scamper home and ring the papers to make a few quid. Now, though, the eldest lad in particular looked frightened. Events had run away from him and he seemed scared. He might also have had a hard time from kids back at the school. There must have been one Bath supporter in the ranks.

The prosecution produced several more witnesses. A woman by the name of Jennifer Booth was one of them. She had a formidable air about her, proper and correct. Her words would carry weight with the jury. 'My interpretation was that it was a violent incident and that the mixed-race man was the aggressor and the white man was doing nothing other than weakly defending himself.' Simple and to the point.

And then it was our turn. From Sally's very first sentence I knew I had the smartest cookie in the business. She was sharp without being aggressive, calm without being passive – the perfect mix. She had a presence that commanded respect and she was well prepared.

It had been her idea to spend more time examining the CCTV video presented by Jones's side. At normal speed the video didn't appear to help my case. I did look aggressive. But Sally wasn't satisfied; every angle, every micro-second, had to be examined. She sent the video to a specialist unit to be looked at in more detail. Critically, they were able to slow it down. And that's where the truth of the matter lay. The slow-motion showed Jones aiming a kick at my car as I passed him.

That's why I was surprised that the case against me wasn't dropped. Surely they too had examined the video in minute detail? Apparently not. However, commencing her cross-examination of Jones, Sally wasn't going to reveal her hand straightaway. She gave him ample opportunity to say that he was unclear on certain points, but he ploughed on, unaware that he was digging himself in deeper and deeper.

'You say that you were on the island in the middle of the road, Mr Jones?'

'Yes, I was.'

'Are you sure?'

'Yes, I am.'

'You couldn't be mistaken?'

'No, I couldn't.'

'Well, let's have a look at this, shall we? There you are, you're in the road, you're not on the island yet, what about now, have you reached it yet? No, you haven't. You weren't on the island at all, Mr Jones. The video clearly shows that you were not on the island.'

Once again I felt sorry for those who were accusing me. First the young lad who squirmed in the focus of such attention. Now it was the tormentor-in-chief I was getting misty-eyed about. But there it was. He was being hung, drawn and quartered and had nowhere to hide. She cornered him about the kick.

'Mr Jones, did you kick there?'

'No, I didn't.'

'What does it look like to you?'

'A leg movement.'

'Moving from the knee, in a swinging action?'

'Yes.'

'Well, that's a kick, isn't it?'

Sue Evans tried to intervene once or twice when she saw the way it was going and raised a couple of technical objections which got nowhere. Jones's shoulders were hunched and he looked miserable. If he could have run I'm sure he would have done. Sally had opened him up from the outset. She pointed out to the jury that a week after the incident Jones had instructed solicitors to work on a possible civil action.

'Is that your real motive – to sue Mr Guscott eventually?'

Jones's case now looked threadbare. All the witnesses called by the prosecution had only seen the outcome and not the start of the incident. Now here was the other point of view – my point of view – and the video backed it up.

The jury was told that Jones ran 'full pelt' with his arm raised and struck my car. Under cross-examination Jones admitted that he made 'the first acts of verbal and physical aggression'.

I could see that in Sally I had a winner. She made her next point forcibly.

'By the time my client took hold of you, you had struck his car, kicked out at his car, shouted at him and were moving aggressively towards it, annoyed, very annoyed and with a large object in your hand.'

Jones had been stripped to the bone. A man had walked into the box and a skeleton walked out.

Sally now had the whip hand, and all the other prosecution witnesses were given similar treatment.

'Ah. So all you saw was the end of the incident. You didn't see the beginning. You didn't see Mr Jones move aggressively towards . . .'

She repeated the line to witness after witness. The jury was getting the message. There were several witnesses called. They didn't know that their testimony had been put into sharp relief by the video, and their evidence sounded flawed.

By the third day I was getting used to the routine and it was now my turn to take the stand. I'd been given a few tips by Sally: she told me to keep it simple and to keep it straight. Her questions to me would be very matter of fact and straightforward. The big test would come when Sue Evans was allowed to get her teeth into me. Sally stressed the need for me to keep control whatever happened. She warned me that Evans would try to rile me, to show me as someone not capable of keeping his temper. I had to be composed and obliging.

There are standard ploys that every good prosecutor will use. They will mix three or four questions in one, jumbling the ideas and details so that you appear confused and uncertain. Worse, you could seem evasive. So, I was to take the initiative, to slow down the whole process by asking her to repeat the question. If necessary, I was to break the question down myself so as to make it clear to the jury that there were several points rolled into one.

We all know that the facts should speak for themselves, that the truth of the matter should be the only evidence necessary. But trials are not like that. The court is a theatre and the jury can be swayed by a performance. The professionals – the solicitors, the barristers and the judge – all know that. The jury might not. So you have to get in on the act yourself. Your body language, your expressions, your gestures and your mood are all key elements. Sally told me to look directly at the jury when I gave my evidence, to be sincere and self-contained.

It sounded easy. But I was wound up inside. We'd only had a short briefing because I'm used to working with an audience, be it a dinner, a press conference or a TV studio. But Sue Evans got really stuck into me. Fair enough. That was her job. It was my job to keep my emotions in check.

I was sworn in and now it was up to the jury to decide whether I was the good guy or the bad guy.

At last I got a decent chance to put my side of the events. We went over a lot of old ground, in particular the build-up to the incident.

'I just missed him,' I told the jury. 'As my car went through the lights they turned to amber. There was a large bang, one single bang. I think it was on the driver's side. I was shaken and shocked. I initially believed that I had hit the man who had just crossed in front of my car. I felt disbelief and sickness. My heart skipped a beat. I unfastened my seat belt and began getting out. My first vision was of Mr Jones coming towards me with his arms raised high. It seemed that he was going to have a go at me. His voice was raised and he seemed very, very angry. I felt threatened and believed that the man was going to attack me. I saw an object in his hands. My instinct was to defend myself.'

What about the strong language? It didn't sound good in the cold light of day. Still, let's not be too prissy about this.

'I know I swore at the time. With the nature of my job and the guys I knock around with, that language is quite common.'

And so it is. They should have been at a training session with Roger Spurrell or Gareth Chilcott in the early days at Bath. Those sessions were not for choirboys.

I was pressed as to why I was so angry.

'The whole reason that I was shouting at him was because I might have killed him when he stepped in front of me. I believed that to risk life like that was a liberty.'

The prosecution claimed that I wanted to teach Jones a lesson.

'There is no truth in that,' I said. 'I am not an aggressive person. I avoid confrontation whenever possible. I am not vindictive. I show a lot of humility in what I do. It's not in my character to be like that.'

And then came the question about the money I

had offered Jones. It was obvious that the prosecution would play on this. PC Colin Williams stated that I had told him that I was willing to compensate Jones.

Sue Evans then used another expression. I struggled to get my tongue round it. She repeated the point. I looked towards the jury. 'I did not . . . I did not . . . I didn't offer them what you were saying because I can't even say it now.'

The line got the only laugh on offer in five very serious days. It didn't go down too well with Sue Evans, who could see the favourable impression it had made with the jury. I drank a lot of water while she was questioning me. Just little sips, very considered – and very irritating if you were trying to move things along. I didn't want my voice to crack at any stage and I also wanted to interrupt her flow.

I could see that I was getting to her and she didn't come even close to cracking me. I was pleased with the way it had gone but Sally, quite rightly, warned me against getting complacent or cocky. A jury can swing both ways and she reckoned that it was still only 60–40 in our favour. I thought we were streets ahead and her words brought me back down to earth.

The CCTV video guy, Alan Humphriss, was called to the stand and went through the technical aspects of the tape. He had been on duty at the Closed Circuit Television Monitoring Centre at the Guildhall in Bath on the day in question. The questioning was standard stuff. Could it have been doctored? Was it selective?

We moved on. We had another witness up our sleeve – a guy by the name of Paul Wheeler who worked for

Wessex Water and had been a passenger in his works van at the time of the incident. He had been following behind and saw what had happened.

His evidence was very favourable to my case, yet we decided not to call him. Sally argued that we were in a good position already and that it was not worth the risk of our witness being cross-examined. Tactics. It's what the law game and the rugby game are all about. She was head coach and I put my trust in her – not that I've always done the same thing in rugby.

It was time for the summing up. Now, who do you think might have seen me in the following way: the bad guy, the aggressor, the man who lost his temper, the guilty party? That's right, counsel for the prosecution Sue Evans.

Still, Sally gave it the treatment as well. Sharp, poised and to the point, she highlighted a few key issues, including my forceful swearing.

'Industrial language – the use of swear words – does not make someone guilty of assault occasioning actual bodily harm,' she said. 'Height, weight, age matter not a jot.'

There was, she said, one question the jury had to answer.

'Could Mr Jones be perceived as a threat to Mr Guscott? If he could have been, then what Mr Guscott did was reasonable self-defence.'

She added that no one knew how Jones had broken his ankle. It could have been caused by him turning and landing awkwardly before I had got hold of him. She went on to point out that Jones had admitted shouting at me and striking my car, thereby verbally and physically posing a threat, making me feel 'under attack' as she put it.

Jones's evidence had been 'fatally flawed', according to Sally, and proven as such by the CCTV footage of the altercation that lasted no longer than five seconds. She then asked the jury to put themselves in my place: driving home and going through an amber light when suddenly my car was struck by a man with something in his hand.

'There's no magic in the name Jeremy Guscott,' said Sally. 'Even rugby players can feel threatened, especially by some unexpected and really extraordinary actions. This was not a rugby match. This wasn't two teams engaged in a fair fight, with a referee to ensure fairness from both sides. This was Mr Guscott going home from work, taken by surprise by a man who, in this court, has admitted that as a result of his physical and verbal actions, he [Guscott] was under attack . . . You feel surprisingly under threat. You feel he may attack you. You are in the throes of being attacked. You get out and push him away. You don't throw punches or kick or lash out at him. It is a perfectly reasonable action.'

She concentrated on the ball of string.

'It doesn't matter what he [Jones] hit the car with. It is still a surprisingly large object that you cannot get your hand around. It is easy to look at it with the twenty-twenty vision of hindsight and say it is obviously a ball of twine. But would you know that in a second?'

Good question. She went on.

Ken Jones was 'a liar' said Sally. His claim that I had held him by the lapels and 'banged' him up and down was not borne out. There had been no damage to the waistcoat and not even any dirt on it. There were no bruises on him either.

'His lies and inaccuracies colour every single thing he says,' concluded Sally.

It sounded good to me but was it enough to convince the jury? I was about to find out.

The jury was out for two hours and twenty-three minutes. It felt like two years and twenty-three days to me. We sat around in the café, trying to make small talk. The moment had finally arrived. This was it. My heart rate was about 200 and I knew that if the verdict went against me I would not be walking out of the same door through which I had just walked in. I would be going the other way. Down the steps. Down in every sense of the word.

Finally, after one abortive attempt to get an unanimous verdict we try again.

'Foreman of the jury. Have you reached a decision?'

'We have.'

I looked round the courtroom and each pair of eyes in the public gallery looked back at me. I was terrified and once again experienced the sensation of not being there but looking on from the outside. It's not a feeling I want to experience again.

'Not guilty.'

How long does it take to say those two words? A second, two at most. They seemed to be delivered in extreme slow motion, but what a pleasure it was to hear them. Without question, they were the two best words I have ever heard in my life.

There was still a bit to do. The jury was released and then a few people approached me to tell me this or that. Did I shriek with joy? Did I punch the air as if I'd scored a match-winning try? I don't think so. I was still in a state of shock. The newspapers reported me as showing 'one quick grin of relief' and that was it.

There were no costs awarded, which I found a bit galling. A case was brought against me, I was found not guilty and yet still had to pay all my costs. Still, that could wait. I walked out and hugged everyone. Jayne, Mom, Dad, Maria, Sally, Tim – a good team. Dad was so relieved that he was in tears. And so was I, deeply so. Throughout my life I'd dreamed of visiting quite a few places in the world – prison had not been on the list. Friends, family and even strangers had been hugely supportive throughout the trial and my postbag had been generally favourable.

'Congratulations,' read one letter from a Jeffrey Holmes. 'You must be thankful that this nonsense has been put into touch, where it bloody well belongs.'

A couple of others were not so sweet. In the early stages of the trial, one chap, a broadminded soul, wrote from Shepley in Yorkshire.

'As one whose fame originates from chasing a ball around it is well appreciated that little intelligence is demanded in your profession, i.e. "strong in the back and weak in head". One can only hope that justice is done and that you suffer appropriate punishment, that is, lengthy confinement. All types of ball games these days seem to attract violent characters far more efficient with their fists and their feet than with the brain section. While certainly not confined to any ethnic type, percentages seem to show that dusky characters are too well represented in violent characters involved in many sports. I often note that the "Collymores" of sport appear to have a large chip on their shoulder which creates these aggressive outbursts.'

Charming. Glad he didn't find his way on to the jury.

chapter three

beginnings

Nature or nurture? Was I born like it or did I become it? Become what, you might ask? Well, take your pick from a whole heap of profile writers down the years who have trekked to my door in search of the real Jeremy Guscott. How the hell they expected to find him I've no idea. Even I didn't know who he was.

Here's their view of me: pretty boy, superstar, pampered, arrogant, difficult, cynical, glamour-puss, self-confident, assertive, bumptious, troublemaker, gifted, cosmopolitan, man about town, family man . . . the list goes on.

I've never felt the need to define myself and have never thought of myself as belonging to a particular class or being any particular colour. I was about six years old when I was first called 'nigger' or 'wog'. It obviously didn't mean much to me. It was just a word but I knew from the tone of voice that they were bad words.

I asked Mom at the time what those words meant. I reckoned I might as well get the difficult things out of the way all in one go. However, colour was never an issue in my life. Of course, I was called things, but then 'fattie' and 'four-eyes' were also common jibes in the playground. The colour of my skin never had any influence on my selection for any rugby team. The time I was affected by it was when I played 'kiss touch' with my schoolmates. The girls seemed to back off from me and I can only imagine it was because of my colour. Couldn't have been any other reason, could it? I did well to come back from such an early snub.

I suppose that if I'd been brought up in a ghetto things might have been different. Perhaps I would have been swept along in some movement or other, become part of a gang or targeted more by outsiders. Bath is no hotbed of racial tension. It's got its problems – and I managed to encounter a few of them myself – but it is, by and large, an easygoing place, very gentrified and very English.

My father Henry (known to most as 'Slim') came to England from Jamaica and met my mother Sue in Bath some years later. It wasn't exactly love at first sight as far as my mother was concerned. She was bombing down a hill one day on her pushbike when she saw this madman standing right in her line, grinning. Mom assumed he would get out of the way. He didn't. She swerved, clipped him and came tumbling off. He then had the nerve to ask her out for a drink the following night. Some style, the old man.

I was born in the Royal United Hospital on 7 July 1965, and my brother Gary followed about two and a half years later. Dad and I were never that close. I'm not sure that many sons and fathers are. It's not that we didn't get on or that we were always at each other's throats. Far from it, although there were a couple of celebrated incidents, notably when he threw me out of the house when I was sixteen and told me to fend for myself.

Perhaps I deserved it. He and I just didn't communicate enough. We get on much better now. It's funny, people are always telling me what a great bloke Dad is: so sweet, so polite and well turned-out. Jason Leonard, Harlequin and England record-breaking prop but more importantly soulmate because of many late-night drinking sessions, often says: 'You know something? Your old fella is the coolest bloke I've ever come across.'

I'm sure a psychologist might make much of my childhood behaviour and my relationship with my father. Yes, I was in trouble several times, kicked out of home and Dad and I were often not on speaking terms. But, for me, childhood was a great time. Dad was strict and I was forever in trouble for minor matters (minor in my book, that is) such as getting dirty or having an untidy bedroom. Occasionally he took the strap to me but it was no big deal as far as I was concerned.

Now that I've got three children myself – Imogen, Holly and Saskia – I can see the other side. Dad worked very hard to make ends meet. He was a carpenter by trade but gave that up soon after coming to England. He had a variety of jobs for a while, from working in a rubber factory in Melksham, Wiltshire, to selling clothes and finally ending up as a porter at the Royal United Hospital in Bath.

Dad usually did shift work and long hours they were too. Mom had been a secretary but then took a job collecting money from fruit machines in pubs and clubs for Bell Fruit. It was only later in life, after Gary and I were off her hands, that she really turned to what she wanted to do and that was to teach. She'd had a good education herself at a private school and had ambitions of going to university. Only later did she fulfil that ambition and now she teaches remedial kids at Speedwell School, which she loves.

Like most kids, I saw a lot more of Mom than Dad for the simple reason that she was at home more often. In many ways, I'm more like her than like Dad. She ought to have raced right through the standard academic route but she didn't – she fancied savouring life a little first. She knew that everything would work out in the end, that life would somehow look after her. I'm like that, not on the academic side I hasten to add, but in believing that things will take their natural course. I don't get too weighed down by life's little problems.

Life began in a flat in Lansdown Road in Bath. The flat was on the top floor so Mom had to hump all the shopping up five flights. They weren't the easiest of times. Then we moved to Ringswell Gardens, where we lived until I was six years old. I have only one significant memory of Ringswell Gardens. There I was, four years old, standing in the garden looking up at Mom who was in the upstairs bathroom, and I was crying because I'd wet my trousers. Er, and that's it.

All the hours I've spent with my kids, all the money, all the presents, all those lovely moments that you think will be with them forever and a day. Then look at what I remember of my early days: wetting myself.

We lived at 2 School Lane in Batheaston until my late teens. Then the family moved to St Saviour's Terrace in the Ringswell area – and I moved into rebel country.

There were three semi-detached houses along a private lane, with a big mill house at one end and the school itself, St Saviour's, two hundred yards away.

Along a path which led from our road there was a council estate called Elmshurst. As far as I was concerned it was a great setting. The garden was about half an acre's worth, with trees and grass and a brook at the bottom. A sewage pipe led across the brook to a playing field and the church hall, which had a youth club. Every summer the Brownies held their summer camp there. Not that I was ever to be caught spying on them of course.

School Lane was considered a step up from where we had been, almost countrified, wouldn't you know. Not that we were particularly well off. Dad's factory was nearby in Melksham and Mom by then was working at Bell Fruit.

I attended Batheaston Junior School and had my own back-door key to let myself in. I'd often make myself bread and jam and then wait for Mom to arrive home. Dad, who was working on the production line, would come in later and then we'd all sit down and eat as a family.

Other kids seemed to have a few more things than we did. My mate Gary Johnson always seemed to have a quarter pound of peardrops or apple cubes on him, sweets that we didn't have. I don't know if that meant that he was rich and we were poor. And I don't really care. These are just unimportant things that you remember when you look back. I have no feeling, though, that I was much different from the friends around me.

My family used to spend the weekends together,

taking walks up to Salisbury Hill for example. Or perhaps we'd drive somewhere. Our first car was a green Capri. I remember Dad standing alongside it complete with goatee beard and black leather jacket, looking very sharp.

Then we moved on to a big old Morris, a tank of a thing which is probably a classic of its kind today. The next car was not quite so desirable: a brown, rusty Datsun 1.4. Dad got a company van at one point and we also had a clapped-out Mini. The Mini proved to be too much of a temptation for me. I was in my early teens at the time and Mom and Dad were out somewhere. We had one of a row of garages opposite our house and the Mini was parked there. But not for long. I figured that Mom and Dad would be away for ages and that one little try-out in the Mini wouldn't do anyone any harm and wouldn't be noticed. So in I went, reversed out, went forward, did a three-point turn, drove back into the garage and thought nothing more of it. Until Mom collared me.

'Have you been in the Mini?' she asked.

'Whatever gave you that idea?' I replied.

'Follow me,' said Mom.

We walked outside into the garden and looked out on the grassy area. There, for all to see, were the tyre marks left by my perfectly executed three-point turn. Perfect except for the fact that I'd left the handbrake on and the locked rear wheels had left indelible evidence of my crime on the grass.

Mom and Dad had a good circle of friends. They were sociable people. I think that was the reason why I was first taken down to Bath Rugby Club. It was another social circle for my parents to move in. Mom's brother, my Uncle John, took us along. He played rugby for a while – not to any great level, perhaps, but he had a huge love for the game. Dad, coming from Jamaica, knew nothing about the sport but it didn't take long for him to get hooked.

Cricket was his first love, naturally enough. He never once tried to foist his preference on me. I played a bit of cricket here and there but was quickly bored by it. I can remember a few of the names from Somerset cricket of the time – Vic Marks, Viv Richards, Ian Botham – but I had no great affinity with the sport.

Football was a slightly different story, and it's about time I came out of the closet on this delicate matter. It will disturb a lot of people – it disturbs me – to know that I had a poster of Arsenal, yes Arsenal, on my bedroom wall. It was a picture of their 1971 double-winning side. Goalkeeper Bob Wilson was my favourite player.

The love affair faded pretty quickly. By the end of the seventies I was a Manchester United fan of sorts and remember being really upset when they were beaten 3–2 by Arsenal in an FA Cup final.

I was and still am a huge admirer of Pele and wish I'd been born a few years earlier so that I could have appreciated him at the peak of his powers. For me, he had everything: grace, style, supreme skill and the killer instinct. I was always Pele when I was kicking the ball against the wall at School Lane.

I was keen on football and played a lot in five-a-side competitions when I was a Wolf Cub. The matches were often held at Kensington playing fields, which are now occupied by a supermarket. One year we did particularly well, getting through to the final. We lost something like 10–8 and I scored seven goals. Did I take defeat on the chin? Did I hell. I blamed all the others for costing us victory and then burst into tears. I think I might have been known as a bad loser.

I wasn't bad at soccer and might have taken it on further if I'd been brought up in, say, Manchester or Liverpool. The two Bristol clubs, Rovers and City, had their affiliated sections and I was invited along to the City junior section once but that was as far as it went. I'm competitive by nature so I liked to think that I might have made it if I'd really tried. To be honest, I don't know. I was also fairly small as a kid, a real lightweight. I'm now over six foot but I was a late developer.

Although I've been known to show a turn of speed on the rugby field from time to time (usually when there's some brute trying to tackle the living daylights out of me), I didn't actually stand out at all in athletics. One hundred metres seemed a long way for a little fellow, while four hundred metres was a marathon.

I took up judo when I was about nine. Bas Lloyd was the teacher and conducted classes in the church hall at Batheaston. He taught us for three years and I moved up through the ranks. The next teacher was Peter Thatcher, a much stricter figure altogether. I was suspended from his classes for a while for insubordination. Shades of things to come. I won a few tournaments and was the West of England champion in my weight division. I competed at Crystal Palace for the National Championships one year but I won only one bout of the three. The Olympic Games never did beckon.

Dad was never pushy about sport – I did it because I

liked it. I played rugby for the same reason. It was more of a social exercise than anything, somewhere to make friends and have some fun.

Most of my friends lived on the Elmshurst Estate – boys such as Gary Johnson, Simon Carlin and Keith Rudland. We used to get into trouble at junior school although at that age the consequences were no more than a telling off. The big bust-ups would come later. There was one teacher at Batheaston Junior, Mr Maggs, who was one tough cookie. He would give us a whack if we stepped out of line. Another teacher got rid of all the troublemakers from his class and lobbed them to Maggs. I was one of those lobbed his way.

It was harmless stuff. He'd give us a smack on the backside from time to time. I didn't complain, I knew the consequences. I was once sent to the headmaster Mr Snell after one of the girls had falsely accused me of kicking her. I've always been able to dish out the verbals, but I've never been physically aggressive. The girl made up the story and I didn't enjoy being grilled over something I hadn't done, although I was eventually believed. Some might say that I've always had a problem with people in authority but that's not really true. I do bristle easily with some people but I also respect those in authority who treat people fairly.

Junior school was a breeze. I see what our children have to do now and know that I wouldn't have been able to cope. Imogen, our eldest, gets two or three homework assignments a week. Me, I was out the door the moment I got home from school, up to the estate with the boys and down to the brook to play. It was a different lifestyle then and seemed a lot safer than it is for children of today. There are so many horrible cases of assault against children in the news these days that Jayne and I would never feel happy about letting the girls out on their own. There's a large park near where my parents now live in Bath, where Imogen is given her little bit of freedom. She's allowed to cycle round the pathway but she's always in our sight.

I was the big brother in the house, both literally and metaphorically. Gary was two and a half years younger and did I let him know it. I would beat him up when Mom and Dad were out and then make him promise not to tell them when they came home or he'd get another beating. Gary was handy to have as a playmate when my other friends were not around, but we weren't that close. Gary and Mom were good pals. I was not exactly a loner, far from it, but I just preferred to do my own thing in my own time. Dad is not like me. He's a great conversationalist and he's the sensible one. Mom has more in common with me: she's easily led, likes a drink and a fag and a night out.

However, Dad did like his cheese and wine occasions. He gets tiddly quite easily, and he's not a big drinker so it doesn't take much. It would surprise people to see him that way because it happens so rarely. He is good company. I remember once at School Lane when Mom's sister, Auntie Nick, was visiting from New Zealand and Uncle John was there too with his wife Vera. We had a big barbecue that went on for hours.

There were some lovely trees in the front of the house which separated our garden from that of Glen and Tony Butcher, our neighbours. They had two daughters, Andrea and Hilary, who we played with, and we would push our way through the trees to get to next door. My room was up in the roof of our house in a loft conversion, and I remember looking outside that next morning. The family had been at it all night and the garden resembled a Red Indian village that had been attacked. Smoke was still rising from the fire and an old tent lay squashed on the ground. The scene was one of devastation and the trees had been hacked down. They'd all drunk so much that they'd taken an axe to the trees in the middle of the night and reduced the garden to a wasteland. I knew better than to ask too many questions.

St Saviour's infant school was followed by Batheaston junior school and then I went on to Ralph Allen Comprehensive. It was around this time, at twelve years old or so, that I started playing rugby for Walcot Old Boys, up on the hill near the racecourse. I'm still a regular there at the club bar and they hold a ten-a-side competition every year for the Guscott Cup, which means a lot to me.

You could say that the academic world was not exactly trembling at my arrival into its senior ranks. In fact, I was pretty much in the top stream for most subjects, but application was not my strong suit. When I got out into the playground I'd find myself with the smokers, the rebels.

I was not a great student and a pain to some teachers. I don't know whether it was a case of my seeking attention or what. That sort of theory is too deep for me. It's more that I can't resist a face-off – if someone hands me a gun I'm only too happy to pull the trigger. I was seen as the troublemaker whereas most of the time it was just me finishing something off. I could always have backed down, but I didn't. Nobody could tell me what was what and I had a problem with that.

I haven't changed much now. I'll make sure that people know what I think of something and I've got strong views on certain matters, as a few coaches down the years will tell you. I don't believe in holding back.

Most of my senior life at Ralph Allen was spent outside the dinner hall at lunchtimes. That was the punishment: wait outside the dinner hall until everyone else had been served. It was pathetic really. Still, good for the figure.

I was suspended three times. In an all-boys school I would probably have been caned and that would have been the end of it, but at Ralph Allen it was suspension or exclusion. My first major run-in was with a teacher called Barney Parr, who taught technical drawing. We did not get on. I swore at him once and that was it: yellow card, suspension.

The second time was for smoking. I was a pillock. When I was caught I lied and made the situation far worse. For some pathetic reason, I can't think what, a couple of us, Simon Carlin and myself, decided that our teacher Mr Bruce wouldn't mind if we lit up at the back of the minibus on a trip back to school. We tried to puff the smoke out of the little windows at the back.

I claimed that it wasn't me, and Mom and Dad were summoned. Dad asked what had happened and I explained that they'd got the wrong boy. He believed me and took issue with the school, fighting my corner for all it was worth.

'My son does not lie,' said my father. 'The others must be lying.'

Poor Dad. Sold down the river by his eldest son.

He was not impressed and our relationship bombed. He was working hard for his family and, as far as he could see, I was not appreciating one little moment of it. In the same way that I look at all the things that my daughters have and compare it with my upbringing, so must my father have struggled to make sense of why I seemed to be frittering away my life. He had not had many opportunities in life and, by comparison, I did.

Once I had a reputation at Ralph Allen as a disruptive influence, I was the first in the firing line every time there was a hint of trouble. The final straw for everyone – me, Dad, Ralph Allen Comprehensive – came at a school football match.

We were playing Broadlands School in Radstock and their teacher was the referee. Fair and objective? Not a chance. We didn't get a single decision in our favour. Not one free kick, not one offside. It was as much as the ref could bring himself to do to let us kick off. Finally, our goalkeeper had had enough and he summed up the situation:

'Ref,' he said, 'you are a fucking cheat.'

There was uproar and the ref was forced to abandon the match. On the way back we were all laughing and joking about it but the smiles were to vanish the next day. Or mine did, anyway. I was the only one hauled up before the headmistress Miss Hayter. She was usually fair-minded was Miss Hayter, but she wasn't interested in my version of events this time around. I knew it was futile, it was all over. However, I pleaded my case: it hadn't been me who had given the final, ringing mouthful to the ref. But Miss Hayter knew from long experience that I would have been giving the ref both barrels throughout the game. As far as she was concerned, I had brought shame on the school.

There was no way back and I was expelled. For all my bravado, I was shocked. I was also anxious, not so much about the school, but about Dad. I was right to be worried. He was furious. But life ticked on by.

I had been due to sit my O-levels but they felt that I would be too disturbed to do myself justice so they entered me at a later date for the re-sits. I had to take them somewhere so I enrolled at Bath Technical College. There was a lot of leeway at the college. Some people are mature enough to respond well to a certain amount of freedom and responsibility, but I wasn't. I couldn't believe that you didn't have to turn up too often. My books didn't get much attention, but the pool table did.

I just wasn't self-disciplined enough to handle the freedom. At the time, Tony 'Chalkie' Wardle, a great mate of mine, was doing a stone masonry apprentice-ship together with a couple of other lads I knew. They were on day release to the tech so, instead of attending classes, we just knocked around together.

The education system and I just didn't get on. I had begun senior school in the top stream, been set for my exams and then frittered away my time at technical college. It was a shambles.

At the back of my mind was the thought that because I was good at rugby that somehow everything would turn out all right. It was naïve and romantic in many ways. After all, although I was doing well I wasn't winning England Schoolboy honours or anything like it.

I can't imagine how I'd feel if my three daughters had the same outlook on education – probably not best pleased. They do seem to be far more driven at their school and more aware of the future. Mind you, I can see bits of my stubbornness in them. There's a look in Holly that is pure me when you're trying to get her to do something that she doesn't want to do.

Mom dealt with the whole situation pretty well. She figured that I would get it all out of my system one day. Dad just despaired. I was using the house like a hotel, lounging around, not paying my way and taking advantage of everybody and everything. In his eyes I had no respect for him or the home.

As for me, I was just being a teenager – life was for dossing about. However, things had to come to a head and they did.

Mom, as ever, was very straightforward about the whole matter. She wasn't too upset, or so it seemed to me at the time. But she did realise that Dad was at the end of his tether. My college tutors had almost given up on my attending at the right place and the right time. Eventually, I did manage to get seven CSEs of varying grades to my name – hardly a haul to make the academic world quake. Finally, Dad had had enough. There had been too many talks down the years and now it was time for action. At the age of sixteen I was out.

I found a home from home with the Allen family. Judy, the mother, lived in Hill View Road, which was about a mile from where my parents lived. There were three teenage daughters: Tracey, Geta and Wendy – all good-looking girls, as was Judy, who had separated from her husband Brian. So, there was I in the middle of them all. Tracey was a friend from school and I remember waiting outside her front door while she went inside to ask her mother if I could stay. Judy said yes and I slept on Tracey's floor for a long while.

There was never anything between myself and the girls except friendship. We were all just young things having a good time. I got my own room when Wendy left home and I was like a brother to Tracey and Geta. Every time we went out together it was a nightmare. Women take so long to get ready. Tracey has long, thick, ginger hair and it took an age to dry. And they'd all be walking around in their bras and knickers, dolling themselves up. It became so natural that I barely even gave it a second thought. I look back now and wonder what was wrong with me.

I wasn't traumatised by being thrown out of my home. It just meant more freedom. My dole money helped Judy pay the rent, and I did odd jobs, such as stacking shelves in the local supermarket. A couple of guys there, Steve Davies and Carlton Dixon, made the hours tick by pretty quickly. I was playing for the Colts team at Bath by this stage and it was going pretty well. We rarely lost. As far as I was concerned, work just got in the way of rugby. That and sleeping off the effects of the night before. Summers were for lazing about down by the weir in Bath. We all used to meet up on the grass, laze about, smoke and have a chat. There was a desperate game we used to play, which was to run through a shop on Pulteney Bridge and jump out through the window and into the river. I gave it up when I saw one of the boys cut his foot to shreds on glass on the riverbed.

It was a good if wayward time and life followed a predictable lads' pattern. We'd all go out after playing on a Saturday night and hit the rum coolers – Bacardi, orange and lemonade. The other lads were working so they'd lend me a tenner, which would never last long. I'd invariably end up crashing out at Pete Blackett's flat. He and Chalkie were my best pals and still are today.

I was away from home for about a year and, at first, wasn't set on mending any fences any more than was Dad. I used to pop home to see Mom when he was at work. Finally, I decided to ask Dad to let me back. There was no fatted calf on the barbecue when I got there. No surprise really, I wouldn't have wasted good meat on me either. I mumbled a few half-hearted apologies and made a few vague pledges to sort myself out. And that was it.

And there was no smart room either. My parents were in the process of redecorating and I was given the room that hadn't been done up. A bed, no shelves and muck everywhere. But it was a start, although the atmosphere was cool, to say the least. I wasn't the most pleasant item, I suppose, full of myself in a teenage way. Even though I had promised to sort myself out I didn't exactly send the employment market into a whirl chasing for my services. I stacked shelves, did some labouring and then did some work felling trees for a man called George Norman, who played for the Spartans, the third XV at Bath. We'd fell the withered trees on the course at Bath Golf Club, saw them up, shift them by tractor and then pile them into the pick-up to sell for firewood around Bath. I was a dab hand behind the steering wheel, so much so that I thought I'd better try and pass a driving test just in case I was stopped on the road.

I had no ambition in those days, but then I never really have had. I'm a competitive swine and have often been accused of being a closet trainer, of putting in a few hours' secret training just to be in better shape than the rest of the team. However, I have never had a particular aim to reach a certain goal in my life by a certain age.

I certainly had no idea at the time of trotting out at Twickenham for England. My only experience of the old stadium had been when I went with Dad to the 1980 match against Wales. It was during that match that Welsh flanker Paul Ringer was sent off. I can remember entering the ground and climbing the steps at the back of the old South Stand. It was packed and the kids were pushed down to the front to get a better view. I ended up right down near the dead-ball line behind the advertising hoardings beside some old Welsh chap. I have no great memory of the game itself – a hard, dirty match apparently, that England won 9–8 (three English penalties to two Welsh tries, sounds familiar) – except this Welsh bloke moaning and taking a swig at his bottle every time Dusty Hare knocked over a goal.

And that was it – noise, people, fun but no tingle inside to get out there one day in the white shirt. Bath's John Horton was at fly half that day. I knew him by name and had a vague aim to play his position for the club one day, but I had no future mapped out for myself. Too much like forward planning.

I know that in those early days I had a fearsome reputation as a big-headed prat, full of myself and letting everyone know it. But that was bravado, a need for attention if anything. I fancied myself and let the world know it. I had my wings clipped eventually, but my bragging and showing off were due to immaturity as much as anything – that and an inclination to wind people up. It wasn't because I had my England career mapped out to the last detail. No, details didn't interest me much in those days. Life was for living not planning.

chapter four

true romance

I was no great shakes in the love game at this point. I was a late developer on that front, slight in build, with an afro haircut and a pathetic attempt at a moustache.

And then came Jayne. I met her at Nero's night-club in Bath when I was nineteen years old. I was there with Pete Blackett. I felt a kick in the back of my leg at one point in the evening. I turned round and saw Jayne. In fact it had been her friend, Sharon Williams, who had given me a nudge but all I saw was Jayne, Jayne Aland as she was then. She was going out at the time with Sharon's brother, a black guy. I was charm itself. I told her bluntly that she didn't have to kick me if she wanted to get noticed, she only had to talk in the normal way. Anyway, we had a dance, something that I didn't normally bother with. There is a malicious rumour put about by sources close to my household that I even tried to avoid the dance, claiming that I'd hurt my foot playing rugby. It was not exactly *Brief Encounter*, soft lights and all.

I saw her leaving at the end of the evening and

took the plunge and asked for her phone number even though she was going out with someone else. I was smitten. Jayne lived in nearby Trowbridge, was studying at college but also working at night in a factory in Trowbridge to earn some money.

We had a secret relationship for about three months, most of it conducted on the phone. Given that I'm pretty curt on the phone these days, it amazes me to think that I used to spend two hours or so chatting to Jayne every night. We sometimes spoke a couple of times during an evening, often during her half-hour break at the factory.

Our first date arrived. I was working at the tree-felling job at the time and arranged to meet Jayne outside Bath station. Jayne did as most women would: she got herself all dressed up, keen to make a good impression. Me? Well, I jumped into the rusty, yellow Datsun pick-up that I didn't have a licence for. Out from the railway station came this vision of loveliness, looking around for the suave boyfriend in his sports car.

I had my dirty old waterproofs on. I quickly shoved some newspaper on to the front seat. As Jayne said later: 'My first thought was to get back on the train and go home.'

It got better. After three months of clandestine meetings, I told Jayne that she had to make up her mind between me and the other man. It was me. We had an easygoing time of it, nothing sexual for a fair while. She would come round to the house – I'd been upgraded to a decent room by this stage – and we'd listen to music or watch television.

It was my first serious relationship and right from

the start it was different with Jayne. We went on holiday together, to Zante in Greece, as a trial run for moving in together. I wasn't sure about such a big step (typical male) but thought that if we could get through two weeks in each other's company then we had a chance.

The big move was to a rented ground-floor flat in St James' Square. It was a neat little place but freezing in the winter. We had a gas fire and one old Flatley heater and that was it. In the winter we'd go to bed wearing our jumpers. It was our place, though, and it worked. For our first Christmas we invited everyone round, both families included. Jayne's parents split up when she was eight years old and she has hardly had any contact with her father since. Her mother Pat remarried, to Richard.

We had good times in the flat and meanwhile I was making a real hit on the job front. I'd trained as a bus driver for Badgerline, got my PSV licence and did the various routes in the little buses that pootle around Bath. The Kingsholm crowd at Gloucester used to give me merciless stick a few years later, chanting 'Badgerline, Badgerline, Badgerline' each time the ball came near me.

Our time in the flat came to an end when I was offered a chance to play in Australia. John Morrison, the Bath lock, had spent a season playing with the Waratahs – not the Super 12 side of the same name, but an up-country club in Wollongong, New South Wales.

I was invited out to follow in John's footsteps. (His sister Samantha was later to marry Andy Robinson, Bath flanker and valued team-mate for many years and now England coach). It was a real dilemma: Jayne and I were on the point of buying a place of our own and yet this was the chance of a lifetime. It meant giving up work (no big deal) as well as the flat (big deal). Jayne couldn't afford the rental on her own so she moved in with my folks for the time I was away. She got on well with my parents and wanted to remain in Bath.

I headed south in April 1987. The flight was paid for – and it was the cheapest ticket on offer, with Garuda Indonesia Airways. If I'd known then what I know now about airlines, I might not have set foot up the steps. Twelve stops and thirty-eight hours later I touched down in Sydney to be met by Bob Kerr, one of the committee men from the club, and Ronnie Wessels with whom I ended up sharing a flat.

We didn't hit the sporting heights that season but we hit everything else in sight: the bottle, the town, you name it. Most of the team were older than me and it was a fairly tight-knit community. The club captain took me back to his place one night for a meal with his wife and kids. Then, after dinner, we set about his drinks cabinet.

After staggering home, I decided to write to Jayne. It was full of tender thoughts and fine words, a love letter that would stand against the most romantic ever written by great poets. At least, I thought it was until I looked at it the next morning in a sober light. It was drivel and I couldn't understand a word of it.

The team didn't do too well during my time there. John Morrison had done a good job for them the previous year, as had Peter Williams at fly half, who was to play for England a year later. But the Waratahs' form took a bit of a dip thereafter. I switched between fly half and centre and did all right.

I had my first experience of South Seas rugby out there. We had a Tongan, Don Tevvy, playing for us. What a nutter. He was a lovely man off the pitch but on it he was a head case, smashing into everyone with his rib-crunching tackles. He was sent off every other week but was back within a couple of matches. I went along to a few of the South Sea Islanders' parties. Wild. There was a real frenzy about them, with booze and women and a lovely, laid back atmosphere. They all knew each other and looked after each other too. Great people.

I had a typical Aussie time out there, not worrying in the slightest about tomorrow. It was very boozy and very male-orientated. I had a lucky escape on one occasion when I misread the traffic lights and an old couple smashed into me, writing off Ronnie's car in the process. It was my fault entirely. I had to report to the police station and, luckily, I had a driving licence by then. I got away with a small fine.

I only ever did about three weeks' work during my time there, in the university mailroom operating the franking machine. In the main, I got by on the few quid put my way by the club. They shared a facility with the bowling club and one night each week there would be a huge meat raffle that raised a decent amount of money. Most of it went to me, about £50 a week. I wasn't sure if amateurism had hit Australia and wasn't too fussed about finding out.

Jayne joined me for six weeks or so before I was due to return and we had a stopover holiday in Bali on the way back. It was while lying in bed one day that we decided to get engaged. No big build-up, no fanfares, not much thought – it just seemed the natural thing to do.

We stayed at my folks' place for a couple of years. In the meantime, I'd really committed myself to bolstering the coffers of the Inland Revenue by becoming a bricklayer.

I had worked alongside a brickie called Roger Hill, who was one of the most chilled-out guys I've ever met. He used to take his time, lay his bricks, casually make his roll-up, smoke it slowly and lovingly, and then go on to the next line of bricks. There seemed to be no stress in his life and I figured that I wouldn't mind that. So, bricklaying it was.

I did a six-month course at Fishponds Training College in Bristol. I got through it somehow, although the old instinct to rebel against authority almost got me into trouble. However, I passed my City and Guilds and went to work for a subsidiary of John Mowlem. Life was going well.

By the start of the 1988–89 season I had broken into the Bath first XV, playing alongside Simon Halliday in the centre. Jayne and I were saving for our own place and, by the end of that season, took the plunge and bought a terraced house in Larkhall, a stone's throw from my parents in St Saviour's Terrace. Mom and Dad helped us with the mortgage as well as with doing up the place. Rugby interrupted a lot of good intentions, notably my surprise call-up for the British Lions tour to Australia in June 1989. But more of that later.

I would quite happily have drifted along like that for many years, but Jayne forced the pace as usual. It's a good job someone does. The church and vicar were booked before I knew what was happening and we were married in St Saviour's Church in Larkhall on 14 July 1990. I had two close friends, Pete Blackett and Chalkie Wardle, and couldn't decide on who should be best man. So I chose both.

A lot of the boys couldn't make it because they were away touring with England. However, Simon Halliday was there too and, obviously, many of the Bath contingent. The Bath mini-rugby lads formed a guard of honour and it was a wonderful day.

Married life soon became parental life. Again Jayne took the initiative when, midway through 1991, she started talking about having children. Our firstborn might well have been conceived on the night of the 1991 World Cup final when we lost to Australia, 12–6. At least some good came from the day.

On 4 August 1992, Imogen was born. Her arrival and those of her two sisters who followed are the most fantastic things that have ever happened to me. I was only present though for Imogen's birth. My folks were thrilled at the thought of becoming grandparents and I remember Dad giving Jayne a big hug when we broke the news to them.

The day of the birth itself followed a typical routine. I came home from work and Jayne said that she had been having contractions. I leapt into action and asked her to cook me dinner, which was scampi and chips as I recall. A twenty-three-hour labour followed not long afterwards.

I was nervous as hell. God knows how women put up with all that pain; I wouldn't last five minutes. I was jumping around, tending to Jayne and trying to see Imogen emerge. It was an overwhelming sensation when she finally did make it. There was one slightly scary moment when the umbilical cord got wrapped round her neck, but the nurses were so calm that it was sorted out within seconds. Imogen's birth brought us all closer.

At that time rugby still had amateur status, but I was already managing to find a few commercial activities to boost the earnings from my current job with British Gas as a sales and PR man. In 1994 I co-presented ITV's *Body Heat* and a second series was planned for the following year. However, by then Jayne was pregnant once more and the production schedule was going to clash with her giving birth. The programme was to be shot in Atlanta, Georgia and I was torn between staying behind and going to the United States. However, given that rugby was not providing a living, it was too good an opportunity and off I went.

We were in Tennessee on Easter Sunday, white-water rafting and mountain-biking, when Jayne attempted to contact me via the production unit's mobile phone. However, the reception was weak and she was unable to tell me that she was having a few contractions.

I phoned as soon as I got back to the hotel and at first Jayne was pretty downbeat and matter of fact. False alarm, I thought. Not a bit of it. Jayne had gone into hospital at five that afternoon, given birth to Holly two hours later and was home by nine o'clock. Two days later I arrived back in England to see my second treasure.

My home life has taken a turn in a different direction in recent months. Jayne and I announced in August 2001 that we were to separate. The decision was not taken on the spur of the moment but had been brewing for some time. It was a process that had its roots in my playing days.

I was forever away from home, either with Bath, England or the Lions. I felt that I would be able to devote more time to home life when I hung up my boots. That has not happened. My workload is such that I still spend a lot of time on the road. My character is such, too, I guess, that I have not felt able to take on that added family responsibility.

It's a great credit to Jayne that she has brought up the three girls, Imogen, Holly and Saskia, so well. She has done so much of it on her own. Jayne has often pointed out to me that I needed to spend more time with the kids. I haven't been able to come to terms with that although, ironically, since the separation, I have done just that. Imogen remarked the other day that she's seen far more of me lately than in previous times.

It was the hardest decision I've ever had to make. Telling the children was not an easy moment. It was very emotional for all of us. We would not have done it if we hadn't felt that it was best for all concerned. It's been tough on Jayne. She felt that enough was enough and I had to accept that.

chapter five

the bath years

Let's get it out of the way early. Yes, I was a complete prat, and, yes, David Trick did tell me that. Nice, mild-mannered Tricky, Bath winger loved and respected by all, told me the bare-knuckle truth one evening on the way to training. It was my Damascus moment. Well, not quite. I still gave as good as I got in the years to come but I have to say – and nearly every newspaper feature ever written on me has told the tale – that Tricky's heart to heart chat did sharpen me up. I became not so much a new man, rather a more guarded one.

I pitched up one evening during the mid-eighties at the Recreation Ground for training. I had barely made much of a mark on Bath, let alone on the rugby world in general. Still, no reason why that should hold me back and I let the world and his wife know about every try I scored. The trouble was that the world and his missus were none too interested.

I may have been a loudmouth in those days but I was not daft and I could sense the bad vibes. Training that night had been switched from the Rec to Lambridge, our other ground on the road out of town. I hopped into Tricky's car for the ten-minute trip. Now was a chance to find out just how bad I was so I asked Tricky what the boys really thought of me.

'Well,' said Tricky in that nice way of his, 'they think you're a bigheaded prat. And you are, aren't you?'

Put like that, who could disagree? Anybody else I might have shouted down but not Tricky. He is one of life's gentlemen in every sense of the word, modest and down to earth. He'd been brought up to Bath from school in Tiverton, Devon, and scored a couple of tries in one of his early games. He saw it as normal and not anything special at all.

And so I listened to him pointing out that I was only one of twenty blokes in that squad who had the ability to skin their opposite number alive in whatever way they needed to.

'Just think about it,' he said. 'They don't need to go on about it.'

And I did think about it, decided that I was an arrogant upstart and toned down my behaviour from that moment on. Well, to a degree. Bath Rugby Club was full of strong characters and you had to stick up for yourself to survive. You could take the mickey-taking on the chin up to a point but then you had to bite back. I was quicker to snap than most and didn't always choose my victims too wisely.

I was once winding up Paul Simpson, a back-row stalwart and a real bear of a bloke. It was the end of season dinner in 1991. We had all piled into Oldfield's club bar after the dinner just in case we'd not already had enough to drink. I was giving him stick about not going on the England tour that summer to Australia. 'Don't blame me if you're not good enough to get selected. I am and I'm going,' said modest Guscott. I just about saw the left hook coming. If it had connected properly I probably wouldn't be here today.

On another occasion I laid into Richard Hill, our scrum half and a great pal of mine at the time. We used to room together on away trips, and our wives Jayne and Karen got on well. Still, I was never one to let friendship get in the way of a good wind-up.

Bath was in Lanzarote for a New Year training camp and I was goading winger Tony Swift, telling him how crap he was and that he should step aside for someone with pace and youth. Perhaps I should mention that I'd had a few drinks. On and on I droned, but Swifty took no notice so I turned on Richard instead. He took avoiding action and went to his room but I followed him. I simply had to let him know that he wasn't really a British Lion as the game he'd played in had been a celebration International Board game and not part of a full-fledged Lions tour.

This was a red rag to Hillie. He walked across the room and clocked me one flush on the jaw. Full back Jon Webb, who is now a surgeon, was also in the room at the time and was listening to all this from under the bed, having dived there when the fur started to fly. He would have had a good view of me as I slid to the floor, out cold. I woke the next morning with an aching jaw and little recollection of what had gone on.

That was the way it was. I dare say to outsiders it may all seem boorish, childish even, and not exactly a recommended item in the team-bonding manual. Well, all I can say in my defence is that it worked for us. No team came near to matching our record across a decade of success – League Champions six times between 1988 and 1996 and Cup winners ten times between 1984 and 1996.

Figures mean nothing to me. I can remember only a handful of games in any detail. One is the Cup Final win over Gloucester on a blisteringly hot day in late spring 1990. The weather was not the only thing that was on fire that day as we smashed our West Country rivals 48–6, scoring eight tries. Another was when we defeated Harlequins in extra time two years later, with Stuart Barnes knocking over a wonderful drop goal in the last minutes. And six years later in Bordeaux against Brive when we became the first English club to win the Heineken Cup. Now that was a game I can recall, or at least the dramatic finale.

As for the rest, they are a bit of blur. They happened, they were a mix of fun and disappointment and they passed. I rarely dwell on what has happened in the past, good or bad – particularly bad. Call it a weakness or a strength, but I always bury the bad times. I just don't want to know. You could argue that I'm poor at confronting unpalatable truth or that I'm strong enough to move on immediately and not be dragged down. It was the same when Dad threw me out of home and again with the court case. I won't allow myself to be plagued by guilt or misery.

There were far more good times than bad with Bath, that's for sure. But triumph was treated in the same manner as adversity. I think Kipling once put that approach to life a touch more poetically than I can manage. Bath to me was a succession of fleeting moments, times enjoyed in the company of others, occasionally fractious and often hilarious. And we won more often than not, which tended to make the beer taste better on a Saturday evening.

I sometimes wonder what made us tick. Did we create Bath or did Bath create us? Was Jack Rowell the man who made it happen or are there other names to put on the roll of honour, men such as Dave Robson and Tom Hudson, who worked alongside Rowell for so many years, planning and recruiting and taking us to new levels in terms of fitness and mental toughness? There is a whole cast list of top players to consider, from the likes of Roger Spurrell in the early days (a harder man you're unlikely to ever come across) to Jon Hall, another back-row man and the greatest player I ever played alongside. Hallie had it all – he was fast enough to train with the backs and matched us stride for stride. He should have been first choice for England for ever and a day, but twenty-one caps is all he managed, although he was held back by knee injuries. He was the complete, all-round back-row forward and the reason that I preferred playing flanker above all other positions. To see him involved in a game, handling the ball, making tackles and driving the opposition backwards was inspirational stuff. Good job he wasn't so hot at three-card brag, or my weekend spending may have been curtailed.

There were any number of backs who tickled my fancy: Serge Blanco, David Campese, Jonah Lomu – all great players in their right but Hallie is right up there with them. The more I played the game the more I appreciated just what he put into a performance. He had the right mix of graft and subtlety, the ability to knock lumps out of the opposition pack and deftness of touch as well as a keen eye to be able to put a back clear into space. Tim Rodber at Northampton used to say that he breathed a sigh of relief when he saw the Bath teamsheet and Hall's name was missing. For him it meant an afternoon in prospect that was altogether a less ferocious proposition.

I didn't have much to do with Roger Spurrell because he was coming to the end of his rugby career when I became a regular Bath team member in 1986–87, but his aura lived on. He came from Cornwall and had been a shepherd, but he then moved on to more glamorous things, owning a night-club and other businesses in Bath. He lost none of his rough edges, mind. He brought a ferocious approach even to training sessions, an atmosphere that was still there when I became a regular.

There was a combination of factors at work at Bath. There was a hell of a lot of talent there: Stuart Barnes, John Palmer, Johnny Horton, Simon Halliday, Tony Swift, Gareth Chilcott, Graham Dawe – a great mix of brawn and brain. Not too hot on the beauty front, however.

I had arrived in the First XV via Walcot Old Boys and Bath Colts. I was fifteen when I first joined the Colts section and it was great fun. I wasn't in any particular hurry to break into the first team, although the prospect of meeting some of the women who always seemed to be hanging around the squad was pretty inviting. I felt that my time would come, probably when someone retired. I also played for Somerset Colts at this stage, with Peter Jenkins as coach. He was a good man whose son Alan was fly half for the Colts. I've not always had a lot of time for coaches but Peter was an exception.

The coaches at Bath Colts were Geoff Pillinger and Tom Martland. I had little sense of being groomed for the future, even though Tom was a former first team coach. I lived for the day: play the game and get stuck into the Guinness afterwards.

I spent three years with the Colts. The first was outstanding, the second less so and the third no more than mediocre. I was sent off on one occasion. It was an evening game at the Recreation Ground and our captain was getting a pummelling from someone. I don't know what came over me because I'm usually happy to hide behind the big boys, but I ran in from the backs and joined in the fight. That was bad enough, but worse was to follow when I gave a false name to the referee when he sent me off. Although I confessed soon after, I was still banned for a month. That was the only time in my career that I was dismissed from the field. The hot blood of youth was quickly to cool in the face of some of the brutes I faced over the next twelve years.

The Spartans, Bath's third XV, was the next step up the ladder for me. The club was just beginning its great run of success in 1984, beating Bristol 10–9 to win the knockout cup, which was sponsored by cigarette company John Player in those days. The dash for the free cigarettes in the changing-rooms after matches would have broken all sprint records.

I was fly half at this point in my career and thought that I would remain in that position because I was still fairly small and slightly built. The Spartans was a great stepping stone, captained in the year I played there by Robbie Lye. Robbie, who had played over five hundred games for Bath first XV, was a wonderful captain and, as it turned out, friend. He gave us free rein to run ball from wherever we wanted. He was good with youngsters like myself. He has remained a close friend.

I got the call more and more often the following year to train with the first XV. There was a line of succession ahead of me. John Horton, England fly half back in the Grand Slam side of 1980, was possibly to retire at the end of the 1984–85 season, while Charles Gabbitas and Alun Watkins also had opportunities.

One day in early January 1985, at the age of nineteen, I was put on standby for the first XV because John Palmer was struggling to get time off from his work commitments to be able to travel north to Waterloo. Palmer was one of Bath's all-time great players. He had so much skill, so much time to tease and torment the opposition and was an all-round footballer. Why on earth he didn't win fifty caps at centre is beyond me. He had to make do with three, which was a scandalous waste of talent.

In the event, Palmer didn't make it and so I was on the bus and on my way. I was apprehensive at first. I didn't fancy that long trip north with blokes I barely knew and I'd have rather been on the Friday night drink-up with the boys in Bath. Or, at least, that was what I kept telling myself. It was a front to cover my own pre-match nerves. I was nervous as hell that Saturday morning, intent only on getting through the game and not making a total ass of myself.

Jack Rowell gave the dressing-room team talk but not a word of what he said went in. Bath won 23–13 and a career was launched. So too was a cuttings book. Mom still keeps one, although there are one or two items she'd rather had not made it into print. However, that day's cuttings were innocent enough. 'Guscott Gusto,' ran the headline in the *Sunday Telegraph*. I'm not sure why; I kicked four penalties and set up Barry Trevaskis for one of his two tries. Perhaps they couldn't work out a snappy headline for Trevaskis.

By and large I've got on well with the media but I've not quite got to grips with their way of choosing a man of the match, or of singling a guy out for special mention. I might play like a pillock for seventy-five minutes (rare I know) and then happen to be on the end of a movement to score a couple of tries in the closing minutes. They don't seem to appreciate the work done by others.

As a mere boy I was happy enough to take the plaudits and I got a few more run-outs for the first team during those months. As the 1984–85 season drew to a close Bath once more worked their way through to the final of the John Player Cup, this time against London Welsh. I was chosen as a replacement at the age of nineteen. The best bit of the experience was getting kitted out for the blazer.

I came on in the second half for wing Barry Trevaskis. Don't ask me what happened in the game, I barely saw the ball. Who'd be a wing? Not me. Chris Martin, our full back, made one break and I was up there in support ready for the scoring pass. It never came.

I've got the photos still from the moment of victory. Me, with a giant afro haircut. There are still a few in circulation that I've not managed to burn yet. The team went on an open-top bus tour round Bath the following day. It might have been the done thing in soccer, but in rugby you felt a fool up on the top deck, glugging champagne as a few hundred die-hards cheered us below.

It took another two or three years until I became a regular in the team. I'm sure I might have been more keen to get there sooner if the game had been professional and money had been on offer. As it was I was happy to bide my time. Palmer and Simon Halliday were the first choice for the team and what a pair they were. Palmer was vastly underrated by England as was Halliday. Halliday was without doubt the best centre of his time. Actually, make that one of the best of any time.

He and I were to play for many years alongside each other in Bath colours. His England career was probably checked by the emergence of Will Carling and the decision to make him captain. Halliday was easily the more talented of the two. He had the rare ability to play the ball out of the tackle at pace and would always commit at least one and often two players, aiming for their inside shoulder before turning out. I fed off him all the time. There is no doubt that he made me a much better player and taught me an enormous amount about space and angles. Audley Lumsden, Bath full back, and I scored many tries courtesy of Halliday.

He was educated at public school and Oxford and was making a name for himself in stockbroking. His background was a world apart from my own and yet we got on. He had a wonderful ability to communicate. You rarely saw him lose his temper but you knew to steer clear on the rare occasions when you saw his finger wagging. He was also as hard as they come, for all his fine words and nice accent. I would like to have played more for England with him alongside and Stuart Barnes at fly half. I think the rugby might have been more productive.

Halliday was a splendid team man, always committed, always sharp. He was generous with me, seeking me out to see whether I preferred left or right centre, inside or outside. I was never as accommodating with new boys. It was a shock when he left at the end of the 1990–91 season. Some of the boys were put out by his departure – to Harlequins of all teams – but it didn't bother me. He'd given his all for Bath as he would for the Quins and was a real force during that last season, driving himself and those around him to new heights. I think he knew that he was on the move at the end of the season and wanted one last hurrah. His wife Suzanne was a GP and was set on moving back to London, where her father had a practice. Stuart Barnes in particular took exception to the move but, loyal as I was to Bath, I could see that Halliday's move was for genuine reasons. Perhaps the boys were upset that he'd not let them in on the secret earlier.

Halliday was on the other side when we beat Harlequins in the 1992 Cup final 15–12 after extra time. He was the first in the dressing-room afterwards to congratulate us. It was a decent gesture but unappreciated by some of the lads, who gave him stick as he left. Bridges were eventually mended although it took Barnes a while to tiptoe across to the other side to shake hands.

The name Barnes was not my favourite. Any vague thoughts I might have had of a long career as the Bath fly half were knocked soundly into touch during the 1985–86 season when a bloke by the name of Stuart Barnes turned up at the club. He'd come from Bristol, our deadly rivals, and eased one of the Bath icons, John Horton, out of the frame. Barnes, a talented schoolboy player in Wales, had worked his way along the M4, first playing for Newport and then Bristol. Now it was Bath's turn.

I didn't take to him. We even had a falling out on my stag night. Years later Barnes criticised me, saying that I couldn't accept anyone from outside Bath. He was right. But he didn't care and, by the force of his personality, he slowly took over – first the card school and then the backs. Within a couple of years he was virtually running the club. To think he was to have the nerve to drop me at one point. The upstart.

It happened the year after the 1989 British Lions tour. I'd come back and nothing seemed quite the same again. I struggled for a long while to get the same feeling back into my play. It wasn't that I thought myself above it all because I didn't. Running out at the Rec has always meant a lot to me: turn left out of the changing-room and out on to the pitch. I always got a kick from it. But that 1989–90 season, something just wasn't firing inside me.

On the outside I looked as if I didn't care, but deep down I did. The final straw was the cup semi-final against Moseley. One name was missing from the teamsheet. Mine. Jack Rowell and Barnesie took the decision between them – and guess who was the one to tell me. Barnes.

Jack hates confrontation. It's a remarkable failing because, when it comes to probing weaknesses, he is one of the most incisive people I have ever met. He was known as the Bath coach, but I never saw him exactly in that light. He was more the overseer, the manager, the guru, the impresario, the agent provocateur, the puppeteer pulling the strings. Technically, he was not that great a coach, especially with the backs. He loved the back row, in his eyes the unit that made any side tick. No, there have been better tracksuit men than Jack: Brian Ashton at Bath, for one, who went on to a troubled two-year spell with Ireland a couple of years back and is now working with Clive Woodward's England. Dick Best is another who I have a lot of time for as a coach, and also Ian McGeechan, with whom I shared many a fruitful time on three Lions tours.

However, Jack had something else to offer. Maybe it was just his towering personality. He was always challenging, isolating you in front of others, wondering aloud what right you had to be in such company. It was a provocative approach and it worked. He would sometimes come to team meetings armed with a list of points and go through them one by one, asking each individual what they had to offer. At other times he would get emotional and speak from the heart. He would fix each of us in the eye.

'This is your stage, this is what you do best,' he would say. 'Now go out and do it as you have always done.'

On other occasions he would be merciless. 'You came to Bath as a nobody, you went on to become a British Lion. Tell me, why aren't you playing like a British Lion?'

I had a lot of respect for Jack although I would never have let him know it. In fact, quite the opposite. It was 1988, we'd just won the Merit table and we were at a restaurant called Maxim's in Bath. We were drinking at the bar and I found myself for the first time beside

Jack. This was the big moment, the chance to impress the main man.

'Jack, I hear you have a way about you and that is to be a complete and utter bastard,' I said.

As introductions go, it wasn't the most diplomatic, but Jack, being Jack, got up and walked away without saying a word. We never did get to have a heart to heart in all those years together and he left Bath to take on the England job in the summer of 1994. Did we get on? In a way. We had respect for each other, that's for sure, but were never soulmates. Barnes was the man Jack related to and bounced ideas off and he was also his front-man. When I was dropped for the Moseley game I immediately challenged Jack about it. He blurted out straightaway that I would be back for the next game but Barnesie stood up and told me that it had been his decision as captain to leave me out. Jack, at 6ft 6in, hid behind the little fellow.

However, he was an amazing character. He juggled his work and sporting commitments superbly. Quite how he managed to be a chief executive at Dalgety on the other side of the country in Market Harborough, and still be there wind, rain or shine for evening training at Bath I don't know.

He was a quirky individual in many ways but also a great team man, not that his love of the collective made him shy about enjoying the spotlight when it came his way. But he knew the value of good teamwork even if he was not always the easiest to get on with. He did not create the Bath myth on his own but he had a significant hand in shaping and developing it.

Dave Robson and Tom Hudson were important lieutenants. Dave was a good talent spotter, always on the lookout for promising youngsters and not slow in bringing them to Bath. He was an accountant, knew lots of people in business in the area and, if there was a job to be had, he would find it. Hudson was more of a front-man, a motivator out on the training field. He gave us hard yakka.

Hudson and I had our fall-outs but secretly I thought he was a great bloke. We fell out over stupid things. He would tell me to bring over some balls during training and I would refuse.

'Go and get them yourself,' would be my mature response, feeling as if I was being victimised.

'Right. I'm the coach, I'm the boss, off you go,' came the reply.

And off I would go. It was trivial, no more than each of us marking out his territory. It didn't last because I knew Tom was doing a good job. We did a lot of endurance training – running, jogging, sprinting – and it was always varied and interesting. They were mainly evening sessions, two, sometimes three times a week and you came off feeling that you'd really done something useful with the time. Tom kept us ahead of the opposition each and every year. Just when they thought they had cracked our fitness regime and caught up, Tom would come up with another strategy for keeping our nose in front. We had mid-winter camps in Lanzarote long before England took up the idea in the late eighties.

Bath had many supremely gifted individuals in the side but ability counted for nothing if you could not get to the right place at the right time. The fitness allowed us to do what we wanted to do at a greater pace for a more sustainable amount of time.

There I am sounding like a fitness freak when in fact I'm one of the laziest blokes around. I enjoy being in shape and although I'm naturally slim like my father I still have to work at getting in the right condition. But I don't enjoy pain, I prefer the long and winding road to fitness rather than the short, sharp shock. I would rather sneak in a few sessions on my own during the summer rather than endure too much suffering when pre-season training starts. The boys have always accused me of that and now it's time to come clean – I am a closet trainer.

I'm not good at pushing myself and can only cope with pain on a gradual basis. I knew what was expected of me and I made sure that I was able to hit the target, but I would never be looking to push myself on to another level. Recently I was chatting to Mike Catt, Bath and England team-mate, be it at fly half, centre or full back, and he was saying that I ought to have been one of the fittest guys in rugby, given my physique. Mike *is* one of the fittest guys around, a natural athlete. But he knew that I'd always look for the shortcut.

I was never a Neil Back, for example, who would smash through a pain barrier just for the sheer pleasure of it. A Leicester flanker, he led the way in the England fitness tests in the mid-nineties. Fitness became more of a serious issue during that period, particularly when the game went professional in 1995. Before, most of the lads would mock those who really went for it. Mike Teague, Gloucester flanker and one of the heroes of the 1989 Lions tour, had a real 'Rocky' type phase, when he really bulked himself up. He would stagger away at the end of his fitness test, groaning and his face twisted in pain. Not for me, thank you very much.

Jason Leonard almost had a rifle taken to him by his fellow England squad props, Jeff Probyn and Paul Rendall. Jason, an eager young thing back in the early nineties, got a low score on a fitness test. Probyn and Rendall, not eager young things, gave him a rough ride for letting the front-row fraternity down so badly.

It's not for me. I find it almost sad that some people push themselves to the point of passing out. When I consider the career of people such as Olympic gold medallist rower Steve Redgrave I am lost in admiration. Five gold medals is a hell of an achievement, but I could not have applied myself as he did – even if I had the talent. Of course you must be fit for rugby, but speed of thought, your relationship with others, the emotion brought on by the physical battering . . . all have their part to play. I relied on my instincts to get me out of tricky situations. I always question how much you really have to do. Look at Kelly Holmes in the Sydney Olympics. She'd been injured and had only been able to do four weeks' track work beforehand and yet won a bronze medal. How much training do you actually need? How much is mind over matter?

I'm lazy and I admit it. I'd always back natural talent over application. Of course, you need to be pretty fit as well, but I don't think rules should be set in stone as to how you lead your life off the field. As long as you deliver, it doesn't matter what your lifestyle is. You might smoke twenty cigarettes a day and drink three or four bottles of wine a week, but if you can cut it on the field, then you've got my vote. Stuart Barnes was a big red-wine man the night before a match and it didn't do him much harm – apart from his shape, hence his nickname of 'the Barrel'. In my early days at

Bath I'd always meet with the lads on a Friday night for five or six pints of Guinness. We'd meet at the Grapes. Pete Blackett and Chalkie Wardle would be there along with Bath players such as Nick Maslen or Steve Knight. If you were really intent on a good drink you'd go on to Krönenburg after the black stuff.

The point is that rugby has never been my sole focus in life, far from it. It's a big part, of course, but I was never driven solely by sporting goals. My years at Bath were enjoyable because of the blokes as much as because of what we achieved together. We enjoyed each other's company and the feel-good factor was a key ingredient in our success. It was a sharp, feisty atmosphere.

Away trips were always great fun. A lively three-card brag school would always be on the go and there were a few casualties from time to time. A lot has been made recently of the England football squad being allowed to play for biggish stakes in their card schools, but I don't see the point in getting too uppity about it. Blokes are blokes. They know when the gambling is getting out of hand and the stakes rising too high.

Mind you, there was an interesting face-off once between Spurrell and a guy by the name of Michel van der Loos. For those who don't know the intricacies of three-card brag you need a lot of nerve, a fat wallet and the ability to lie with a straight face – the merest hint of emotion and you're done for. As for the rudiments of the game, it doesn't take a genius to work them out. You bet on your hand, the order of prominence starting with a single card through to a pair, a flush, a run and finishing with three of the same kind, which is known as a prial. The sequence for this

ight: Early days with my younger brother, Gary.

elow: Imogen gets an early look at the sporting world.

ALLSPORT

Above: Jayne and I just after the birth of our daughter, Imogen.

Right: A lovely family moment: Saskia gets a kiss from her dad after the 1997 Lions' tour.

REX FEATURES

COLORSPORT

COLORSPORT

Top: Chasing the ball, despite the wind resistance created by my afro, during the 1985 John Player Special Cup final against London Welsh – my first trophy in the big time.

Above: Two years later and I had become a regular in the side, and was able to help Bath to their fourth successive Cup title.

Above: Signing autographs for the Bath faithful in 1994. Although the rugby league scouts came calling many times, they never offered me anything like enough money to abandon my home, or my sport.

Right: In action for Bath during the 1996–97 European Cup against Dax, our first season as a fully professional club and a PLC.

Left: The tension and drama of our 19–18 win made this final as close to an international match as any club game I ever played. The celebrations were only just about to begin – at McDonald's!

Below: A rare moment of freedom during the European Cup final against Brive in 1998.

VANDYSTADT

Top: My England debut against Romania on 13 May 1989 couldn't have gone much better as I scored a hat-trick in our 58–3 win.

Below: Battling it out with John Jeffrey and Tony Stanger in the 1990 Grand Slam decider. That defeat helped create a win-at-all-costs mentality in future seasons.

Above: The third Grand Slam in five years is completed after beating Scotland at Twickenham in 1995 – it was a glorious period of success for England.

Below: Celebrating Rory Underwood's crucial try against France in 1991 with my long-term centre partner Will Carling. This time there was no missing the Grand Slam.

Right: Scoring a try for England against South Africa in December 1998, but Phil Larder was much more impressed with the fact that I got in some good defensive work that day.

Below: Running out onto the pitch for my last Five Nations match, against France in 1999, a game we won 21–10 thanks to the boot of Jonny Wilkinson.

COLORSPORT

Lloyds TSB

last much-treasured category is as normal, starting with three twos and running through to the ace card. However, the little quirk of the game, is that three threes is the top hand.

What had Spurrell and van der Loos drawn? The odds on it must been several hundred thousand to one. Van der Loos was sitting pretty with three aces, only for Spurrell to be sitting even prettier with a prial of threes. It got very heated, shall we say. Words were exchanged, if not punches, and the row rumbled on for months.

The biggest pot I ever saw was about £300, enough to do some damage to the back pocket but not to make you bankrupt. International gatherings in later years might see that figure double to about £600. In the early days we were sensible, knowing that the team were all in different financial situations. It was reasonably friendly, with 'best that you see me' advice given if the cards were stacked too heavily in someone's favour. That worked for the most part.

We knitted together at Bath. There was no real mystique, we just played hard in every way. We were not so outstanding as individuals as, say, the great Welsh side of the early seventies. Players such as Gareth Edwards, Barry John, Gerald Davies, JPR Williams and Phil Bennett were geniuses when measured against any rugby generation. Bath was different, a combustible mix of many elements.

A key figure for the club and for my own development was Gareth Chilcott. He was a mentor in my early days and has remained a close associate and friend ever since that first glimpse of him on the back seat of the coach on the outing to Twickenham with Dad to watch England and Wales in 1980.

'Coochie' was a loveable rogue and I really related to him. He was born on a less than salubrious side of the tracks and was a real handful as a teenager, standing as one of the Bristol City faithful on the terraces of Ashton Gate. He fought with the best of them. Like so many rugby players he was a beast on the pitch and a real softie away from it. He has time for autograph hunters for example, be it a child or a granny. He never just scribbled a name and walked on by. He was the same man whether he was talking to a politician or a West Country local.

Lord knows how many times he was sent off – at least half a dozen, I reckon. I remember his England debut against Australia in 1984. Nigel Redman, Bath lock and longstanding butt of many of my feeble wind-ups, made his debut on the same day. All I can recall of Coochie's great moment in a white shirt is of him leathering Australian scrum half Nick Farr-Jones. Everybody saw it except the referee and Coochie got away with it on that occasion. These days of videotaped evidence would have blighted his life.

He's also a sharp operator. His humble beginnings and his broad Bristol accent have not held him back. He runs several companies, is an accomplished after-dinner speaker and has even done a few seasons treading the boards in pantomime. There have been times when the Chilcott caricature – the roly-poly, fun-loving prop – has been in danger of taking him over but he's always spotted the danger in time. He's never short of a word but people make the mistake of taking his open, affable approach for naivety. That's the last thing he is, he can weigh up people in a flash. As for spotting an opening, be it in the transport business or corporate hospitality, both of which he's made a success of, he'll see a crack of opportunity and make it a chasm.

However, he was a mean so-and-so on the field and I would have hated, but hated, to have trotted out for my Saturday afternoon of so-called relaxation and seen Chilcott, Dawe and Richard Lee, both farmers, lining up against me in the front row. What a terrifying sight. Who the hell could call that relaxation? Coochie won fourteen caps between 1984 and 1989 and if he'd applied himself more to training then he'd have won many more. He was underrated as a player. His hands were unbelievable if only he'd ever got into a position to use them for passing a ball. When the game went professional, he was involved in the club as marketing manager but during the years of turmoil, 1996–98 when the club made a pig's ear of it all, Chilcott fell out of favour with the new powers-that-be.

If Barnes was the brains of the operation, then Chilcott was the brawn, the bedrock of the pack alongside his grizzled mates. Pre-match meetings used to crack me up. We'd all gather early at Dukes Hotel in Bath for toast and honey and a pep-talk with Jack Rowell, and the routine would go like this.

'Barnesie, tell us what cup games are all about,' Jack would say prior to every cup game.

'Winning, Jack,' would come the reply.

'Coochie, what are the opposition like today?'

'They are big and strong and robust,' said Coochie.

It's not a bad line the first time you hear it, but when you hear it for seven seasons in succession it begins to wear a bit thin. I could hardly contain myself every time Jack swung round to Coochie to ask him for his assessment. 'Big and strong . . .' Stifled giggles all round.

I rarely thought of leaving Bath. There were regular rumours that I might sign for rugby league, most of which had about as much substance in them as a Jack the Ripper alibi. The first tall tales from the sporting north began to circulate in the 1988–89 season, which was the year that I finally made my mark for Bath. We had won nothing the previous year, which didn't sit too well on the lofty shoulders of Jack Rowell; Stuart Barnes was captain, and pre-season training was intense.

As the season kicked off I was by then the established choice alongside Simon Halliday. We had toured the Far East in the summer and then won a tournament in Leiden, Holland, which was notable for beating Toulon in the final in one of the most brutal games I have ever played in.

Our first match back home was at Pontypool, not the easiest game on the card. They had lost only twice the previous season but we defeated them 50–9. It was not a bad afternoon at the sporting coalface. I went well, but don't take my word for it, listen to the media.

'Glittering Guscott,' purred the *Sunday Mirror*. 'Glorious Guscott,' was another alliterative effort from the *People*. The *Sunday Times* took a stab at where it all might lead: 'Bath were simply magnificent. This was the first match of the post-David Bishop era at Pontypool. However, it also may well have proved the first match of the Guscott era. It was he, more than anyone, who undermined Pontypool's morale because he simply cut their midfield to pieces.'

For once, it was not a bad effort from the *Sunday*

Times. However, even if they had an eye on the future, I still only had an eye on next week. But I was aware that rugby was well and truly falling into place and that my life was taking shape around it. It became the focus of the week as opposed to a mere Saturday distraction.

It was a good back line to be part of. Barnes orchestrated everything and he was a master at committing the opposition flanker, while Halliday would always, but always, take care of at least one centre. I made hay. The poor old wings – Tony Swift, David Trick, Barry Trevaskis and Pete Blackett – rarely got a pass as I or full back Audley Lumsden were in the clear and on our way to the try line. I scored twenty-eight tries that season. I was the new kid on the block and I ran free. We did the double that season, beating Leicester 10–6 in the cup final and winning the league. By the end of the season I had won my first cap for England and had been a surprise call-up for the British Lions.

It's only when I look back that I realise just how special that era of Bath dominance was. At the time I didn't take it for granted because the team was always looking for ways to keep one step ahead of the opposition. Jack Rowell was always challenging us to explore the full range of our abilities, and we were also ruthless about letting each other know of any individual's weaknesses. If you came through a Bath training session with ego unscathed then you could survive anything that came your way in a match.

I suppose there was an arrogance about us but not in an overbearing sense. It was more a supreme feel-good factor at work. I remember driving to the ground on a Saturday morning feeling totally at ease with life. Any top sportsman will tell you the same: it's as if you're in your own world of make-believe, it's all coming true and nothing can pierce the bubble. I'd arrive at the Recreation Ground or Dukes Hotel and there would be seven or eight other guys arriving at the same time, all with the same vibes. It was a powerful feeling.

It would have taken a huge amount for me to give up such a place, such a setting and such a burgeoning success story. Not that the rugby league boys didn't try – or, at least, kick-start the rumour machine. If I had a hundred pounds for every story of my going north, then I could have retired rich a long time ago.

Hull Kingston Rovers was to be my first supposed relocation. I hadn't even played for England at this stage but Hull KR, apparently, were going to make me the richest man on planet rugby. It was all nonsense. I had no idea at first what people were talking about when they asked me, players and journalists alike. And then two days later Hull KR actually did phone.

The whole sport seemed to work as a rumour mill. Someone – either a club in need of publicity or a journalist in need of a headline – would set the hare running. The invention became a half-truth, others followed up the story and suddenly I was selling out to rugby league. The supposed bidder got acres of publicity and I or other targeted players got hours of grief from the media. It's called a PR machine – and once it clicked into gear, it was almost impossible to stop.

Wigan courted me several times. They used to send me a tape every season of their Challenge Cup victories, telling me that this was what I was missing. I'd also have been missing tours to Australia, South Africa, New Zealand and several other exotic locations round the world if I'd ever taken the rugby league shilling. Wigan's Maurice Lindsay, however, was a good bloke – persistent and credible.

I was with the Lions in Australia when the rumours started with a vengeance, suggesting that I was on the brink of signing for St Helens. At one point on the Lions tour I was sharing a room with Donal Lenihan, Irish lock and manager of the 2001 British Lions tour to Australia. The phone rang in the hotel room and Donal picked it up.

'Jerry, it's Ellery Hanley for you,' said Donal. Ellery, Wigan and Great Britain captain, was an icon of rugby league.

'Piss off, Donal,' I said. 'If you think I'm falling for that pathetic wind-up then you're dafter than I thought.'

The phone was passed over.

'Hello, Jeremy, it's Ellery Hanley here from Wigan. Please don't sign for St Helens. They are our deadly rivals I know, but I can assure you that Wigan have far more to offer.'

Ellery was playing in Australia and the penny finally dropped that it wasn't a joke. I thanked him and told him that the timing wasn't right and that I had a bit of business to attend to out in Australia.

There were some serious offers made and there was a point at which I would have been tempted. Mind you, it would have taken a million-pound deal, that was the figure I had in mind. I was very rooted in Bath and still am. I didn't want to up sticks just for sport and there would have to have been a serious incentive to get me to move. My family is there and always has been, my two best mates Chalkie Wardle and Pete Blackett offered me a lively social outlet and I didn't know how I'd fare in Wigan, Manchester, Leeds or Bradford. Perhaps if someone had taken the trouble to give me a guided tour, shown me properties that I would have been able to afford, then they might have had a chance. As it was it was often no more than a phone call. They didn't give it the hard sell.

Balmain in Sydney did actually make an offer but it was while I was out in Wollongong. I was barely making an impression there let alone in top-flight union back home with Bath. A few years later, after I was established with Bath and England, I was called by Manly-Warringah, one of the top rugby league outfits in the world. Graham Lowe was their coach at the time and he wooed me with talk about the hard, fast surfaces and how my talent would flourish in such conditions. I said I'd think about it and so did they.

Even then I was only vaguely tempted and only because I fancied the idea of a few years in Sydney. Perhaps I was being cowardly about change but I was happy with my lot even though I wasn't earning much at the time. But it just didn't feel right. I didn't want to take the risk of going into a new sport and perhaps not doing that well, when I felt I had a good future before me in union.

The genuine offers came at regular intervals from Widnes, Wigan, Salford – the usual suspects. Dougie Laughton had pulled off a major coup in snatching Jonathan Davies and bringing him to Widnes and Doug went for the double whammy with me. Or I think he did. He did phone, or his intermediary did, and suggested a meet. You could tell they meant business by the proposed location: a lay-by outside Bath. Secretive, yes; lavish and impressive, no. Still, I turned up, which is more than anyone else did. I waited twenty minutes and then went home. I never did find out if Doug had a million to offer.

The two genuine offers came from St Helens and Bradford Northern. Joe Pickavance, the St Helens chairman, contacted me and suggested that we meet. In the early nineties Bath were up north to play Liverpool-St Helens in a league match. After the game, I went my own way home. Or so everyone thought. As the lads piled on to the team bus, I headed instead to Pickavance's home. Alex Murphy, that man of a loud voice and no little repute on the coaching field, was also there.

We sat and talked and succeeded only in skirting round the subject. Money was never mentioned. Why the hell I didn't just blurt out that I wanted a million I don't know; I was so naïve in those days. If I had known then what I know now I'd at least have had some fun. They made all the right noises – suited to league, Great Britain beckoned etc – but they didn't nail their colours to the mast.

The next time we met they did. On this occasion we were on my territory, the Compass Inn at Tormarton, close to the M4 Bath turn-off. Pickavance and Murphy had the club treasurer with them this time and at last they meant business: £150,000 for a four-year deal. It was far more than I was getting as a bricklayer, but they were asking far more for their money and it was not enough. I wasn't going to give away Bath for that. They actually handed over a pen, expecting me to sign there and then. They had another think coming. Thanks but no thanks.

Bradford Northern were the most polished operators when it came to trying to tempt me across the great divide and they were persistent, contacting me at least once a year between 1988 and 1994. Their chairman was Chris Caisley, who was a good operator. If only he knew how close he came to signing me. In the early nineties I was first wooed by phone and then met with him and Peter Fox, the Bradford coach, after one of our divisional matches. The pair of them praised my sidestep and swerve, saying that it was wasted in rugby union because I rarely got the ball. They had a point there.

We met again, this time at a Heathrow hotel, and this time it was serious. They offered me £300,000 for a four-year deal. I pushed harder, pointing out that sport was a precarious business and that I needed some security, a career perhaps, because I'd have to give up my position with British Gas to move to Bradford. Caisley asked what line of work I was thinking about. Marketing and PR seemed to be the catch-all phrase of the time so that's what I went for.

Bradford were back within a week with a top-up offer of £27,000 a year with a local PR firm. Unlike Widnes and so many of the others they had put flesh on the bones and they were talking money. Now I would have to make a real decision. It was not a bit of fun any more, sparring to see how far each other was prepared to go. I was pulled up short and reverted to the usual tactics, saying that I would have to think it over. Caisley phoned again on the 1993 Lions tour and upped the ante once again, adding £25,000 to the signing-on fee. It was a substantial amount of money, although not as much as the papers claimed.

'Guscott turns down a million,' shouted the head-lines. A Channel 4 comedy show of the time called *Drop the Dead Donkey* did a short sketch about it: Guscott turns down a million. He's a bright bloke, isn't he?

In fact, I would have gone for a million. As it was, good offer though it was in their terms, it was not enough for me to go North with all that that entailed – and have my head torn off by those league players into the bargain. I'm told that Will Carling claimed that he was once offered a million to sign. In the first place, I find it staggering that he was, given what he had to offer. And secondly, what the hell was he doing turning it down?

The big offer never did come and by 1995 the whispers were already beginning to sound that union might be awarded professional status. That was enough for me.

chapter six

the professionals

R ugby union finally went professional in August 1995. Good old union. No gradual build-up to the big moment, with time to get the groundwork done so that everyone could get proper structures in place. No, it was the Big Bang. The fall-out was pretty devastating, with casualties everywhere, and Bath was hit as hard as anyone.

The year before, 1994, had been a significant year. Barnes retired and Jack Rowell moved on to England, so we began the 1994–95 season without two of our leading lights. Another one, me, was operating on pretty low wattage. It had not been a great twelve months for me. I'd come back from the 1993 Lions tour with a niggling back and hip strain. I wasn't sure what had caused it. I had wrenched a muscle in the groin area just before the second Test in Wellington but thought of it as a routine injury. Think again.

By the time the summer was drawing to a close I was back in training of sorts and put the ache down to the fact that I'd been carrying my two-year-old daughter Imogen around a good deal. The Bath physio Julie

Bardner didn't think it was that serious, although she did warn me that the groin area was complicated and prone to playing up. She was right there. I managed the first three games of the season and that was it.

Julie continued treating me with ultrasonics and massage. One day she mentioned the phrase 'Gilmore's Groin', not a term I was familiar with. By the time I got back on to the playing field, against West Hartlepool in October 1994, I was sick to the back teeth with the phrase. In November I went to see Harley Street specialist Gerry Gilmore who had identified the complaint, which was common to sportsmen. He'd operated on a few million pounds' worth of footballers in his time.

I visited him just as England were taking on the All Blacks, the first international I had missed in four years. Nice bloke Gilmore, although he did stick his fingers up my scrotum during our first meeting, which sent me up to the ceiling.

It was to be a long, long road. Gilmore didn't want to operate straight away, his advice was to aggravate the problem first. I spent two weeks at Lilleshall. Liverpool footballer Jan Molby was there and he gave me the low-down on all the Anfield dramas. Just as well, for the routine was deadly dull: breakfast, exercise, tea, biscuits, more exercise, more tea and more biscuits.

Time slipped by but there were no miracle cures on offer, no guarantees that an operation would do the trick. Finally, in March, with the Five Nations in full swing, I went into hospital in London for an operation.

The rehabilitation period was six weeks. I was walking again after a week and, on the surface, was making some progress, but deep down I knew things were not right. I went to La Manga in Spain to finish off some filming for *Body Heat*, the TV show I co-presented with Mike Smith and athlete Sally Gunnell. Rex Hazeldine, the RFU's fitness advisor, was there as consultant for the programme and we did some light training together. But light was the operative word.

England's summer tour to South Africa was looming but I wasn't going to make it. Rowell had just been brought into the England set-up to succeed Geoff Cooke, with Dick Best carrying on as manager. I told Bestie that it looked bleak and it might be best if I backed out and tried to get fit for the following season. The outcome was that I did pull out, Leicester's Stuart Potter taking my place. Seven caps went begging and one cup final appearance against Leicester that Bath won 21–9. They won the Courage League too, by six clear points from Leicester. It was the fourth year in succession that Bath had taken the title.

It didn't mean all that much to me. I don't believe in hanging out with the boys just for the sake of it. They did well in my absence but absence it was.

However, the club did push the boat out for the players. After years of penny-pinching over expenses, they finally dug deep and paid for a ten-day trip to Barbados for players, wives and girlfriends. It was there that things did start to wear me down. It was probably seeing the players go through their paces for the new season, while I had no goals, no dates and no real hope of a comeback. It was a big season, too, with the World Cup in South Africa at the end of it.

The season began without me and I was not best pleased. I was frustrated and moody and wondered if I'd ever play again. I was liaising with Nigel Henderson, the RFU's honorary consultant surgeon, among others. Nigel is a lovely guy but I was getting impatient. Along with Rex Hazeldine we worked on various programmes of recovery. It was slow and uncertain and I was feeling frustrated.

However, time was to be the healer and my groin did eventually settle down. My comeback was against West Hartlepool in October 1994. It is not the most glamorous place on the planet but it felt good to me.

The 1994–95 season saw Bath finish runners-up to Leicester by four points, the first time for four years that we'd not won the title. The campaign ended on a really low note when we lost 18–13 at home to Sale. Nevertheless, there was some silverware in the cabinet because we beat Wasps 36–16 to win the Pilkington Cup. Jon Hall, who was the captain that year, was forced to cry off with injury two days before the final, but we made him go up the steps to accept the trophy. It was the least that he deserved.

Jon was to feature strongly in the Bath story over the next eighteen months as the game and the club struggled to get to grips with professionalism. Bath, so self-confident and dominant in the amateur era, were suddenly vulnerable. Jon was to have a variety of roles: from chairman of selectors to coach to director of rugby. There were many arguments and departures. A vote was held to decide whether Jon or Richard Hill should coach the club. Jon was the winner and Richard left to join Gloucester. Coochie had a stint as commercial manager but became tired of the political infighting, the bitching and confusion, and eventually chucked it in. It was not a good period, although we somehow won the double in 1996. Little did we know that we were in decline and they were to be the last domestic honours that we won. Professionalism was to level the playing field. Other clubs were to buy what Bath had spent years grooming.

As ever I was fairly self-centred. If I was playing well then I wasn't too bothered about what was going on around me. And I did play well up to the 1997 Lions tour to South Africa.

First, I needed to get my contract with Bath sorted out. I didn't get many offers to go elsewhere. In fact, I got only one – from Bristol. And I sure as hell wasn't going there. Perhaps people assumed that I'd never up sticks from Bath, or that I was too expensive. That wasn't the case, I wasn't the worst paid player at Bath but nor was I the best.

I looked after myself in these matters. Mind you, it was a lively old market. There was a moratorium on professionalism in England during the 1995–96 season. Good old RFU. Turn the clock back. First we're professional and then we're not professional. Sir John Hall came in at Newcastle in September 1995 and other big spenders followed suit: Nigel Wray at Saracens, Ashley Levett at Richmond in February 1996, Chris Wright at Wasps. At Bath, the waiting game went on. And on.

We were all shooting in the dark. In the early months there was talk of £20–30,000 contracts and by mid-season those figures had escalated wildly. Bath did not lose too many players. The biggest name to go was Ben Clarke, who is a good friend of mine. Generally, the team didn't confide that much in each other but I remember Ben and I chatting the whole professional thing through at one point. The Kerry Packer project, the rebel circus that was going to sign up players from all over the world to break away and play international rugby, had been in the air through the summer of 1995. It was a few months later that Ben asked: 'What do you think you'd be worth on the market, Jerry? Two hundred thousand pounds?'

'Not sure, Ben,' I said in my naïve way. 'If you did that you'd cut yourself off from England, your club, all your commercial rights. You've got to be sure about what you're doing.'

On and on I droned. Shortly afterwards we were all together after an England match in a room set aside for players and partners. There was a band playing and we all struck up: 'If I were a rich man, la-di-da-di-da . . .' and so on. I looked across at Ben and he had a twinkle in his eye. The next week he'd signed for Richmond. It was a brave move by Ben. He signed a seven-year deal in May 1996 for a reputed £200,000 a year but he gave up his England career for that because he dropped down into the Second Division.

Bath eventually got their act together, which was just as well. Richmond had come after Mike Catt as well and if he'd gone then I would have had real problems staying with Bath because it seemed to me that Mike was central to what we might achieve over the next few seasons.

He stayed and I signed. Andrew Brownsword, a Bath-based businessman came on board in July 1996 and Bath lost only a few players apart from Ben: full back Audley Lumsden to Gloucester, lock Andy Reed to Wasps, and prop Darren Crompton to Richmond.

In March 1996 the club became a PLC, with 806 voting in favour and only six against at an emergency

general meeting. Brownsword's arrival at least gave
Bath some financial security, which was just as well
because we were rocky on so many other fronts.

I don't blame any one individual for the upheaval.
Hallie was thrown in at the deep end with no clear
job description. Was he coach? Was he manager? Was
he director of rugby? Brian Ashton became coach,
Tony Swift was appointed non-executive chairman,
and then, in January 1997, chief executive. It was a
fast-changing scene and I kept out of it.

Once the game went professional I made a conscious
decision to treat the club as my place of work, to clock
on and clock off. I would never have dreamt of hanging
around the building site after a day's bricklaying. It was
to be the same with rugby, I did my training and left.

There were hiccups, that's for sure. There were new
faces around and new ways of doing business. There
was also tension, even given my restricted presence
at the club. One of Brownsword's men, Ed Goodall,
was brought in to oversee the running of the club. He
wasn't a rugby man but I had no argument with that.
Rugby had become a business so there was as much of
an onus on the sport to merge with the business world
as the other way round.

However, I wasn't quite so evenhanded when Goodall
approached me in the clubhouse one evening and
asked me not to smoke.

'I'm surprised to see you smoking,' said Goodall. 'I'd
rather you wouldn't.'

'I beg your pardon,' I said. 'What did you say? This
is me and this is what I do.'

There were a few words and that was that. He carried
on with his life and I carried on with mine – the

occasional cigarette included. Our paths didn't cross too often after that.

I had relationships, of course. Jon Hall was a good friend but in my business dealings with him, it was business. I'm good at divorcing the two things. My contract was sorted out in a businesslike fashion and I left Jon to get on with the struggle of running the club. He was welcome to it and was learning as he went along. He wasn't given enough recognition for managing to hang on to the number of players that he did. A lot of the boys had offers from elsewhere but stuck with Bath even though the Brownsword money was not there until very late in the day. True, we didn't go wild in the transfer market ourselves for the 1996–97 season but there were two additions to the back row when former Wales and Salford rugby league flanker Richard Webster signed, along with the American Eagles captain Dan Lyle. In addition, lock Brian Cusack came over from Ireland along with another flanker, Bridgend's Nathan Thomas, and Argentinian hooker Federico Mendez arrived in October.

There were also two other new faces: Jason Robinson and Henry Paul, who signed on short-term contracts from rugby league. The contact with Jason and Henry had come from when Bath played Wigan in two cross-code games the previous May. I'd missed both games, it just wasn't my scene. I didn't consider them to be proper games of rugby and so I opted out. I had no regrets – rugby is not a pantomime. These were strange times in rugby with so many things changing so quickly.

The season was a mixed one. There were some high spots, an 87–15 victory over Swansea being one of them. I didn't play in that game but the boys certainly played some rugby that night. But the old Bath aura of dominance had faded and tension built as the season spluttered along. I did have a word with Hallie from time to time and pointed out that there were a few cliques building that he needed to sort out.

There was another cloud on the horizon. In early December 1996 we played Harlequins at the Recreation Ground and won 35–20 after trailing 17–3. I scored two tries against my old mate Will Carling. It was a good game and a good night afterwards. A few of the girls – Jayne, Jon's partner Kirsty and Ben Clarke's Michelle – were having their own weekend away in New York doing a spot of shopping and sightseeing. While the girls are away . . .

Yes, we had a few drinks. It started in the Teachers Stand in one of the sponsor's bars and then carried on to the Beehive pub in town. We were drinking this luminous-looking cider. Evil stuff. From there we went to a club called PJ Peppers. By this time I was wasted and was standing in the corner, leaning against the wall and trying to get my bearings. The next thing I knew someone told me that Jon Hall was in trouble and that he was in tears. The crying bit was not as unusual as it might sound. Jon is an emotional guy and does get weepy from time to time.

But then I was told that he was in bother with a woman. That brought me round – it didn't sound like Jon. I finally found him, and he told me that he'd been accused of messing about with some girl. It was near closing time and I went outside to freshen up, but the night air hit me and I was all over the place again.

The club was set above street level and there was a police car parked at the foot of the steps leading to the entrance. It was too tempting, particularly in my state. I ran down the steps, across the top of the police car and off down the street, shouting back at one of the policemen:

'Catch me if you can. I'm Jeremy Guscott and I'm as fast as lightning.'

I headed off down Milsom Street. I had no idea what possessed me to do it. I got halfway down the street before I realised what a silly prat I'd been. I turned and came back to try and retrieve the situation. I approached the young policeman.

'I can't apologise enough,' I said. 'I don't know what came over me. Please accept my apology.'

Thank goodness, he did. I don't know exactly what happened after that because I was swept up with a few others and headed off to a party. The next day I rang Jon and told him that I would help him whatever happened. The girls were due back on that Monday and I headed off to an England training session before Jayne arrived home.

I was sharing a room with Ben Clarke when the news came through that the story had hit the *Bath Chronicle*. Jon had been accused of assaulting a twenty-three-year-old woman. I was mentioned as being there and that was enough for Jayne, she wanted to know what was going on. I made my excuses with England and headed home. The kids were in a Christmas show so we had to sit through that first. The air between us was frosty and Jayne wasn't too impressed with my story, innocent though I was.

The club at this time was in upheaval. Relations

between Jon and coach Brian Ashton had come to a head over that Christmas period and Brian had officially taken a week's leave just before Christmas. Results hadn't been that bad although we had dropped a couple of league matches, losing 28–25 at Leicester after having the winning of it, and then slipping to a 40–36 home defeat to Wasps the week after.

However, we did score 76 against Bristol in late October, with yours truly scoring a couple of tries. But in the big matches we came up short and lost in the quarter-final of the Heineken Cup at Cardiff 22–19. That match really showed up the tension between Jon Hall and Brian Ashton, who disagreed over selection. Jason Robinson was fielded instead of Jon Callard and, needless to say, we missed kicks at goal during that match. The final straw was the home defeat by Leicester 39–28 in the sixth round of the Cup. It was our heaviest defeat in a decade.

Three days later Jon was fired. When his case finally came to Bristol Crown Court in September 1997, he was found not guilty and cleared of a charge of indecent assault. After a two-day hearing the jury took only forty minutes to reach their verdict. But by that time Jon had long since left Bath. He had been sacked on 11 February 1997 and charged with indecent assault on 19 February. Not the greatest eight days of his life.

Andy Robinson and Clive Woodward were to form the new coaching team, with Tony Swift confirmed as chief executive and, for the first time, there seemed to be a clearer chain of command. It paid off for we eventually ended up second in the league that season behind Wasps. We finished at a gallop, smashing

Leicester 47–9 at home, then putting 84 points on Sale and 71 on Gloucester. What might have been.

Jon Hall had taken us to a double the season before, yet was associated with failure. It was harsh. He'd spent fourteen years at the club, and his father before him. Jon made 276 appearances for the team and yet was to become persona non grata. It's an unforgiving world.

It was strange, given that I was close to Jon, that the upheavals didn't affect my own game. In fact, I was playing as well as ever leading up to the Lions tour to South Africa in 1997 and I felt a freedom in my game that I hadn't experienced for several years. That was my best year in club rugby. I just played how I felt. You get fed an awful lot of stuff by coaches and much of it just swamps you. I don't listen to most of it.

Perhaps my form was due to the switch to professionalism. It suited me, I could do my stuff and move on. The criticism that I'm selfish is true as regards my rugby – I do what I think I need to do and that's it. All the behind-the-scenes stuff with Brian and Jon left me cold and I didn't get involved, even though I know both of them well. The rest of the team didn't confide too much in me either, perhaps because they thought I was close to Jon. But Jon didn't share his thoughts with me either. That's just the way we are. Business is one thing, friendship another.

Considering that I was in good form that season, it was ironic that I didn't get a look-in with Jack Rowell's England. Jack opted for Carling alongside Phil de Glanville, whom he'd made captain. But more of that later.

I was injured when I came back from the 1997 Lions tour. Just as well as I needed the rest. I had broken my arm just before the end of the tour, which seemed straightforward enough. But then came real disaster when I ruptured a disc in my back. Since my groin problem in 1993–94 I'd become very twitchy about any injury in that lower back area.

I had an operation in late October 1997 and was told it would take six weeks' rehabilitation. I was concerned about the surgery because the area in question was very close to the spinal cord. I took a lot of soundings as to what I should do.

'I'm ninety-nine per cent certain that you'll be able to play rugby again,' said the surgeon who eventually operated.

Thanks very much. What about that one per cent, I thought. The operation was successful but it wasn't the easiest convalescence. When I came out of hospital I couldn't walk. We were moving house and there I was, a complete invalid. That went down well at home.

I worked my way back to fitness gradually, doing a lot of physiotherapy with a specialist in Bristol. The club was not having the happiest of times. Clive Woodward took up the England job in September 1997, Jon Callard coming into work alongside Andy Robinson on the coaching front at Bath. There were some bad performances in the league, notably a 50–23 hammering at Saracens. We scraped a third place finish on points difference by the season's end, behind Newcastle and Saracens. We lost nine league games in all though, a far cry from the glory days. Still, we edged out the Tigers on points difference, so there.

There were two major talking points of the season – one wonderful, the other not so. I was almost back to fitness in early January and Bath was drawn against

London Scottish in the Tetley's Bitter Cup. I was watching the game and nothing that untoward seemed to have happened. There was a bit of a fuss at one point during the match but that was nothing unusual. It was only afterwards that it all hit the fan.

On the Monday, London Scottish called a press conference and revealed the damage done to the ear lobe of their flanker Simon Fenn. It had been bitten and there was a chunk missing. It was dramatic stuff. We all do things in frustration, but it's a low act to bite someone's ear, as low as you can get. Andy Robinson was away that day at a Heineken Cup media gathering in Bordeaux, where we were to play the Heineken Cup final a few weeks later against Brive. Talk about triumph and disaster going hand in hand.

It was a difficult issue. London Scottish were demanding a full inquiry. They cited our entire front row: Victor Ubogu, Federico Mendez and Kevin Yates. Quite how they arrived at three blokes biting one ear lobe I don't know. The incident created a huge amount of friction at the club. There was a two-day hearing at Twickenham. But there was no evidence – no TV footage, no photographs. The whole thing got out of control.

Nobody came forward. I'm not surprised because they would have been banned for life. There were rumours and there was a split. I wasn't at the club that often as I was still working my way back to fitness but Adedayo Adebayo kept me briefed. But he, too, was not sure of the truth. I don't think anyone was.

In the end it all came down on Kevin's shoulders. To this day he denies it and that's good enough for me. How the hell the RFU tribunal found him guilty

I don't know. He was banned for six months and ran up costs of over £50,000. No wonder he eventually decided to give it all up as a bad job and head down to New Zealand. He's done well there in the Super 12 with the Wellington Hurricanes, one of the few overseas players to appear in the competition. When the storm broke I gave him some advice about dealing with the media. Boy, did he need the advice. It was a huge story and he was pursued for weeks. I told him to trust no one and not to talk to anyone if he didn't want to.

From the low to the high in one swoop. Two weeks later we were in the Heineken Cup final against Brive. It was to be one of the best club weekends in my career. It was touch and go as to whether I'd make it at all. I'd planned to warm up with a comeback game against Newcastle, but the match was called off at the last minute. Robbo had told me that he wanted me to play in the final so that was it. I had to get myself ready. I'd had a few run-outs so didn't feel too bad about it. The lads had done well to get to the final given that the season hadn't gone too well in general. We'd played Brive in our group and had mixed fortunes, winning 27–25 at home and losing 29–12 in France.

In the quarter-final we beat Cardiff 32–21 and then saw off Pau 20–14 in the semi-final. Brive had come through by the narrowest possible margin, a last-gasp penalty from Christophe Lamaison which enabled them to draw 22–22 with Stade Toulousain after extra time in their semi-final. Brive went through by virtue of having scored two tries to one.

Brive, champions the year before when they'd demolished Leicester 28–9, had a formidable side.

Lamaison was paired with David Venditti in the centre, Alain Penaud was full back, Lisandro Arbizu was outside Philippe Carbonneau at scrum half, with the Carrat brothers Sebastien and Jerome flying down the wings. The pack was a scary-looking act too.

We'd been knocked out of the Tetley's Cup by Richmond the week before 29–17 after extra time. It was not the best preparation but we were in good heart. We stayed outside Bordeaux and my lasting memory is of the drive to the stadium, Parc Lescure, on the morning of the match. It was how I imagine the pre-match atmosphere of big football matches to be, although there was no nastiness in the air. Far from it, it was one big party.

I've played a few international games in my time but nothing prepared me for the scenes that day. There were flags flying and klaxons sounding everywhere. The whole city seemed to have been taken over by both sets of supporters. It was fantastic.

We must have had more religious believers in our side than they did that day. That's the only way to explain our win: God was on our side. We trailed from the second minute to the eightieth but somehow came through to win 19–18, Jon Callard scoring all the points. The game itself was not a great exhibition of flowing rugby but it was hard and tense, quite the equal of any international game I've played in.

There are only a couple of memories of the game itself. The goal-line stand by our scrum in the second half was awesome. Seven times Brive went for the pushover; seven times the boys held on. That would have been Victor Ubogu's worst nightmare. After the second one he'd have come up asking how many more.

He, 'Ronnie' Regan and Dave Hilton were incredible in that front row.

Callard kicked our last goal in the last minute to sneak us in front and even then the drama was not over. Brive came back at us and were awarded a penalty about thirty-five metres out, halfway to the touchline. It was not that difficult a kick, certainly not so for someone of Lamaison's calibre. It dropped just under the posts, straight into the arms of Andy Nicol. And straight out again. If looks could kill. A scrum under our posts, five metres from the line. All they had to do was hook the ball back, fire it out to Arbizu who would drop kick it over the posts. A blind, one-legged donkey could have kicked it over from there.

Down went the scrum, back went the ball, Arbizu swung his leg – and the blind, one-legged donkey missed. Still it wasn't over. There was then a mad, heart-stopping chase to touch down the bobbing ball and Richard Webster got there by inches. Final whistle. Cue pandemonium.

We all ran to the tunnel and embraced each other, shouting congratulations. None of us could believe that we'd nicked it in such dramatic fashion. This called for celebration of the highest order. We dined in style at McDonald's. There we were in the gastronomic heartland of France and we all had Big Macs.

There was no function, no dinner organised for that evening, but it was a great night. We hit the champagne in the dressing-room and then headed into Bordeaux. The place was jumping. There were fans in the street, in the bars and in the cafés. I remember leaving a bar to get some food and passing Phil de Glanville and Ieuan Evans being carried out as

I came back in. Good stuff. I'd barely touched the ball all afternoon yet I can say that it was one of the best rugby experiences of my life.

It was to be the high spot of Bath's performances during those two years. The club was reinventing itself and so was I. The 1998–99 season was not a good one. We finished sixth in the league and were knocked out of the Tetley's Bitter Cup in the fourth round at Newcastle. There were comings and goings in the background, with Tony Swift stepping down as chief executive. He backed away altogether by Christmas. I don't think Swifty was best suited to all the politics of the new game.

Nigel 'Ollie' Redman ended a sixteen-year associ-ation with the club when he left to take up a coaching post with Richmond, and Ben Clarke returned after the Richmond affair ended in tears when the club owner, Ashley Levett, pulled out. English First Division Rugby then put the boot in by refusing a stay of execution in winding up the club.

It was good to see Ben back at the Rec, he was an old friend and was to become Bath captain during the 2000–01 season, although my time there was limited. I retired from international rugby during the 1999 World Cup and I decided to rein back on my involve-ment with Bath for the next season. I reached an agreement initially with Andy Robinson to that effect. He then took over as coach with England, with Jon Callard filling the director of rugby role at Bath. The arrangement was fine by Jon. I wanted to concentrate on my commercial work and testimonial and only turned out when the club was in real need of my services.

Bath took time to get its act together in the professional era. I think most clubs did in their different ways. There's no doubt that Bath was in the spotlight more than most because the club had been so successful in the amateur era. Leicester have had the whip hand in the last few years but that's because they already had a decent commercial operation in place and have built on that. Saracens? They came at it with a big bang and have a powerful PR machine that tells the world how successful they are. But how many trophies have they lifted for all that investment? And how many have Northampton, for that matter? A Heineken Cup, as did Bath. It's a much tougher world in the professional era. The margins are that much finer.

I never captained Bath for a season. Part of me would love to have done it but I know what I'm like, I have outside distractions. I might also be too sharp or outspoken for some people's tastes. I'm not good at giving of myself although I've mellowed in later years. In the early days I was selfish, less so as I got older although I wasn't at the club as much for various reasons.

Too much responsibility rested on the captain's shoulders until recently. Things got better at Bath when we set up a players' committee to liaise with the club but I still think that the business side of Bath needs someone with a rugby background to be in there really driving it. Perhaps Phil de Glanville might like to take it on now that he's about to retire.

It's not for me, however. Bath has been good to me but it's time to move on.

lights, camera . . . action!

The rugby was great – but it wasn't paying the bills during the early years. I had always had to work in one way or another since the day I left school: tree-felling, bricklaying, driving a bus for Badgerline and so on.

But the attraction of being a bus driver somehow wore off. At the back of my mind I felt that rugby might eventually look after me in some form or other, but at that time the game was not professional – and the Bath expenses system did not exactly have me rushing to set up an offshore account.

My first break did come through rugby, however. Dave Robson, who was coaching alongside Jack Rowell at Bath, knew John Day, who was deputy chairman of British Gas South-western, and through that contact I got an interview for a job in public relations with the company.

Bill Edwards was public relations manager and I duly joined him in January 1990 as a PR assistant. It was goodbye to the bricklayer's hard-hat and roll-ups and hello to the world of suits. I was a glorified office boy in those early days, taking telephone messages and processing invoices. It was fine. Not mind-blowing but then my mind wasn't too bothered about blowing in those days. The post gave me scope for training, doing interviews, golf days and the like. It was a loose arrangement and I like loose.

There were several people at British Gas who reckoned I'd be gone within six months. There were also several people at Bath Rugby Club who reckoned that I'd be gone within six months. And there were times when I was one of then.

Christine Foster, who was a work colleague, used to ask me the same question every other week. 'When are you leaving us all behind, then, Jerry?' she would say. 'Three months' time? Six months?'

Gradually, though, I saw the possibilities. I began to realise that there was something I could offer the company. I suppose I began to grow up.

I did different types of work within British Gas, eventually moving into the sales and external public relations side, working under Trevor Cooper. I was given a grand title – marketing co-ordinator (housing promotions) – and various responsibilities. My role was to promote British Gas with housing developers and to help sell the company products into various housing projects in the south-west. It wasn't a hard sell as such, but it was certainly more stimulating than pushing a few invoices round a tray and certainly less taxing than knocking up cement in the freezing cold.

I learnt to interact with a variety of people, from salesmen to chief executives. My mouth was finally getting me into positive situations rather than into trouble.

I worked for British Gas for six years rather than six months, only parting company with them when rugby became fully professional in the mid-nineties. Other opportunities had come my way during that time. There was an early appearance on the fashion cat-walk, which was set up by local businessman Malcolm Pearce, who was a great benefactor of Bath Rugby Club and is now owner of Bristol Rugby Club. He did it to help me out and it did. It also spawned a hundred piss-takes from the lads at the club and gave the impression that I was mincing along the cat-walk every other week. As if.

As my England career got under way and my name found its way into newspapers and television I began to gain what I suppose could be called celebrity status. This led to offers of various kinds of commercial work, a steady drip at first rather than a flood, I have to say. Fairly early on I was paid £300 for opening a showroom in Bristol. At the time I couldn't believe that you could make so much money for one hour's work.

Then came the agent. Some of the boys were to eventually end up with shifty-looking types looking to cut deals. But, in 1991, I signed with Maria Pedro, who was a different act altogether. We were introduced by David Gay, the former Bath and England number eight, and my contract with her consisted of a handshake – long contracts are not my thing.

My portfolio grew. There were deals with Rover and a modelling contract with Littlewoods, which involved an eight-day shoot in Miami. Tough or what? As my celebrity status grew so the offers increased. My name began to appear on newspaper columns at one time or another in the *Mirror*, the *Observer* and the *Express*.

But I had to balance it with British Gas, with rugby and with my family. Work is a means to an end for me, enjoyable and rewarding, but only a part of my life. I don't want to be dominated by it, no matter what the returns.

I did more and more glossy magazine pieces, each interviewer traipsing down to Bath in search of the real Jeremy Guscott, and then got my first television break in 1992. It was an eleven-part series for HTV called *Let's Go* and was basically a leisure and travel show, which I co-presented with Jill Impey, one of the HTV weather girls. I had no experience, no training and I found it really tough. There were many times when I was in front of the camera, with the lights on full beam, wondering what the hell I was doing there.

But it was exciting, although scary at times – far more so than running out at Twickenham in front of seventy-five thousand people. You become comfortable with a game that you've played since the age of seven, you know what to expect. Of course, there are tough and tense occasions, but you know that you've got the ability to cope. With television I had little idea as to whether I could handle it. That's why I enjoyed it so much and that's why I did it.

I graduated from *Let's Go* to *Body Heat*, a Carlton TV production which was essentially a competitive mix of sport and outward-bound-type activities. I co-presented the programme with Mike Smith and Sally Gunnell. Sally and I brought our own bits of sporting expertise to the show and Mike brought his broadcasting professionalism. We did three series in all, with seven shows for each series. I learnt so much from Mike and all the other people involved on the project. The first rule is to do your homework. Television looks easy from the comfort of your armchair at home – but that's because the people on the screen are professional.

Mike researched everything properly and rehearsed it well. I was working to a script and occasionally I would stumble, not be able to get my tongue round phrases or words. The trick is not to be afraid to divert from the script, to ad-lib as you go along. I do it naturally on a rugby field when a move breaks down but it took me a bit more time to learn how to do it in front of a camera.

There was one bit of television I did steer clear of, and that was the fly-on-the-wall documentary on Bath Rugby Club. Maria advised me that I could only come out of it worse than when I went in and she was right. Bath wing Jon Sleightholme has constantly been the butt of jokes about being a fashion icon ever since he was seen asking whether shirts should be worn in or out that summer. It was a good piece of television but it was not good PR for Bath. I stayed in the background.

I took most of the offers that came my way and they were nearly all good projects, different and challenging. During the amateur era they were a legitimate way of earning money on the back of rugby fame. Some guys did make more out of it than others, myself included, but my conscience didn't keep me awake at night. I don't go touting for business, claiming that I'm the only rugby player worth considering. It's the companies' money and they set the ground rules.

As rugby moved towards professionalism, the England squad was allowed to set up a fund for off-field commercial earnings. This all went into a pool which was to be shared out among the squad, depending on the number of games played, training sessions attended and so forth. It was called Playervision. There was another deal doing the rounds with a company that was fronted by former England fast bowler Bob Willis. I didn't sign up to this short-lived arrangement, preferring to do my own thing. However, I did put pen to paper with Playervision and the operating company, Parallel Media. It hardly yielded a crock of riches, no more than £5,000 or so, but it was a step in the right direction, a nudge to the administrators that they had to get their act together and recognise the needs of the players who were giving up so much time for their sport, a sport that was bringing in millions of pounds. In 1995 they did the decent thing and made the game professional.

By then I was getting more breaks in television. I did a couple of series of *Top Score*, a radical, imaginative attempt to get kids interested in opera. It was a great initiative and I was right behind the concept. Why Jeremy Guscott? Good question, and one that I asked when the proposal came through. The idea was that I would front the programme – essentially a beginner's guide to opera – from the same set that the BBC used for *Grandstand*. I was there to give it a light touch and take away some of the mystery surrounding opera. It was a bright and breezy series and a lot of fun. It also involved the use of an autocue, which I'd not used before. That was another little step forward: reading from camera while not looking as if you're reading from camera. It was a good experience all round.

So was *Gladiators*. I used to joke that it would be a great laugh to do *Gladiators*, never really thinking that the call would come. When I was contacted, in 1998, I thought it was a wind-up but it wasn't. John Fashanu had stepped aside and the producers were looking for another face. I was the man. And Ulrika Jonsson was the woman.

I remember arriving for the first time at the Hyatt Hotel in Birmingham, near to where the shows were recorded at the National Indoor Arena. Ulrika arrived just after me, the blonde with sunglasses and designer gear roaring up in her Saab and jumping out to give me a great big hug. She is as she is on screen: a bundle of laughs and energy. Ulrika was very friendly and very open and she couldn't do enough to help.

The shows were all recorded within a two-week slot, often two shoots a day. It was hard going and they were recorded live in front of an audience of seven thousand. The producers were very keen on keeping the momentum going in the audience so there was a lot of pressure not to make any mistakes. There were a few slips, however.

'Let's hear it for Julie,' I would yell to the crowd.

'Jerry, her name's Sasha,' would come the producer's voice in my ear.

I got on well with the crew and the Gladiators themselves were a lively gang: Wolf, Rebel, Hunter and Lightning. It was a first-rate production. My TV credits also included a two-season stint on *Out and About*, which was shown on BBC2. The first series I presented with David Gower and Suzanne Dando, and the second with Suzanne alone. This second series was broadcast in 1999, the same year that I had a cameo role in ITV's *The Grimleys*, which also featured Amanda Holden, Noddy Holder and Brian Connolly. I was a flash James Bond-type character called Rick Speed. It was only a walk-on part but it was fun.

Where to now with the media? Ideally I'd like to combine radio and TV work. People may think that I prefer the bright lights of television, the so-called glamour life. I do like television but I prefer radio and always have. It has a more relaxed atmosphere and, in many ways, is a more genuine medium. In television there are so many other distractions: how you look, what the backdrop is, what the other people in shot might be doing, the lighting . . . it all affects how you come across. In radio it's simply you and your voice. You can actually miss a lot of what is being said on television because the eye is taken elsewhere. In radio you have more control on the impact. The tone of your voice is there to project the meaning of what you say.

I've had a relationship with the BBC for about five years and I'd like it to continue. There was a time when I fancied the idea of following the likes of Gary Lineker into straightforward presenting but now I'm not so sure. I actually like getting out on the road to do interviews, to go to an event and see what's happening and make the piece work from there.

Over the last year I've done more and more work on *Grandstand*, usually as a studio pundit. That's fine. There's been more rugby on the BBC in recent times and we had a busy year with the Heineken Cup and the non-Twickenham internationals. Again, you can't just pitch up and expect to spout great pearls of wisdom. You have to do some homework. If you don't know your stuff it shows.

In my ideal world, BBC and Sky would stop fighting

each other for rugby TV rights and come to some sort of arrangement, perhaps like they used to have for football. Also, in my perfect scenario for the way things should be, I'd like to be hosting a regular rugby show on BBC radio. However, I don't think that the game is quite big enough yet to sustain the programme. I've had a few shots at such a programme over the last twelve months and enjoyed it hugely.

My first radio show in 2000 was the evening before the England–Australia game at Twickenham. It was a two-hour programme and, as it was the first production of its kind, I agreed to have the script written for me. It was a mistake and I came over as forced and flat, a fatal combination for radio. By the time we'd come to the end of the Six Nations it was all much slicker and livelier. You have to sound natural on radio, as though you are chatting in someone's car or living room. That's not easy to do if you're reading from the page. It's far better just to have an outline and go with the flow.

I actually took myself off to have some radio training early in the New Year and went to a woman in Bristol called Mary Price. She was good for me, in a headmistress sort of way, and kept me in check and made me appreciate the subtleties of the voice. As with sport, so with the media. There's talent and there's practice. You need both to succeed.

I'm hoping to develop all these aspects in the next couple of years but this last year has been all over the place. I was still playing at the beginning of the season, had my testimonial year to attend to, various commercial work for my prime sponsors Adidas and Zurich, and an increasing amount of TV and radio. It was hectic. I don't think I'm a 9 to 5 man but I do need a bit more shape in my work. I'd like to dabble in other sports too, particularly golf and athletics. I'm also opening a bar called Blue Rooms in Bath, in partnership with Ben Clarke, Victor Ubogu and John White. I'm also a director of a local radio station, Bath FM. Somehow I don't think I'll be back on the buses.

field of english dreams

Ah, the fame. The adulation. The recognition. It all goes with the England territory and is what makes the hard work worthwhile. I'd just won my first cap for England against Romania in May 1989. We won 58–3, I scored a hat-trick and now the world had come to worship at the feet of the new genius. Which is why our coach, Roger Uttley, spent twenty minutes at the post-match reception in Bucharest telling my brother Gary what a good game he thought he'd had.

So began an England career that was to span a decade, three World Cups, nine Five Nations championships, sixty-five caps and thirty tries – not to mention a couple of drop goals. My England career began on a baking-hot day in Bucharest in front of a few thousand and ended before a Twickenham full house, playing against Tonga in the 1999 World Cup. I scored in both my first and in my last games for England.

But it might have finished before it had started. One day earlier that year I stood looking at my reflection in the changing-room mirror. It was not a pretty sight:

my nose was all over the place, rearranged courtesy of some French brute. I was playing for England B, as it was known in those days, at Welford Road on a Friday evening before the main game at Twickenham the following day. I'd been brought down by a tackle and smashed my face into someone's knee. Gingerly, I prodded my nose. It moved a bit and seemed to want to go back into place. 'Mirror, mirror on the wall, who is the . . .'

Not me, that was for sure. My nose looked like something Phil de Glanville has been carrying around with him for the last decade. They eventually managed to fix me up at the Ear, Nose and Throat Department in Bath's Royal United Hospital, where the doctor told me that it was touch and go. He said that he would stick two rods up my nose and give them a yank. If that worked, then the nose would fall back into place. If not, then I was stuck with the deformed monster. Well, I might simply have finished there and then. I wasn't going to be taken for a pug-nosed forward for the rest of my playing days. Luckily, the procedure worked. Think of all those modelling assignments I might have missed.

My England career just happened. There was no great scheming on my part, no dropping off to sleep every night to dreams of the white shirt and red rose. I was content at Bath. I'd grown used to seeing the Bath lads head off after Christmas for England trials and then come straight back again, whingeing about this and that, particularly the horrible purple tracksuits they wore in those days. I wasn't particularly impressed, which perhaps showed the limit of my horizons. Perhaps it was also my built-in safety mechanism, protecting me from possible failure. However, it was more likely simply to have been due to the way I still am today: competitive but not desperately ambitious. The local paper caught my mood early in the 1988–89 season.

'My goal is to stay in the south-west divisional side for the season,' I told the *Evening Post*.

Reach for the stars, my son. I didn't have much time for divisional rugby in those days. It seemed a cut below the standard that Bath was playing at and I didn't have to dwell too long on the merits of divisional rugby against club rugby, because the call came from England B. The Australians were touring and I was in the squad.

The game was at Sale and the England B coaches at the time were Alan Davies and Dave Robinson. I didn't know much about them, although both had been involved with the full England side on the previous summer's tour to Australia. What I did find out was that Robinson was a fiery customer, straight out of the old school of bruisers, rather like Roger Spurrell at Bath. Now, I appreciated Robinson as a coach but I can't take the old macho, head-banging routines too seriously. I never could.

Robinson was all heart and soul, spit and thunder. I remember him getting stuck into Andy Mullins, a prop from Harlequins. Robbo was doing the brimstone bit in the dressing-room just before we went out on to the pitch. He gave Mullins a slap across the face and then a fierce pinch in the soft fleshy bit under the armpit as he walked past. You could see the routine: Robinson was the big, hard northerner, psyching up the big, soft lad from down south for the battles ahead. Well, there was one very soft southerner from Bath just about to go past Robinson as well – it was my finest sidestep of the afternoon. Thank God the rough stuff was all over, I thought, the Australians couldn't be any harder than this.

Think again. They won 37–9, with David Campese scoring a hat-trick. My chief memory of the game was of our big, tough number eight Dean Ryan steaming into a maul in midfield with mayhem on his mind. The only thing on Campo's mind was the ball. He sneaked it away and stole down the other end of the field to score. So much for being macho.

It was a quiet day in the England midfield and the media interest was located a long way from yours truly. Scrum half Dewi Morris was the focus of the lenses and notepads. Dewi was born in Wales but had switched allegiance to England. He had been a sensation early in the season and the defeat in the B match didn't harm his chances. He got the full call-up after the B match and was at Twickenham the following week. And look where he's ended up: as a BSkyB pundit alongside Stuart Barnes. You can't win them all.

I got an England call-up of sorts. Along with the now mentally and physically scarred Andy Mullins, I was invited to attend the build-up for the England–Scotland game early in the New Year. It was glorified tackle-bag duty. I was honoured but knew deep down too that I was to be the spare part at the wedding. I was not wrong.

We met up at the Petersham Hotel on the Wednesday evening, England's training base for many years and set high up on Richmond Hill. It's a fabulous position with great views out across the Thames one way and the City of London the other. I knew the landscape by heart by the end of the week as I had little else to do except stare into space.

I roomed with 'Coochie' Chilcott, the idea being that one of Bath's old hands would look after the new boy. All Coochie did was look after his stomach as he loaded up with the Petersham special breakfast at all hours of the day. He guided me through the few days all right. It didn't take great navigational skills because not much happened.

England drew with Scotland 12–12. We all trooped back on to the team bus after the game, bound for the dinner at the Hilton Hotel in the West End. Well, most of the lads were. I came close to not making it on to the coach at all when the RFU lady, Carmen McDonald, almost didn't let me back on because she didn't have my name on her list. It wouldn't have made much difference, I wasn't invited to the dinner in any case. The bus stopped a couple of miles down the road at Richmond roundabout to drop me off. The rest of the players headed off into town to get slaughtered and I walked back to the hotel, picked up my car and drove to Bath. It's a thrilling experience is international rugby.

However, it was to get better, much better. It would be nice to record that I kept on eye on the future throughout that 1988–89 season. In fact, I could barely focus one eye on the bottom of the bed when the news came that I'd been selected for England.

The call came from Don Rutherford early on Sunday 30 April. The ringing of the telephone went straight through me. The day before, Bath had beaten Leicester 10–6 in the final of the Pilkington Cup to win the Cup and league double. We were a hot item that season and we weren't too slow in the drinking stakes either. It took a few minutes for Don's news to penetrate the fuzz that was my brain that morning. Will Carling had shin splints and needed to rest, he told me, and I was in. Bucharest next stop.

Only one thing for it: more celebration. It has become a post-Cup final ritual to have a champagne breakfast at Jack Rowell's house. Jack must have had mixed feelings at every Cup final: joy at winning offset by terror at what we were going to do to his wine cellar.

I spread the news that day and the lads were delighted for me. We partied long and hard. (The next morning, hungover and feeling desperate, I was to receive news of my call-up to the British Lions tour to Australia. Two nights of heavy drinking; two great pieces of news. There must be a moral there somewhere.)

All the Guscott troops wanted to share my England debut. Mom and Dad flew to Bucharest, and so did Jayne, brother Gary, his girlfriend and my grandmother and great uncle. Some turn-out. The *Daily Mail* figured that the bill must have come to £4,000.

Bucharest is not the sexiest place on earth. It was pre-Revolution and everybody was on edge. They were good people, but it was a spooky country in those days. The streets would empty at about 4.30 in the afternoon and you heard nothing except the occasional car hammering by with a few guys and girls hanging out of the window, whistling and laughing. God knows where they were going. The hotel was enormous but dingy and we had to take our own food over as there were concerns as to what we might have to eat. The bottles of Coke the hotel served up were covered in cobwebs and dust. We all played 'spot the secret service man'. Mind you, there were so many shifty, brooding blokes with moustaches and dark glasses hanging about, it was impossible to nail down the Securitate bloke. There was a whole nation of them.

I was roomed with Simon Halliday. It was great that my England debut was to be alongside the guy who had helped shape my early career and for whom I had so much respect. He always had my best interests at heart. On the Friday night he told me to get myself up to where Jayne, then my fiancée, was sleeping a few floors above. I didn't quite know how to handle it. I crept upstairs then crept straight back down again, thinking I ought to be with the lads. In the morning I went back up again. You could tell I was really on top of events.

'Jayne, tea or coffee?' I asked.

'Jeremy, what do you mean?' said Jayne.

'Tea or coffee? It's a simple question, isn't it?' I snapped.

'It is for most people,' said Jayne. 'But not for me. I've haven't drunk a cup of tea or coffee in the three years we've been together.'

Mr Cool was getting nervous. I sought out Kevin Murphy, our physiotherapist, who is well-versed in the latest scientific methods for getting a man to calm down. Out came the cigarettes. That was better.

The match was held in the August 23rd Stadium, a vast concrete bowl, and the temperature was in the low nineties. Most of the boys hacked off their shirt sleeves, but I wasn't going to deface my first England jersey. I just rolled up the sleeves and got on with it.

I hadn't been burdened with too many instructions from manager, Geoff Cooke.

'You've been picked because of what you've been doing with Bath all season,' said Cooke beforehand. 'Let's see some of it out there today.'

Simple to say. And, as it turned out, not too difficult to deliver. I scored three tries, one from long range in the early stages, and wing Chris Oti trumped my hat-trick with four tries. I never quite hit it off with Oti. He was his own man and it showed. He told me that I could have passed more often to him. He should try playing for Bath: the wings and full back don't get a look-in. I thought his comment was out of order but, for once, I let it pass.

It was a good weekend. England won at a canter, 58–3. It wasn't an overwhelming experience and was business as usual as far as I was concerned. I'd merely played the way I had been doing for Bath. Just as the good man had requested. Romania weren't too tough a nut to crack either. I knew it wasn't the real deal. England had come out of it well despite the fact that it was an alien country and unusually hot for us.

There were three new caps that afternoon: Wasps scrum half Steve Bates, Nottingham full back Simon Hodgkinson, who kicked 19 points, and myself.

RFU president John Simpson presented us with our caps after the match. I'd trimmed the afro but the cap still didn't fit. However, everything else about the England set-up did – I wanted more.

I took nothing for granted. I had a horrible feeling that the England shirt was only on loan to me. After all, I'd come in for Carling, who had been injured. He was Geoff Cooke's man, captain of England and a certainty for his place. By the time we next met up for England duty I'd got another little honour to my name, a British Lions tour. The trip had gone well, I'd scored a decent try in the second Test in Brisbane and my name was up in lights – and yet I was as nervous as I've ever been when it came to selection for the Fiji game in November.

I was sure that I'd be the one to drop down, with Halliday and Carling resuming in the centre. Instead it was poor Hallers who got the chop. His first thought was to congratulate me, which was typical of the man. I was relieved at my selection but disappointed at the same time – I'd have much rather played with Halliday alongside. And so began my long-running partnership with Will Carling. We were to play forty-five times together for England and once for the Lions, a world record for a centre pairing. And yet I felt we never fulfilled our real potential.

Carling and I were efficient. We did the job but no more than that. I didn't realise it at the time and, given that we won three Grand Slams together, you might argue that we achieved a fair bit. And you'd be right, but it could have been so much more.

I'm sure also that a midfield trio of Stuart Barnes, Guscott and Halliday would have brought more out of England and would have set the tone for the rest of the decade. We never did play together, were never given the chance to show that what we did at Bath we could also do on the international stage. There was something instinctive about the way we gelled at Bath, often playing intuitively. If Barnes made a break, then Halliday was on his shoulder. If Hallers went through two tackles, then I'd be there to take it on. There were no strict guidelines, just a freedom of expression and a certainty that we would be there for each other. We had an understanding that far outstripped anything that I ever achieved alongside Carling, or he for that matter with Rob Andrew at fly half.

That's not to say Carling was a bad player. Far from it; he rarely let England down. But his natural instinct was to turn inside, to look for support from his flanker, be it Peter Winterbottom, Gary Rees or Andy Robinson. Carling rarely took the outside line, which is where I liked to operate.

Who knows where we might have ended up if we'd won that flipping game at Murrayfield in 1990? The 13–7 Grand Slam loss to Scotland didn't bother me unduly. It was a defeat, sure, and I don't take too kindly to losing, but it didn't change my outlook on the way the game should be played. We'd played some fantastic rugby up to that last game against Scotland. Ireland had been beaten 23–0 and I scored one of the four tries. I was on the score sheet again a fortnight later when we beat France 26–7 in Paris, Carling and Rory Underwood getting the other tries. We were still in form when Wales came to Twickenham and were blown away 34–6. We scored four tries, making a total of eleven tries in three championship games. Heady stuff for those times.

And then, against Scotland, it all went horribly wrong.

There was huge hype surrounding the match, the first Grand Slam shoot-out. All the fuss washed over me. It was just another match and I went about my business, getting training over with as quickly as possible so that I could give Dean Richards a pasting at cribbage at the Peebles Hydro in the Borders where we were based. I wasn't aware of any hostility in the air, far from it.

Some of the boys get too superstitious, setting too much store on how training went on a certain day and what the omens meant for the future. We had a good session on the Friday with not a ball dropped – so what did that mean? To me, not a thing. The Friday sessions were usually no more than a showcase, good for giving the press boys a few quotes and the photographers a few snaps.

I've never lost any sleep before an international, never worked out why everyone goes so quiet on the bus on the way to the ground. I was always dying to have a chat with someone but didn't dare pipe up in case one of the forwards thumped me for breaking into their silent, staring routine. Brian Moore was really winding it up for the match, feeding on the hysteria that was building in the Scottish press. It all seemed a little unnatural.

There was a lot of anti-English, anti-Thatcher stuff in the media in the days leading up to the game. There was supposed to be hatred in the air and Murrayfield was to be a poisonous, intimidating place. It all passed me by. I knew a lot of their lads from the Lions tour only nine months earlier: John Jeffrey, Finlay Calder, the Hastings brothers Scott and Gavin, Craig Chalmers and Gary Armstrong. I knew them better than some of the English guys because I'd been living cheek by jowl with them in Australia for two months. So I didn't line up that day seething with fury and wanting to beat the opposition because they were a bunch of horrible Jocks.

The famous long, slow walk out into the middle of the pitch by Scotland captain David Sole was supposed to set the tone for the whole afternoon. I didn't even notice it at the time. Sole had been at Bath so his presence was certainly nothing out of the ordinary to me. What was unusual, however, was the appearance of Scott Hastings.

He looked almost demented, eyeballs bulging, away with the fairies. What the hell was going on here, I wondered. He gave me a bit of lip during the game but nothing that fazed me at the time. Scott was a loud character, too loud for my taste.

Scott did admit in his own autobiography that he indulged in some sledging during the game. I'd taken a bang from Calder and was down with a dead leg. He leant over and said: 'Get off, you English black bastard.'

I didn't hear it at the time but Carling did and pointed it out to me at the dinner after the game. Scott was mortified and apologised. It was no big deal for me.

'No hard feelings, Scott,' I said.

Nevertheless, the Scots won the day and the Grand Slam and they let us know it for years to come. I never felt that we were swamped by any great force that day, we just got beaten in a close match. It's sport. It happens. We were always in the game but they took their chances. We didn't and paid the price. I managed to get us into the game with a first-half try, triggered from the back row by Mike Teague and taken on by Richard Hill and Carling. But we were always just slightly off the pace, all the more so just after half-time when Tony Stanger touched down for Scotland after a chip ahead by Gavin Hastings.

There was speculation after the match that Brian

Moore and Carling had fallen out. Moore had taken the initiative during the game by opting for scrums rather than kicks at goal. I wasn't aware of it at the time. Of course there were things we should have done better, but it was a defeat and that was that. A lot of the team were in tears afterwards. I'd come off the field early with the dead leg and was sitting in the dressing-room with an ice-pack on my thigh.

I just wanted to get out of there. I can't stand too much soul-searching. I'm very competitive but only up to the final whistle and then real life takes over. I care, but only in context. Jayne feels the same and she was relieved to see me coming in to the tea-room afterwards, limping along like a war veteran. The atmosphere among the wives and girlfriends had been as sombre and edgy as in the England dressing-room and Jayne burst out with relieved laughter at the sight of me. Perhaps if I'd been in the team for years I might have felt the same hurt as some of the others.

Coach Roger Uttley looked devastated. The Lions tour had ended in bitterness between him and the Scots so his disappointment was all the more acute.

That was the end of an era in its way. England teams came to value victory over everything from that point on and performance and style became secondary considerations. We could beat teams through the power of our forwards so why worry about anything else? Why concern yourself about the development of the game when the only thing that meant anything was winning? It was a powerful argument and one that I bought into as much as anyone at the time. England became cussed and determined. They did occasionally break free, but only for the blinkers to come on as soon as defeat loomed.

Scottish games in future seasons also took on an altogether different feel and became a much nastier experience. Not because of the players, who were fine, but because of the Scottish public. They got carried away by the manner and mood of that 1990 victory and really went for the anti-English 'Bannockburn' stuff.

It got to the point where I stopped going out of the team hotel when I was up in Edinburgh. What was the point when you were likely to be abused by some moron calling you an 'arrogant English bastard'. I suppose it was a convenient idea for their small minds to buy into. I always seem to be labelled as an arrogant bastard, yet I've never imposed my views on anyone or sounded off about being better than an opponent.

Two years after that Grand Slam defeat Jayne and I were dining in the Carlton Highland hotel with Mike Teague and his wife. It's a four-star hotel and the dining room is as you would expect; very discreet and proper. Yet still we get a guy coming over to our table to give us stick along the same dreary lines. We'd won that day 25–7, and were having a quiet time. We took it for a while and then Mike Teague stood up. That shut the pillock up.

I don't mind people being emotional about their sport but it doesn't mean that they have the right to bad-mouth others. How David Beckham puts up with it on a weekly basis I don't know. I love the singing at football matches and the way fans get behind their team. But the rest – the tribal taunting and the filthy abuse – just isn't for me. There were a rough few years north of the border but things have improved now and it's more the way it used to be. Perhaps I'm no longer seen as just an Englishman but also as a British Lion.

chapter nine

the game's the thing

England were dominant during the early nineties. Our pack was bigger and stronger than the opposition and they won matches for us time and time and again. Paul Ackford and Wade Dooley ruled the roost in the lineout, while Dean Richards, Mike Teague and Peter Winterbottom blasted the opposition away in the back row. Brian Moore led the charge from the front with Jeff Probyn and Paul 'Judge' Rendall alongside. All big men in every sense, strong characters with a view to express. Usually a forward's view. At the time I went along with it and it brought success to the team with back-to-back Grand Slams in 1991 and 1992.

We even scored a record number of points in the 1992 Five Nations championship – 118 in total – but still there was a sense that we were holding back. There was no feeling in those days that we ought to see how far we could go, what horizons we might explore. Victory was the be-all and end-all of everything and Murrayfield 1990 was seared into the minds of each one who had played that day. That feeling of having let something precious slip from our grasp was to shape much of what happened in the following years.

We are down in the record books as winners and that is no mean achievement. But in terms of developing the sport and playing exciting rugby, it was a step backwards.

Will Carling has to take much of the responsibility for that. He was the captain and very influential. If he had told us to give it a lash we would have done but his goal was simply to win. Of course, it was the correct view for the time. Previously, England had underperformed for so long. The team had only won one Grand Slam in thirty-three years – Bill Beaumont's in 1980. England had been the butt of much criticism for not delivering. They had the biggest media following of all the home countries and much was expected of them.

Geoff Cooke and Carling were determined to put that to rights and they did. We won three Grand Slams in five years, two of which Cooke was directly involved in and, in my opinion, laid the foundations that were to last for a good few years.

Geoff Cooke took England a long way, but to a certain level and no further. Perhaps it was impossible to go much beyond that at that particular stage in our development, but he didn't take the big risk and really reach for the stars. I suppose you can compare it to the business environment. There are thousands of businessmen in the country, many of them successful in their own right, but there are only a few big-time entrepreneurs, guys who have really gone for it hell for leather. The template is there for all, the basic strategy is common, but only the entrepreneur, a Richard Branson for example, has the balls to really go for broke. And while we don't hear too much of the failed entrepreneurs, the many who went bust in the process, we have heard of Will Carling and Geoff Cooke's successes. It was a fair enough deal.

Geoff did a huge amount to shake up and shape the administration. The friction between players and the Rugby Football Union, the 'old farts', as Carling was to call them, had been a running sore for years.

Geoff took on the old brigade. He didn't exactly champion our cause like a Red Robbo at the barricades, he was more moderate than that, too shrewd to go for the full frontal assault. He told us that he would back us in a bid for better expenses, improved conditions, travel and the like. Geoff knew his own worth and our value. He told us that the best way to get what we wanted was to go out there and win matches. That way we got leverage and the public would be on our side. That way the old farts would have to listen. Win and we could stick it up the establishment.

And he was right. Geoff knew his business. He was a manager as well as a coach, equally comfortable in tracksuit or suit. He was very controlled and self-contained and didn't lose his temper very often.

Mind you, he didn't need to rant for us to know when he was cheesed off. There was one year in the early nineties when we'd met up on a Saturday evening for a Sunday squad session. We'd all played that day and gathered at the Petersham Hotel. There was nothing scheduled for that evening as the boys were coming from all over the country so we thought we would provide our own entertainment. We knew where to find it: The Sun in Richmond, a fine pub just set back a little from the main road. Several pints later we struggled back up the hill to the hotel and a few hours' sleep.

The next morning – in fact, the same morning given that we didn't get to bed until the early hours – we were out on the pitch at Twickenham. We'd done no more than a couple of warm-up lengths of the field before we all broke out into a sweat. Balls were going everywhere, passes were dropped and the whole attitude was dreadful. Fair play to Geoff. He twigged straightaway what had gone on. He could probably smell the booze from where he was standing.

'Right, gentlemen,' said Geoff, all calm and matter-of-fact. 'I know some of you have come a long way for this. But we're wasting our time here because of the activities of some. You're all grown men, I'm not going to give you a lecture, you know what the problem is. That's it. Off you go. See you on Wednesday.' Good man-management in my book. He made his point without getting hysterical and shamed the lot of us.

Geoff had a clear vision of what should happen behind the scenes and that was half the battle. That's also what Clive Woodward has managed to do in the last few years. If you get it right off the field then there's no excuse for not delivering on the field. I have nothing but admiration for Geoff in that regard.

Perhaps I'm biased. Geoff never dropped me so I had no cause to disagree with him. Players do take a one-dimensional view of managers. If they pick you, you like them; if they leave you out, then they're the biggest fool in the kingdom.

He had a very close relationship with Will Carling, which got on some people's nerves. Jeff Probyn in particular took exception. And didn't we know it. Jeff felt Carling was privileged, with his selection never being in doubt. Jeff has never stopped banging on about it. It didn't bother me too much. Geoff Cooke was good for the game and good for England. As for Will, I always viewed him as competition, he was a centre and so was I. The fact that he was captain cut down the options as to how many centre places there were on offer and I had to make sure that I played exceptionally well to be in the frame.

Will and I were never close – he was not my type of bloke. I always had more affinity with the forwards, blokes such as Dean Richards or Mike Teague. Bighead that I am, I always figured that I could match them in the drinking stakes. Talk about over-estimating yourself. Still, it was good fun trying.

Will kept himself to himself. He had his own room as captain for a start, which meant that he was apart from the rest of us. I roomed a lot in the early days with Rory Underwood, the perfect teetotal foil to my late-night social inclinations. He was good company, always friendly and obliging. Will was a man apart most of the time. He took the role of captain very seriously. I suppose he saw it as part of his future career. Fair enough; it worked for him and it worked for England.

Will had a lot going on. He was getting out of the Army and trying to establish his own business. He put a lot of time and effort into the England captaincy, planning speeches, finding ways to get the lads to focus on the job in hand. He was into motivational gimmicks, team building and all that sort of stuff, which wasn't my cup of tea although I could see its value. Will was setting up his own company on similar lines, organising corporate sessions for businessmen. It was in his interests to make sure that England went well and he realised pretty early on the commercial advantage of being England captain. Some, like Jeff Probyn, took exception to that. I didn't. Good luck to the bloke.

Remember too that this was the amateur era. We didn't meet until Wednesday evening, had two days' training, followed by the match itself and then away we went back to our clubs. England players now spend the whole week together and get to know each other well. Will didn't come to me for any advice on playing or working on strategies. Rob Andrew was his sounding board and feed. They'd work it out, pass it on to me – and then I'd do what I liked. Well, not quite, but too much pre-planning left me cold.

Will was not on my wavelength. Prep school, public school, university, Army officer – we didn't have much in common. It wasn't that I was cold with him or he with me, it was just that we didn't mix. He didn't drink or socialise much. He had his speeches to do at the post-match functions and so he had to stay sober and on top of things. Meanwhile, down the other end of the room the boys were getting stuck in. By the time the dinner broke up I'd find Jayne and we would be off to a disco, rocking until the early hours. Actually, when I think about it, the fact that Will and I weren't close had nothing to do with background. Halliday had a similar upbringing to Will and yet he and I got on like a house on fire.

Perhaps the fact that Will didn't have many close

friends or allies in the England squad goes with the territory of being England captain.

Cooke was the main man, of that there was no doubt. He knew his own limitations, however. He was okay with the backs but didn't know his forward play as well – and that was why he had Roger Uttley working as coach with him for the first few years and then, from 1992–94, Dick Best.

Roger was the unsung hero of those early nineties. While Will and Geoff got most of the plaudits, Roger just got on with the job. At the time not many of us really appreciated quite what he'd done nor quite what he was doing for us. A few of the boys used to take the mickey out of him for his 'giving it large' attitude, but Roger gave his heart and soul to England. You only have to take one look at his face to see that. It's the classic lived-in face, one scarred by battle. He wasn't a prima donna who ponced about the field with locks flowing and getting all the attention.

Roger was involved with England for three years, from 1988–91 and with the successful British Lions in 1989. You don't have that sort of record by chance. A lot of what the England pack did in those years was filtered through Dean Richards and Brian Moore, but, for me, Roger was an important rock, a solid figure in the midst of it all.

Geoff Cooke was not a bad coach and did set us going in the right direction. He wasn't top-drawer in the same way that Ian McGeechan was with Scotland or the Lions, but then not many are. The best coach of that first half of the nineties was Dick Best. He was brought in by Geoff when Roger retired after the 1991 World Cup. I knew Best only by reputation: that of a sharp-tongued, witty individual, never happier than when laying into some poor hapless soul. Just my type. I was never coached or managed by Dick at club level, where some say that his man-management skills were over the top and damaging. I can only judge him as a coach and I believe that, along with McGeechan, he was the best I've had.

Bestie would probably have gone down well at Bath because he was confrontational in a verbal sort of way. That's what made us tick down there, a spot of vicious mickey-taking.

'I'd rather stick needles in my eyes than play along-side you,' was one of Bestie's lines.

He was a bully with his tongue. We had our face-offs but they didn't really come to much. A dropped pass and it would be: 'Round the posts for you, my boy.'

'You're bloody joking mate,' I would reply. 'Life's too short for that sort of carry-on.'

That occasion was with the Lions in New Zealand in 1993 when Bestie was assistant to McGeechan. He looked at me. I looked at him. I told him that it was the pass that was poor not the catching and I never did get to jog round the posts.

Bestie's great strength was that he taught you to be a better player. He didn't just shout or use a blackboard or expect you to know it all, he broke the skill down, worked out what was going right and what was going wrong, and then devised a drill to make it better. It was constantly challenging. and I always came away from a Bestie training session feeling that I'd achieved something.

Bestie is not a dictator but he is all-consuming. He has had big fall-outs, notably with Harlequins and Will

Carling. I don't know the ins and outs of all that but I can imagine how it might have happened. Remember that Will was made England captain at the age of twenty-two and then had years of being the centre of attention, of people looking for his view on this, that and the other. It's easy to begin believing your own publicity. He had also made England his number one priority and club rugby was a secondary consideration, something he had made quite clear from the start. In the amateur days that was fine. That attitude wouldn't have cut much ice down at Bath but it was okay at Harlequins. And then the game went professional and suddenly the control was no longer quite so much in the hands of the captain. As Harlequins' director of rugby, Bestie would have made that quite clear to Will and it must have been a shock to him. Will liked control, but then so did Bestie. The row was a thing waiting to happen.

I don't know how it would have worked out between Bestie and myself over the long haul, because we only had a relatively short time together. Perhaps we too might have fallen out.

England's Cooke–Uttley era moved fairly seamlessly into the Cooke–Best period and the Grand Slam of 1991 was achieved without too much fuss. The tone was set in Lanzarote at the New Year. England had the bright idea of going there for warm-weather training each year, which had the added advantage of keeping us away from temptation during the festive period.

The mantra was repeated again and again during those few days. We were fed up with being runners-up, we would not be also-rans, no more the under-achievers. We wanted to be in the record books and if that meant that we had to be dull and boring, then dull and boring it would be.

We would play a restricted game, planned in advance, all possibilities prepared for. There was a fair amount of apprehension bubbling under the surface that it might somehow get away from us again. In truth, we were too good and the opposition not good enough. If we played to our strengths – the pack – then we would be home and dry.

Of course, theories sound simple on paper. On grass it's usually another matter entirely. Take Wales. Why had England not won there in twenty-eight years? Factor in a decade or so of rugby geniuses like Gareth Edwards or Gerald Davies and half a dozen others such as Barry or Bennett or JPR doing their stuff, then another ten years of solid sides, home advantage, England below par and you're still eight years short of a proper explanation. We just couldn't win there.

Well, the Cardiff Arms Park bogey was not going to do for us this time and we pulled out all the stops to make sure it wouldn't. Geoff Cooke came up with the notion that England teams had been fazed by the hostile environment, put off by the passion of the Welsh public, especially when they sang their songs. And so, for three entire days of build-up, we had the Welsh anthem playing everywhere. At Kingsholm where we trained 'Land of My Fathers' blared out from the loudspeakers. On the coach to and from the hotel 'Land of My Bloody Fathers' swirled around us. There was no escape and by the time kick-off came I knew every last syllable by heart and was sick to the back teeth with it. Personally, I'd never had a hang-up about playing in Wales. Bath had crossed the Severn Bridge often enough and won.

A conscious decision was made to stay right in the heart of Cardiff, beside the Arms Park itself. You could see it from the hotel window and we even walked to the ground on the day of the match.

The night before, we'd had our final team meeting, which is usually a straightforward affair. Will says a few words, Brian Moore says a few words and then someone else lobs in their two-pennyworth.

That evening Will did his bit, Mooro did his bit: 'We have to present the ball well and make tackles,' said Mooro.

Then Will turned to Richard Hill. 'Now, what do we have to do, Richard?' asked Will.

Hillie and the Welsh go back a long way. He'd been banned for a game after leading the England side that got involved in a massive punch-up there in 1987. He'd had it drilled into him all week before the 1991 game of the danger posed by Wales's scrum half, Robert Jones.

Hillie was sensible in his analysis for about thirty seconds. Control this, play down their end, draw their sting ... And then it came out, all the months and years of frustration and venom.

'When I get hold of that bastard Jones I'm going to rip his fucking head off,' growled Hillie. And off he went.

'Tear his fucking limbs off. Wring his neck ...'

I was at the back of the room and was the first to go. The tears started rolling down my cheeks and I could see Mooro's shoulders start to shake in front of me. John Olver was about to burst. Here was one of the seminal moments for the 1991 Five Nations championship, the moment that the mood was set, and we were all about to collapse in a heap of hysterical laughter.

Geoff Cooke, who was smirking as well, moved in swiftly and cut it short. Richard had another mini-eruption just before kick-off and Rob Andrew had to take him to one side. It was the only time that we looked like losing control.

It was a clinical, methodical performance and we won 25–5. Wales were never at the races. Mike Teague rumbled over from short range and Simon Hodgkinson kicked a record seven penalties. I chased some kicks, made some tackles and, er, that was it.

'England's efforts were about as exciting as watching the tide turn in Swansea Bay,' wrote the *Daily Telegraph*.

Did we care? Did we heck as like. Geoff Cooke went round the dressing-room congratulating the boys. The pack, especially Wade Dooley and Paul Ackford, had been enormously impressive. Dooley was a colossus, or 'Dipper' as we knew him after the Blackpool Big Dipper where he was based. I never socialised much with Wade but not for any particular reason. I saw him as a forward's forward, with no quarter given and none expected. He had a walk and a presence and the international stage was made for him. He played his little bit of rugby with Preston Grasshoppers, at a gentle pace and with no great limelight. But he stepped up his game every time he played for England and was a huge bloke in every sense. You knew the opposition pack would think twice about messing with you with Dipper around.

Ackford had been playing senior rugby for almost a decade before he finally decided to get serious and make it count. He won an England B cap in the late seventies and then had to wait another nine years before making his debut against Australia in 1988. He had a better grasp of what it was all about than any forward I have come across, with the exception of Jon Hall. He could take in the whole picture and see what the forwards needed to do in order to help the backs function. He could reason things and not just think in terms of bish or bosh.

Ackford got out of the game while the going was good. During the three years of 1988–91 he won a Grand Slam, got to a World Cup final and toured with the Lions. He got off before the magic carpet fell to earth and I admire him for that. He now works for the *Sunday Telegraph* as a journalist.

At that time, on 19 January 1991, all we had to do was celebrate the first English victory in Cardiff since 1963. Except that we didn't celebrate it. Well, not properly. We had a good night and all that but the history books present that day in a different light.

There had been talk during the build-up to the match of not cooperating with either the BBC or the press. It was to do with money and also what some players felt was excessive intrusion. The decision was that there would be no post-match interviews given. We were going to make a stand.

It seems pathetic looking back and it probably was. Poor old Simon Hodgkinson. He'd kicked a record number of points, helped lay the Arms Park bogey to rest and no one was going to record the moment in its full glory. The boycott wasn't all player-driven,

Geoff Cooke was also involved. He wasn't going to be terrorised by the grey-haired blazers. He knew the power of the victory and this was an opportunity for a symbolic gesture.

I was not too fussed either way. I showered and rushed off to do a spot of glad-handing at the hospitality box of my employers, British Gas. There was no three-line whip to do so but I felt I owed it to them to meet a few clients and chat for a while. I wonder why the RFU never took it upon themselves to pop into some of the boxes in those days. After all, in the amateur era these guys were effectively sponsoring English rugby by employing players.

By the time I got back to the hotel, the lobby was a scrum of demented press men looking for an interview and failing miserably. Tony Roche, then of *Today* and a fine figure of a man, approached me: 'I suppose you're not going to bloody well talk to us either,' barked Roche.

It was only then that I realised that attitudes must have hardened in the changing-room after the match. One for all and all for one. I made my excuses to Roche and went to find Jayne. She is not particularly mad about rugby although she loved the international gatherings because they were fun times. Some of the girls were into the rugby itself but Jayne wasn't and she didn't come to the Recreation Ground that often. She wanted England to win but probably only because she wanted to avoid us all being miserable sods afterwards if we lost.

That season we were happy and so she was happy. Scotland were beaten 21–12 in the next game and then it was off to Dublin, where the welcome is warm and the on-field battering heartfelt. It was a bruising affair, with the Irish back row, led by Phil Matthews, intent on mayhem. Dean Richards steadied the ship and got the initiative back in the final quarter. Rory Underwood's try inside the last ten minutes broke the resistance and Mike Teague got another to give us victory by 16–7 and our first Triple Crown since 1980.

Three down and one to go: France, who were going for the Grand Slam as well. The French are the most frightening rugby nation on the planet. Sure, the Blacks, the Aussies and the Springboks are formidable opponents, but you know what you're going to be getting from those sides every time you play them. With the French you never knew for the simple reason that they never know. They could play rugby of the gods or rugby of the dogs. Beauty or the beast.

It was summed up on that day at Twickenham on 16 March 1991, the day that England won the Grand Slam, their first in eleven years. We'd spoken all week about the threat they posed from deep. We knew that we would play it tight and that they would play it wide.

It was going to plan. Our pack was on top, grinding out territory and putting pressure on the supposedly brittle French. The plan was that they would crack and Hodgkinson would bang over the goals. And so he did, four in all that afternoon. One of the shots went wide though and we all took our eye off the ball for a split second, expecting a French drop-out 22. That was all the French needed, a glimmer of an opening.

Scrum half Pierre Berbizier fielded the ball behind the posts and stood still for a couple of seconds. Full back Serge Blanco came looping behind him and the break-out was on. Blanco headed towards Rob Andrew. I suddenly spotted what was going on. Help!

I thought Blanco was going to waltz round Rob so I stepped infield to tackle. The ball went wider. Jean-Baptiste Lafond and Didier Camberabero combined down the right. France were still only just outside their own 22 but the force was with them. Philippe Sella hared down the right touchline.

I tracked back downfield thinking that our cover defence was bound to squeeze them out and shepherd them into touch. Think again. Sella linked with Camberabero who chipped ahead. What the hell was going on here? This couldn't be happening, but it was.

Camberabero caught his own chip, made yardage and then cross-kicked infield to where I was. It was also where Philippe Saint-André waited. By this time I was sprinting back for all I was worth. I wasn't worth enough as it turned out. Saint-André gathered, I made a despairing attempt at a tap-tackle but he was in under the posts.

It was French rugby at its best and all I wanted to do was stand and applaud, but I'm not sure it would have been quite the done thing. The French are just awesome when they play rugby like that. Forwards and backs just merge as one. However, there's another side to them as we were to see the following year when two of their players, Vincent Moscato and Gregoire Lascubé, were sent off.

Despite their brilliance, however, I never felt we were going to lose. Our pack had them under control, although they scored two more tries that day, through Camberabero and Franck Mesnel. Rory Underwood got ours, with Hodgy kicking the conversion and four penalties. Rob Andrew also dropped a goal.

We finally won 21–19 but France won the hearts and minds of all the neutrals and they had scored one of the greatest tries ever seen at Twickenham.

Will Carling was carried off shoulder-high at the final whistle and I made straight for the dressing-room. It ought to have been a really overwhelming moment but it wasn't. The feeling was one of relief more than anything. There was also a real sense that our forwards were so much better than anything else on offer that we could only beat ourselves. The truly sweet moments in sport are when you win against the odds or come through in a very tight battle – 1991 wasn't like that.

Nor was the Grand Slam the following year. It sounds a terribly arrogant thing to say but I figured that we had another Grand Slam for the taking. And so it proved. Ackford had retired after the 1991 World Cup but the rest of the side was pretty much intact. Martin Bayfield stepped forward into the second row, another giant but more brittle-looking than Dipper. Bambi with a few muscles. Dewi Morris came through for Richard Hill at scrum half, and Jon Webb was to get the full-back shirt. It was good to have Simon Halliday back, my great mate showing what a footballer he was by coming through to play on the wing. Coach Dick Best took over from Uttley.

It was a canter. I know, I know. Easy to say in hindsight but I genuinely felt it at the time. I remember turning to Will with about twenty minutes to go in each game and telling him that I couldn't believe how easy it all seemed.

We opened the championship at Murrayfield. A few

ghosts to slay? Well, we'd won there in the semi-final of the World Cup a few months earlier, a 9–6 dirge as I recall, but this was the Five Nations and the pipes would skirl, 'Flower of Scotland' would bloom and all that. It never happened. We won 25–7 and we all savoured every last point. I even dropped a goal to really rub it in.

Ireland were hammered 38–9, Jon Webb scoring in the opening seconds and finishing with twenty-two points in all. I got on the scoresheet with one of the six tries scored by England on the day and altogether it was an impressive afternoon's work.

A trip to Paris at this stage ought to have brought us out in a cold sweat. but the measure of the side was that we crossed the Channel in confident mood. We'd won there in the World Cup quarter-final, a thrilling, edgy contest. However, this game was different. We were in control up front and moving towards victory. Perhaps it was our confidence and aloofness that got to the French or perhaps they just got to themselves. The match had been hard but reasonably clean and then, with ten minutes left, it all went haywire.

Lascubé trod on Bayfield and was ordered off by Irish referee, Stephen Hilditch. That wound the French up even more and they went ballistic. Their captain, shaggy-haired flanker 'Jeff' Tordo, came up to the hooker position and lashed out. Moscato followed Lascubé down the tunnel a few minutes later for head-butting at a scrum. We won 31–13 but the mood that night at the dinner was chill. There were mutterings of Anglo-Saxon conspiracies having it in for the French. We drank to Anglo-Saxon conspiracies, whatever they were, and we didn't give a damn.

We finished off against Wales back at base. They posed no threat and we ran off easy winners 24–0. Carling, Mick Skinner and Dooley were the try-scorers. It was England's first batch of back-to-back Grand Slams in eighty years.

Skinner on the scoresheet was a revelation. We used to take the mickey out of him for always going over to the try-scorer and pulling him up from the ground. It was the only way that he'd get his picture in the papers. He was a larger than life character and I got on well enough with him although I thought he played to the image of the 'Large Boy' too much at times, with his big bashes on the pitch and his laddish tendencies off it. Skins was supposedly a big drinker. Supposedly. I have a sneaking suspicion that he would throw it down that great gob of his and then go to the loo to throw it all up so that he could start again. However he couldn't lace the boots of Jon Hall as a blindside flanker in my book. Hall was a footballer. Skinner spent too much time looking for the big hit.

The forwards, as ever, were the nub of the team. Paul 'Judge' Rendall, Dooley, Teague, Richards, Winterbottom, Moore and reserve hooker, John Olver – they were all big characters. The banter was fierce. If you dared step out of line, or even trip over a word, then the stick was merciless. It got to the stage where you'd be frightened to say anything, even at team meetings, for fear of the lads sending you up. Will was the only one talking by the end of the season.

It was like a playground, big men behaving like little kids. It was childish and right up my street. Olver was the instigator of much of it. He didn't use up too much energy on the field, given that he was on the bench so often, but made up for it off the field. Before the Wales match, Olver did a great stitch-up on Martin Hynes, the Orrell prop who had just been called into the squad. They were rooming together and came in one day to see two brand-new shirts wrapped in cellophane on the bed. Hynes asked Olver where they'd come from and he explained that it was all part of the England set-up. You simply rang down to reception and asked the girl to send out for a couple of shirts from the shop in Richmond where the RFU had an account. It would then be charged to their bill. Olver explained that it was the RFU's way of looking after the lads, a means of rewarding the players given that there was still no money in the game.

Hynes fell for it hook, line and sinker. Olver had primed the receptionist as well as Geoff Cooke and Will Carling. At breakfast the next morning Cooke stood up and asked for silence, saying he had a serious matter to address. It appeared that someone had been abusing the system and defrauding the RFU, and it was likely that all player expenses, for travel and so on, would be stopped forthwith. Heads might have to roll.

Geoff did it convincingly. Too convincing for Halliday, who was not in on the joke and exploded: 'Olver, this has got to be something to do with you.'

One or two others began to twig what was going on as poor old Hynes sidled up to Cooke and apologised. Olver, meanwhile, was in stitches.

We finally got our revenge. We were on the team bus one day when an ambulance went past, siren blaring.

'Neeh naah,' said Olver under his breath.

'What was that?' asked Winterbottom from the seat behind.

'Neeh, na . . .' started Olver before he realised his mistake.

He knew instantly that he'd blown it and he became a target of our mature humour for weeks afterwards.

'John, noise number sixteen, a door shutting, how does that one go, please? And what's that I hear? A hammer? Noise number seventy-three, please, John. Can you do it for us?'

On and on it went and I'm still tempted to break into the routine when I bump into him these days. Sad, I know.

The mix of characters was important. Most of us were pretty loud, but Peter Winterbottom was the silent one. But what a devastating player, one of those horrible buggers to play against, who would keep coming at you all game. You could put six bullets in him and Wints would just keep getting back up. England should have made more of him. Wints did keep himself to himself but I actually got to know him better the year that I missed through injury, when I hooked up with him and former England number eight Chris Butcher for a few social excursions. He wasn't so quiet on those nights.

There were so many loud types in that England set-up that it was no easy thing to get yourself heard. Brian Moore was the self-elected spokesman and he loved being the centre of the action. He should have been an actor – centre stage seemed to suit him. He was a bright guy with a view on most matters.

He got right under the skin of the other countries, especially the French. It was tongue-in-cheek in the end and they fell for the wind-up every time. 'Fifteen Eric Cantonas' was a brilliant line of his and it captured them perfectly.

Moore was a winner, a bundle of all-consuming passion and the rivalry he had with Graham Dawe was the stuff of legends. I wasn't there for that famous episode in Australia when he and Moore did a spot of extra fitness work after the training session. It was meant to be a gentle warm-down and they began just jogging round the pitch. Within a couple of laps they were going full pelt, each desperate not to let the other get a nose in front. Within a few minutes everyone had come out of the showers to watch these two lunatics tearing round the field edging each other out at the corners.

I knew Dawe well from Bath. He was the harder man and there were times when he was definitely playing better than Brian but his face did not quite fit. He was too loose a cannon for them, too aggressive. Rather like Barnes and Andrew, Dawe never got an extended run to show what he could do.

And now it was time for us to show what we could do. A hat-trick of Grand Slams was on offer. Could we pull it off?

a trying time

The drifting years were upon me and upon England, a time when our game and my body were not quite in kilter. There were moments when it seemed as if it was all going to plan, moments when the mood was right, the play spot-on and luck was on our side.

That 1993 championship season contained one of my favourite moments in international rugby. It came in the match against Scotland at Twickenham in March. We were hemmed into our 22 and from a defensive lineout Dewi Morris managed to fire the ball away to Stuart Barnes, who had got one of his rare starts in an England shirt. We were under pressure but I knew, I just knew, what was about to happen. Sixth sense. Instinct. It was what we had done for years down at Bath: playing it on the hoof.

Barnes was on the back foot and the Scottish defence was closing in for the kill. Perfect. A little jink and Barnes was away. I followed, wide to his left. The 'Barrel', as our not so perfectly formed mate from Bath is called, may not be the fastest thing on two legs over seventy-five metres, but over twenty-five metres his scuttling action can be devastating. It's what he had over Rob Andrew: the ability to find space up there in the traffic. It was part nerve, part eye and part pace.

Twickenham opened up. Could 'Barrel' get the pass out? Inch-perfect. I didn't have to check my stride at all, I was at full gallop. Scott Hastings fell away in the rear-view mirror and there were only two to go: Gavin Hastings and Tony Stanger. I thought about chipping Gavin because Stanger was still out wide, marking Underwood. Suddenly he came infield. I couldn't believe it: draw the man, send the pass out and there was Underwood on his way to the line. It was a great score and Twickenham rose to salute it. We hadn't done that too often at HQ.

I jogged back feeling pretty pleased with myself. Such perception. It was one of my strong points. I then trotted over to Tony Underwood to congratulate him on the try itself. I smiled and winked at him thinking he'd be feeling grateful for Barnesie and myself setting up his try. His reaction was a bit muted I have to say. I'm not surprised. It was brother Rory who had scored.

Barnes and Andrew. How often that little head-to-head cropped up down the years. My inclination is to go for Barnes, but then I played far more often with him. However, I genuinely feel that he was more my type of player, better suited to my own strengths. Barnes was unquestionably the more talented player and in attack he was far more threatening. In defence there wasn't too much to split them because Rob was always a solid tackler. Barnes was quicker on his feet, which was an advantage in attack and in defence.

Tactically, however, it becomes less black and white.

Do you want a man who plays by the book, who fits in with the coach's outlook, or do you want someone who plays the field, who sees what's happening and reacts? One way is not necessarily better than the other, but rugby is a complex team sport and all the bits have to fit together for it all to work.

Barnes just wasn't a conformist, he couldn't play by the book all the time. His nature was to rip up the instructions and call it as he saw it and at club level it was devastatingly effective. At international level it didn't always come off. In Geoff Cooke's grand scheme, win was always going to be the better bet.

I don't know how Barnes feels about his international career. He only won ten caps and four of them were as a replacement, whereas Rob would win seventy-one caps. I don't think the respective totals are a true reflection of their talents.

The 1993 championship was a patchy affair. The focal point of the English game in the early nineties had been the pack, where no one could match us. So what did the lawmakers do? They found a way to try and neuter us. That season, the International Board introduced a law that was to change the shape of rugby for many a year to come. In short, the new law meant that the team taking the ball into a ruck or maul would lose it if the ball didn't come back. Beforehand the team moving forward in the loose was given the put-in to the scrum if the ball didn't come out.

The upshot was that rugby union started to resemble rugby league, with so many players strung out across the field in a defensive line, forwards as well as backs. The forwards tended to become all one shape and size – there was no longer any great incentive to commit big, lumpy forwards to mauls, so let's make them all the same sort of athletic-looking size and stick them out among the backs.

That was the essence of it although it took a few years fully to evolve to its present form. It also took a few years for England to evolve: our momentum was lost. We had to adjust our strategy, the forwards had to alter their thinking, and it took time. The playing field was levelled.

We bumped along through that season. Before Christmas we beat Canada at Wembley, and then South Africa on a gloomy day at Twickenham. The Five Nations was a mixed bag and we ended up in mid-table, losing two matches – to Wales and then to Ireland. The old air of superiority had vanished.

There were some novelty items that season. There was a dummy called Will Carling for a start. Madame Tussaud's brought one of their new items to one of our training sessions: the England captain in all his motionless glory. It was a good likeness and I gave the press boys a quote to the effect that I wondered if this Will would actually pass the ball more often to me than the real one. It was headlines the next day and Geoff Cooke had a word with me about it.

The rebuilding work at Twickenham was still in progress so we upped sticks to Wembley in north London to play Canada. It was great to be in such a famous stadium and the lasting impression was of how good the surface was. Twickenham still insisted on having grass up round your ankles, which made running much more difficult. We had lobbied for years to have it trimmed but it wasn't until the start of the

1994–95 season that they finally saw sense and gave the Twickenham turf a proper crop.

Canada were seen off 26–13, with Ian Hunter scoring a couple of tries. The Springboks were a sterner test although after so long out of the international game they were still working their way back to full power. It was a dreary day at Twickenham, with low, black clouds full of rain – a Rob Andrew sort of day. He turned the screw on the Springboks. We trailed 16–8 at one stage but came back strongly to win 33–16. I managed to score, catching a chip ahead from Rob and breezing to the line.

We had our usual Lanzarote jaunt to the La Santa complex, although this time it was to take place over New Year itself, which didn't go down too well. At midnight on New Year's Eve I remember standing in the square watching all the fireworks going off. I'd not touched a drop and I was with Stuart Barnes, who assured me that he had not touched a drop either. We were about to head home when we both happened to look towards a night-club on the edge of the square. Not a word passed between us. Jason Leonard caught our glances. 'I'm coming too,' he said. And he did.

It was a major night and we got in at 4.30 a.m. Four hours later we were out doing our VO2 fitness tests. Somehow I recorded a PB, a personal best. Barnes recorded his worst ever, a WE. I don't think he has ever forgiven me.

The 1993 Five Nations staggered along and we were fortunate to beat France at Twickenham 16–15, thanks to a lucky try by Ian Hunter.

We came to grief down in Cardiff, a familiar tale. Yet this was not the old Cardiff Arms Park bogey at work, more that we didn't seem to really want it enough. Wales tackled like men possessed, and Rory was exposed dreadfully for the Welsh try, failing to clear the line when Wales kicked downfield. For some unaccountable reason he dithered, Ieuan Evans swooped, hacked it on and over the try line. Neil Jenkins kicked the conversion and we were done, 10–9, our first defeat in the Championship for almost three years.

The chief casualty of the Cardiff defeat was Rob Andrew, who didn't take it lightly. The best thing in those situations is surely to swallow your medicine, but Rob, so squeaky clean on the surface, let rip and demanded a showdown with Geoff Cooke. I've no idea if he ever got it.

Andrew was out and Barnes was in. There was a bit of friction in the air. Barnes had been critical in the past of the England set-up and he and Will Carling were certainly not bosom buddies. I think Will felt a bit threatened when Stuart was around. I was hoping that Barnesie would have a good game and he did. We won 26–12 and engineered that great try I spoke about earlier.

'It was the rebirth of Stuart Barnes, the man who should never have been away. It was the rebirth of England and the return of excitement,' according to one newspaper.

So much for newspapers. We went to Ireland a fortnight later and were well and truly turned over, losing 17–3. Dublin is one of my favourite places. We were based about ten miles out of the city at the Fitzpatrick Hotel in Killiney – the perfect place to lull you into a false sense of security. The staff bend over backwards to help you, everyone is charming and says that their lads will do so well to hang on to you big fellas come the Saturday. And every time without fail, the Irish emerge at Lansdowne Road to kick the living daylights out of you roared on by the most enthusiastic crowd in Christendom.

Everything that could go wrong that day went wrong. Balls were dropped, passes were off-beam, the lineout ball was spilled and all the while the Irish just came steaming through on to our mistakes.

The Lions party for the tour to New Zealand was to be announced two days later on Monday. Did the boys have their minds on that? I don't know. Certainly Ireland's win did for Jeff Probyn, who didn't make the squad. Cooke was the Lions manager, and Best was the assistant coach to Ian McGeechan. They didn't have enough influence at court to save Jeff.

That Lions tour was to be the end of my big-time rugby for twelve months. I came back with a groin problem, not that I realised it at the time. It was to cost me a year and the chance of victory against the All Blacks, which the boys were to achieve that November. That was the only time that I've sat in a stand and really wished that I was out there. Most of the other times I've managed just to put up with my lot. It's life. Injury happens. But this time it was different.

There was a lot of tension in the air, a mood that intensified almost immediately when All Black flanker Jamie Joseph stamped on Kyran Bracken's leg early in the match. Jon Callard kicked his goals, Rob dropped a goal and we were home 15–9. It was a great day in all respects bar one. I wanted to be out there.

It was a frustrating period, there's no doubt about

that. I missed England's tour to South Africa, one that I wanted to go on for all sorts of reasons. Nelson Mandela had taken over in South Africa and Jack Rowell had taken over with England. Big changes were in the air.

jack rowell's england

The call came early and the voice was familiar. So was the tone. I'd been dropped. What did I think of it? There was a pause – a theatrical five or six seconds. It wasn't good news but nor was it totally surprising news and I wasn't going to get up in arms about it. 'I don't think anything, Jack,' I said. 'It's happened. It's what you think and what you've done.'

And that was it. My five-minute non-showdown with Jack Rowell. The man I knew so well from my days at Bath, the man I'd gone through hell and high water with at club level in the days when it was Bath against the rest of the world, the man who helped forge the tight-knit, cussed squad that was Bath, the man who'd just left me out of the England side for some bloke from Harlequins by the name of Will Carling. Jack Rowell, thank you so much.

It wasn't until months later that we finally had it out, and even then it wasn't a great slanging match, far from it. Jack had made his choice for that 1996–97 season, beginning with the autumn games against Italy and the New Zealand Barbarians, and there was a certain logic to it. He'd made Phil de Glanville skipper following Carling's decision the previous season to step down from the captaincy, and so yet again there was only one centre spot up for grabs.

It was me or Carling and Carling got the nod. Bad news, as I've often said, is there to be deleted as quickly as possible: hear it, scrub it, move on. Jack's view was that Carling was stronger at taking the ball up and more solid in defence. It was as simple as that. There was even a certain logic to it and in a way I respected him for his decision. Not many other people did.

There was a real fuss when the news broke. There was even a bit of a fuss in the car travelling up to England training from Bath that morning. Jack had called at about a quarter to nine and forty-five minutes later I was sitting alongside the England captain, Phil de Glanville, as he drove me, Mike Catt and Jon Sleightholme to Bisham Abbey.

'Oh, he's bottled it then,' said de Glanville.

We all knew that dropping Carling would have been a big step for Rowell. The press might well have rallied to my corner but they would have made hay if Rowell had decided to bump Will. It would have been big news. In rugby terms it might not have been a total surprise. In celebrity terms, the dropping of Carling would have been a huge story, if only for a short time. Jack might not have fancied all that and he wouldn't have wanted all the stick if it had gone horribly wrong. The feeling was that he went for the safer option.

Jack Rowell and England was not a great success story. Sure, he won a Grand Slam in 1995, beat Australia in the 1995 World Cup quarter-final only to get flattened by the All Blacks in the semi-final, and he did manage to put together a record-equalling run of ten successive victories shortly after taking over properly in autumn 1994.

But England in that era never really clicked, never really set the rugby world on fire. Jack made all sorts of noises about playing expansive rugby, about moving the game forward and taking it to a new level but I knew him better than that. Winning was his sole objective. That was what it had all been about at Bath and that was what it would be about with England. All other considerations would be secondary.

In addition, Jack struggled because of the changing nature of the job. He presided over the change from amateurism to professionalism which came in August 1995. He'd been in charge for just over a year by that stage when, suddenly, the whole system needed to be overhauled. Jack had to work out just how long England should be together, how much contact he had with players who all slowly switched over to being full-time sportsmen. It took a long time to settle down and for working practices to evolve. Jack was caught in the middle of all that, a difficult place to be, especially given that it was not his own full-time job. And never would be.

Jack has always been a busy bloke. During all those years at Bath he would be dashing across the country from some high-powered business meeting and striding into the changing-rooms at the Rec, demanding to know what was going on. It worked there because of the sort of people we were and the type of gathering it was. It was a club full of strong, independent characters who knew each other well. We may not have liked each other all the time but we got on with it as any family would. We argued, we shouted, we fell out, we made up and we partied. We knew Jack Rowell inside out and he knew us: what made us tick, what wound us up and what spurred us on.

It took the England boys a long time to tune into that wavelength, and, in fact, many never did find the right frequency. They never knew quite how to take Jack. At Bath he gave out and we gave out back to him. It's called constructive friction by all accounts in management manuals. It's called taking the mickey in my book. It's about fighting your corner, standing up to the piss-taking and the criticism. It was a Bath thing and it worked. It could be hurtful and even demeaning. But it was just a front, a means of triggering the competitive animal within.

Right from the start the England boys struggled to come to terms with Jack's style of management. He was brought in for the tour to South Africa in summer 1994 after Geoff Cooke stepped down. It was a logical choice because Jack had been the pre-eminent figure in English club rugby for a decade.

I didn't tour with England that summer because of injury. Dick Best was coach and Jack was manager but that arrangement was never going to last long. Dick was too much of a threat to Jack, too much of a challenge to his authority, and Jack wanted to do it his way. He wasn't a great hands-on coach himself and had done very little coaching at Bath. He was good on the big picture, on getting us all to somehow fit together. Clive Woodward would have recognised what Best had to offer and found a way of working him into the structure. In fact, Clive tried to do exactly that.

But Jack belonged to a different era and had a different mindset. There was to be one man in charge and that was to be him, so Best got the cold shoulder and was dumped in an unceremonious fashion. Jack distanced himself from all that as he would and brought in Les Cusworth to do the hands-on stuff. I had a lot of respect for Les as a player. He was an inventive fly half for Leicester through the seventies and eighties, full of tricks.

He brought some of that with him to England but you never felt that he was given full rein, seeming to be in Jack's shadow, metaphorically as well as literally: little Les and big Jack. It had a certain ring to it. It was almost as if Les was Jack's fag, at his beck and call. He was too nice a bloke in many ways and he should have been more assertive. I also felt that Les was a bit intimidated by some of the figures there: Will, Rob, even me. Not that I was uncooperative, far from it. I know that I can be with certain people in certain situations but not with Les. I respected him and his views.

It was Jack's show. And did Will Carling know it. The pair of them never got on. In Geoff Cooke's time, Will was very much part of the inner sanctum, involved in all the big decisions and shifts of thinking. Geoff picked the side, of course, but Will had a major input to it all. But Jack slowly moved Will aside. There was never a showdown when they both ripped into each other, they were both too shrewd for that. But Will knew that he was being marginalised. He got the same treatment as all the others.

'Do you think you're good enough for England?' Jack would ask at frequent intervals.

It was a real struggle for many players. They couldn't get their heads round it at all.

'Hang on a minute. You're the bloke who's just picked me for England and now you're asking me if I should be picked for England. What the hell is all that about?'

The Bath boys knew not to take Jack seriously but the England lads couldn't get to grips with it. Nor could Carling – he couldn't work out where Jack was coming from and he just gave up in the end and accepted it.

Jack felt the pressure as England coach as I think most would. It's a massive job. England are expected to win every time they step out on the field and when they don't people want to know why and expect instant answers. At Bath, if Jack lost then he knew that we'd bounce straight back. With England there were no guarantees – and that's what got to him.

I remember one television shot of him coming down the tunnel from the changing-rooms at Twickenham and a cameraman pursuing him for a close-up shot. Jack was trying to walk up to his seat in the stands and didn't want the intrusion. Think again Jack, you're on a public stage. He did the classic thing, the one thing you shouldn't do when any camera is near and that is put your hand out to try and block it. It looks terrible even though the gesture is natural. It makes you look shifty and evasive, and it was when I saw that image that I realised that Jack was feeling the squeeze.

It's a shame that England didn't lay down many foundations under Jack. However, it was a time of great change in the game and that perhaps made it difficult to react. Take Clive Woodward as a point of comparison. There have been some wobbly moments under Clive, occasions when the team has been beaten and the media scrutiny quite intense. But Clive has always had an idea of where he wants to end up. He may get lost now and again but he knows that the ultimate destination is out there. He's had, or has managed to extract, great back-up for his ideas. It's the difference between being full- and part-time.

Jack led a double life. He could only give over a certain amount of his time to England. He was still the main man at Dalgety, a multi-national company based in Market Harborough. There was no sense that Jack was cutting corners, but it was obvious by the end of his tenure in summer 1997 that the new man needed to be full-time.

For all the hiccups we moved fairly seamlessly from the Cooke to the Rowell era. There was respect for Jack because of what he had done at Bath and that bought him a lot of time. I was trying to make my own mark after my groin problems and the star-studded setting for my comeback was that glamorous part of the sporting landscape: West Hartlepool. The media circus rode into town to record the moment and, of course, the locals rose to the occasion. They really stuck it up us, scoring one brilliant try from behind their own line. Bath came through, the groin held up and I answered a hundred original questions all along the lines of 'How does the groin feel?'

How do you describe a groin? It was okay and that was good enough. The following week was a far bigger test, against Leicester, the usual shoot-out. I knew that if I came through that without making a complete prat of myself then I really was mended.

Jack rang the night before the game and asked if I

would be ready for Romania a fortnight after that. I told him that I would be ready. I wasn't going to turn England down because I knew that once a side got into its rhythm it was very hard to dislodge the guy in possession. That's what I kept telling my partner in the Bath midfield, Phil de Glanville, all afternoon. That I wanted to get through this game in good shape, to make the best impression possible on Jack Rowell just so that I could take de Glanville's place in the England team.

In the event I came through. There were no twinges, no signs that I had spent a desperate twelve months on the sidelines.

The build-up to the Romania match was a little strange. Jack's sessions were nowhere near as structured as Cooke's had been. We met at 2.30 p.m. on the Wednesday, bringing forward the congregation time by a few hours. International rugby was spreading further and further into the week. The boys still had jobs and I remember Victor Ubogu struggling to make the meet-up time because of work commitments. The same difficulty befell Jack Rowell himself when he had to miss the Friday morning session at the Stoop Memorial Ground because of a business meeting at Dalgety.

After the Friday evening team meeting Dean Richards made a presentation to Will Carling to mark his fiftieth cap the following day. Deano handed a picture to Will, saying that it was a shot of Will and his friends. It showed Will and about twenty other players, all of whom were Jeff Probyn. Jeff had given Will merciless stick in his book for being so commercial and so close to Geoff Cooke. We're an affectionate lot.

We saw off Romania 54–3, but it wasn't a hugely impressive performance. Canada were next up and number eight Steve Ojomoh and scrum half Dewi Morris were the fall guys. They were left out and Dewi didn't take kindly to it. We had gathered for a squad weekend at Twickenham with wives and girl-friends invited along for an evening boat trip down the Thames, and Dewi opted for a spot of personal drowning of sorrows. Just as well. He'd have probably chucked himself overboard otherwise.

The Canada match was an altogether more positive experience. We won 60–19 and were much more fluid all over the field. Mike Catt came on in the twenty-sixth minute after Paul Hull was injured. It was the last Bristol and RAF full back Hull was to see of an England shirt. Catty added a real attacking edge to the side. He scored two tries, really exploiting the blindside and helped us stretch clear in the second half after we'd gone into the break at only 15–0 ahead. Rob Andrew kicked twelve goals from twelve attempts to equal the world record for most points in a major international. No one has ever doubted that Rob could kick a ball.

We celebrated in style that night at London's Hilton Hotel. The champagne flowed and then the vodka. Jack is a great one for unwinding, especially if it's on someone else's account. Colin Herridge, the team's media liaison man and the RFU treasurer, was a very popular man. He was the man who picked up the tab. The two things might be related.

We were on our way to our record-equalling run of ten victories, which was only finally brought to an end by some nightmare in black by the name of Lomu. I don't know what it was about that international season. It ought to have been a very big deal indeed leading as it did to the World Cup in South Africa. Jack had returned from a manager's briefing there before the Canada game to inform us that there was one hell of a buzz down there and that all the other teams were hell-bent on giving it a real blast in the tournament. Jack was up for it and, for him, the vibes were strong and positive. For me, they didn't exist.

Carling had also weighed in, handing out questionnaires asking us for our views on all playing matters and how we could improve. He felt that we weren't focused enough on the World Cup and what it would entail to win it. Of course, the boys gave the questionnaire their full serious attention.

The Grand Slam came and went but I didn't get much of a thrill from it at all. Perhaps the novelty factor had worn off. Or maybe it was because the opposition weren't up to much, or that we weren't up to that much ourselves.

I was going through the motions. It was strange because I'd been so desperate to get back into action after my groin problems and yet the reality didn't do too much for me. We rounded off that Five Nations championship by beating Scotland 24–12, Rob Andrew scoring all the points with seven penalties and a dropped goal. That about summed up my own state of excitement.

We were a close enough squad and actually went through that championship unchanged: Will and myself in the centre, the Underwood brothers Tony and Rory on the wings, with Mike Catt at full back. Kyran Bracken and Rob Andrew were the half backs and the pack was a mix with the likes of Brian Moore and Dean

Richards alongside Ben Clarke and Martin Johnson, who was beginning to make a real name for himself.

Jack didn't tamper much with a winning side, he knew when he was ahead. We performed efficiently and well in Dublin, with Will, Tony Underwood and Ben getting the tries in our 20–8 victory.

France were next up and all the old clichés were trotted out by the media. The high-flying French always had the capacity to cut us to ribbons. They'd had a great series win in New Zealand the previous summer, scoring one of the game's greatest ever tries. Against us, the French had Philippe Sella and Thierry Lacroix in the centre with Bernat-Salles and Saint-André out on the wings. Danger men. They only broke out once, Sebastien Viars rounding off one of those typically extravagant French moves.

It was the only sighting of our try line they got all day. I managed to get on the scoresheet, so quietening the lads from their mind-numbing whistling of *Mission Impossible* at every training session to mark the likelihood of my ever scoring a try again. Tony Underwood scored two tries and it was an impressive performance all round.

We were due in Wales next and, given that the manager was a resident of the place and that several members of the squad hailed from there, it was inevitable that we should base ourselves in Bath before heading across the Bridge into Wales. We met on Wednesday at the Bath Spa Hotel, a second home for me that week as I had a few business meetings there not to mention a fashion shoot for the *Sun*. That was a great laugh but I was dreading the publication itself because it would lead to no end of mickey-taking.

I needn't have worried too much about my stuff for the *Sun* appearing. Victor Ubogu beat me to it. We'd headed into Wales on Thursday afternoon and there on Friday morning was Victor spread across the *Daily Express* Money section banging on about how he likes to spend his money, especially on designer labels such as Versace and Ralph Lauren. He took more stick that morning than he did the following afternoon from his opposite number at the Arms Park.

Victor had the last laugh on us all, coming away with one of the three tries we scored, and Rory bagging the other two. Or at least he thought he'd had the last laugh. He'd instructed a friend to put £100 on him to score the first try at odds of 18–1. If I tell you that the friend is now an ex-friend then you'll realise what happened to the original stake money.

It was a fractured match, one devoid of real intensity. Welsh prop John Davies was sent off for stamping and that was about as heated as it got as we ran out 23–9 winners.

Somehow Scotland had come through all their matches unscathed and were due at Twickenham on 18 March for a Grand Slam shoot-out. Shades of 1990.

The media build-up was ferocious, with every hack in town looking to exploit the old enmity. Craig Chalmers stirred it up at the Scottish end with some derogatory comments but we all stayed silent. We knew that we had the edge on the opposition and we didn't want to let that advantage slip because of a daft remark.

What a desperate anti-climax the match turned out to be. The Scots came to kill the game, to cut us off at source, and they did just that. Brian Moore got a huge barrage of mail, all with Scottish postmarks, for saying just that on television after the game. But he was right, Scotland offered nothing and were afraid to go looking for victory. We took our chances and that was it – a third Grand Slam.

I was still feeling flat and I needed to get things off my chest. The World Cup in South Africa that summer, which I deal with elsewhere in the book, did little to quieten my unsettled mood. I still didn't think that England was getting the best out of me or its rugby.

It's not often that I feel the need to open up, but I could feel the frustration building and I knew that it would all come out wrong and at the most inappropriate time if I didn't confide my frustrations to someone. That someone was to be Jack Rowell. I gave him a call at the end of that summer, August 1995. He would have guessed that something was on my mind for I'm not the type to give someone a ring just for the sheer hell of it. I met up at his house in Bannerdown and we rambled on for two to three hours.

I needed reassuring that things were going to happen with England, that we really were going to try and take the game forward. We'd been dumped out of the World Cup in no uncertain fashion, hammered by the All Blacks who seemed to be light years ahead of us in what they were offering.

I also wanted to know where I stood in the great scheme of things. Were we just going to muddle our way through each and every match, picking up a good amount of victories, but with no clear goal in sight? Was I to be used more? Were we ever going to play the expansive game? Questions, questions. What were the answers?

Jack agreed with all the points I was making. There

was a need for a radical overhaul, we did need to be more ambitious and we did need to expand our horizons. And what was the upshot of all this? I'll tell you how much of an impact my soul-searching chat made – zilch. England recorded the lowest ever return by a side winning the Five Nations championship. We managed just three tries in the 1997 tournament, pipping the Scots for the title on points difference. Oh well. At least Jack had the grace to listen for three hours or so one sunny August afternoon.

Perhaps my complaints made some sort of superficial impression. The world champions, South Africa, came to Twickenham that autumn, in their pomp after their great victory in June when all the world looked in and admired some little bloke with a Springbok shirt and number six on his back. François Pienaar wasn't bad either.

Rowell brought back Andy Robinson for that match, the ferreting, creative Bath flanker, just the type to bring the best out of me through our close understanding built up down the years. We were never in contention, losing 24–14, with the icon of the 1995 World Cup, wing Chester Williams, scoring two tries and only being denied a hat-trick by a dodgy refereeing decision. It was not the best of starts to an international season.

It wasn't to improve a few weeks later when Western Samoa were beaten well enough on the scoreboard at 27–9, but the Twickenham crowd actually took to jeering us at one point. We lacked shape and momentum, struggling to get fluency into our game. Two tries within two minutes of each other midway through the second half were each triggered from a scrum. Imaginative stuff.

Lawrence Dallaglio made his full debut after having come on as a replacement against the Springboks, while Northampton half backs Matt Dawson and Paul Grayson also took a bow. Grayson kicked his goals, five in all. A safe bet was Grays and that suited Jack.

The 1995 World Cup had excited a lot of interest in rugby what with those two blokes of different shapes and backgrounds, Mandela and Lomu. A lot then was expected of the 1996 Five Nations championship. But there was no Mandela, no Lomu and no excitement. It was a middling tournament won by a middling team: England.

Jack blooded a few names during that championship campaign: Dallaglio, Dawson, Grayson for starters as well as front-row forwards Graham Rowntree and Mark Regan, lock Garath Archer and wing Jon Sleightholme. Another bloke got a run too – well, 'run' might be too strong a word for it; let's call it 'rumble'. Chap by the name of Dean Richards was brought back for the final game, against Scotland in Edinburgh. The Scots were going for the Grand Slam and Jack didn't want his name to be associated with that sort of failure. So back came Dean. So much for the youth policy.

The one thing Scotland had to do was keep the ball away from Dean. So what did they do from the kick-off? They booted the ball straight to him. Giant mitts reached into the air, grasped the ball, thank you very much, game smothered. Six penalty goals from Grayson, an 18–9 victory and our seventh win in a row over Scotland, matching the series record.

Dean and I skipped the team banquet that night and did the town together. Luckily, we decided to leave the Calcutta Cup behind, a notable excursion a few years earlier between Dean and Scotland's John Jeffrey having seen the trophy returned as the Calcutta Shield after a fearful battering round the town.

Dean is one hell of a competitor. One hell of a drinker too, if the mood is right. My Bath team-mate Eric Peters was up against him that day. It was an unfair contest, just like the times when Dave Egerton would try to get the better of Dean in our Bath–Leicester battles. Egerton was a classy player in many ways, good hands and athletic round the field. Yet it was always Dean who came out of any maul with the ball. He may not have looked the part in his shambling way, but he was the man all right.

England still had one more match to go in that championship against Ireland at Twickenham, and we were going for a Triple Crown. The opening match of the tournament had been lost in Paris 15–12, Castaignède doing for us at the death with a cheeky drop goal captured on camera with him sticking his tongue out.

Wales were beaten 21–15, yours truly pulling off one of the most creative tries of his career. Well, not really. I charged down their full back, Justin Thomas, the ball bounced kindly and I flopped on it over the line. It was that sort of season.

The Ireland game was Carling's last in charge and the game was billed as a farewell extravaganza. It was tempting fate and fate appeared on cue to spoil the party. Carling caught his studs in the turf after half an hour's play and crumpled to the ground yards away from the action. He was stretchered off with damaged ankle ligaments. The grand entrance and the low-key departure.

Will got his ovation as he disappeared down the tunnel and he deserved it. He was the most successful England captain, with forty-four victories from his fifty-nine games in charge. He brought a sense of order to the job as well as a sense of importance. It was an extraordinary period for English rugby, the side finally delivering on its potential and Will played a big part in that alongside Geoff Cooke.

I don't know why he announced his retirement so publicly. He did of course play on, as I know to my cost, but even then he mapped out when he was going to stand down. That was right for him, but it wouldn't be my way. I don't believe in fixing a precise moment when you're going to bring the curtain down. Sport doesn't tend to obey too many pre-set ideas.

I also felt that if you have your mind fixed on retiring in the future then you'll train as though you are retiring at some point in the future. You send out the wrong signals to your body.

I always felt that I would get to one match, one session when it would just not feel right and that would be it. Time to call it a day. No fanfare, no fuss, just an acceptance that it was over.

chapter twelve

the summer of '96

The summer of 1996 was fantastic: no tour, nor rugby, just a few weeks in the sun in Barbados. I actually trained well. If only we had a summer off most years you'd see a hell of an improvement in standards. The boys would have a chance to get properly fit and recharge. Not that my laid-back summer did me much good because I was left out of the next England game.

Once Phil de Glanville was announced as captain, I knew that I would be back to scrapping for the one place in the team. Mind you, Carling had started that season playing fly half for Harlequins so he wasn't bursting to get in the frame.

I was actually going well for Bath, enjoying both my life and my rugby. Phil as captain was a natural enough choice. Jack and he had got on well at Bath and Phil was also a good centre, a hard footballer and good passer. He'd been around a long time and was respected by the lads. He's a bright bloke and had never been afraid to have his say.

We were good friends if not bosom buddies. We got

on well and still do and enjoy giving each other stick. I liked playing with Phil because he was a selfless player, always prepared to do the graft, as you can see from the shape of his nose. If my nose had taken as much stick as had his I'd have given up years earlier.

He came under pressure when he was captain and didn't have his best year in the shirt as a player. That's just the way it goes. My form had dipped down the years as had Carling's and yet we kept our places, while Phil had had to put up with warming the England bench. He deserved his spot.

Phil is a really gutsy player, underrated and under-valued because he does a lot of the unglamorous duties such as chasing and pressurising. He would never let you down, never give you a dodgy pass or drop you in it. He's rather like Richard Hill in the England back row, who doesn't stand out because of his looks, his name or his hair and yet he's the best player in there, just getting on with his job. He's not a superstar, just a bloody good rugby player. That was Phil as well.

He got the nod and I got the chop. Nevertheless, the sun still shone, the world didn't fall off its axis and life went on. I wasn't happy about it but nor was I devastated. I had to bite my tongue that day in front of the press at Bisham Abbey. One little slip and it would have been headline news. It wasn't easy facing all the notebooks and cameras but I had to do it. I did it when things were going well so I had to front up when things didn't go my way.

I just got on with my rugby and, ironically, I was playing as well as I'd done for a good few years. I really enjoyed it and I suppose at the back of my mind was the thought that it was a Lions year and that not playing for England might have some bearing on that selection for the 1997 tour to South Africa.

The Lions were a big deal for me and I wanted to be on that plane south. I didn't seek any assurances from anyone because that is not my way, but I did have a conversation during that season with Ian McGeechan. Geech had already been named as coach a full twelve months before the tour began.

We get on very well and we just chatted – about the Lions, about what South Africa might offer, about what it would take to beat them. During the whole conversation Geech used 'we' in the Lions context. Did that mean that I was in on the act, already pencilled in? I didn't dare ask but it made me feel a bit better. I wasn't over-confident but I sensed that Geech had me in his plans and that made the England bench seem a bit more bearable.

I only got two run-outs that year. England came within a few points of a Grand Slam, losing 23–20 to France at Twickenham after leading 20–6, so you could hardly call Rowell's decision to go with Carling and de Glanville a failure. They also managed to rattle up a good number of points along the way and Scotland were seen off 41–13, a late three-try blitz in five minutes giving England a record score for the Five Nations. We hadn't scored a try in the Calcutta Cup for four years and suddenly we were steaming across the white line. Carling had a good game, even scoring a try. Phil scored too. The swines.

I played against Ireland in the next game at Lansdowne Road, sent on with four minutes to go on the clock, although there was a fair bit of injury time. Austin Healey went on just before me and I remember Les

Cusworth giving Jack a nudge all the way through the second half to send me out there. I wasn't that interested at that point. I hate it on the bench. You're not warmed up, you're not in the mood and time is running out. You've also only got a short time to make an impact, so there's always a danger that you will try too hard to make an impression.

We did score four tries in that last eight minutes so I suppose it wasn't a bad return. As far as I was concerned it was the others who had done the hard work in softening up the Irish. You don't wander on to the field at Lansdowne Road and stroll through the opposition unless someone has done some serious groundwork first.

Sleightholme got a couple, so did Tony Underwood and Richard Hill, with Andy Gomarsall bagging the others. Will was going pretty well that season and also enjoying himself a bit more off the field. He could loosen up a bit now that he wasn't captain, sit with the boys at the dinner and get lashed liked the rest of us. He even seemed like a normal bloke. Funny that.

France did for us at Twickenham, in a game that we let slip away after being fourteen points clear after an hour's play. It wasn't that France really let rip with some classic rugby, more that England rolled over meekly and let them sneak through on the blind side.

And so to Cardiff for the final game of the championship. It was to prove the final game for a lot of people – Will Carling, Rob Andrew and, for Wales, Jonathan Davies. Golden oldies day. Jack was criticised during the build-up for bringing Rob back into the frame. He should have gone for Alex King, who was part of the England squad at the time, but brought Rob back when there was an injury. Jack doesn't take risks, people should have known that by then.

It was a poor first half in Cardiff and we were leading 6–3 at the break. I was in the dressing-room at half-time and Sleightholme was moaning about his eye. He'd taken a finger there from a tackle and it hurt and was swelling a bit. I told him not to be such a namby-pamby and to get back on the field. Was he a rugby player or what? In fact, I had an ulterior motive. Once again I couldn't be bothered to get my tracksuit off and get out there from cold when everyone else was warmed up. And certainly not on the wing.

Well, that's where I ended up. It went well although I didn't feel too comfortable in that position. You're much more vulnerable and exposed as a wing, particularly if you haven't a clue where you're supposed to be in defence. However, I enjoyed the second half because I saw a bit of the ball and a few things happened.

Rothmans Yearbook reckoned that I 'brought colour and excitement to a drab canvas'. That might be stretching it a bit, although a couple of runs I made did lead to tries, first for full back Tim Stimpson eight minutes after the break, and then for Richard Hill a bit later. We won 34–13 and the lads who were retiring got a standing ovation.

And that was as far as Jack Rowell and I were to go. He did call me when I was with the Lions in South Africa to see if I would fly down at the end of the tour to Australia to join up with England for their game down there, which I thought was a daft fixture. The side had already toured Argentina while the rest of us were on Lions duty. And yet the administrators still wanted their pound of flesh. Another game, another pay-day.

I had no intention of playing. Saskia had been born while I was away and I was desperate to get home at the end of the Lions tour. Jack made one last pitch and I gave him one last refusal. As it was I broke my arm during the tour in a match against the Springboks and wouldn't have been available anyway.

That was the end of the era. Jack was part of a dying breed – one which combined work and play. He juggled the balls as well as anyone, but it was only a matter of time before they fell to earth. By the end of that summer Jack Rowell was on his way. The players were full-time and it was time for the coach to be full-time too.

the woodward years

It was the black bags that did it. The black bags over our heads that meant we couldn't see what was going on around us. Then, with a whip of the hand, off would come the bag and away we would go. React. Move. Size up the opposition in an instant. Rely on your instincts. Make it happen. Don't be programmed. Be different. Be radical. Be Clive Woodward.

We never did get to put that training drill into practice, although it wasn't for want of trying on the part of Clive. It was just that the boys at Bath didn't think it would work. Clive spent a few months with the side in the latter part of the 1996–97 season, after the club had parted company first with Brian Ashton and then Jon Hall.

By September 1997 Bath had also parted company with Clive Woodward when he became the first full-time coach of England. He wasn't a great technical coach, but he had good ideas, he was enthusiastic and he was persuasive and positive – perfect for the professional era.

Here was a man who could see in which direction

England needed to go, who was not afraid to spend money to achieve it. He played a great game in the committee rooms, arguing his case and fighting his corner with the men in suits. He got money out of them and convinced them that if they didn't speculate then England would never accumulate. Given England's recent results, who would deny that it was the right way to go about things?

The players appreciated that he was on their side. On a trivial level, it meant that we had single rooms in hotels from the moment Clive took over. Or, at least, the option of them. Some of the younger guys, like Jonny Wilkinson, preferred company rather than brooding alone. The old lags such as myself, family men with kids, craved the peace and quiet.

There was a much-publicised incident on Clive's first tour in the summer of 1998 – the self-styled Tour from Hell to the southern hemisphere when a weakened England squad lost every single game – when he moved the whole squad out of their dingy hotel at Newlands on the day before the Test against South Africa and took them to Cape Town's most famous and expensive hotel, the grand Mount Nelson, slamming his credit card down at reception. I wasn't on that tour (nor were many other senior players) but the gesture showed that he did care about the facilities for his team. It also showed he had an enviable credit rating.

Clive's view on England has always been very simple and clear-cut: he leaves nothing to chance and wants the team to have had every chance to win a game. He will lay on the best facilities, the best coaches, the best video analysis, the best fitness back-up – the best of everything. There are to be no excuses after that, no 'what ifs'.

Clive was a breath of fresh air. He might change his mind within the same sentence, but you soon got used to following his train of thought round the scenic route it tends to take. And he was English.

As the RFU pondered what to do with Jack Rowell, they weighed a few options. They even went down to New Zealand to talk to Graham Henry. It was just as well they didn't land him for I don't think that Henry has got that much out of Wales. And he's not English. The RFU also approached Ian McGeechan, a coach I do have the highest regard for. I'm sure he would have done good things for England. However he's a Scot and I think that would have tripped him up some way down the line. It's not that he doesn't care, for he is a very proud man and of course he would care when his players didn't perform, but it would not have been right emotionally. For all that rugby is a very scientific game in many regards these days, emotion is still a key element. And with a foreigner in charge some players at some point would feel that it doesn't mean as much to the coach as it does to them. I know because I feel that way and I'm not untypical.

The Celts in particular take great pride in their country and use that passion as a motivating tool. Sometimes they go over the top but at least it's there. England, too, ought to have pride in what it is and what it represents. It would have been an admission of failure to have gone for a non-English coach.

Clive is a passionate Englishman. He's a rare breed. He used to play a good game as an England and Lions centre and now he talks one. He could lose his cool and fly off the handle, but he could also take a joke. I remember when he first pitched up at Bath banging on about how appearance was important, that you are what you wear. All that sort of stuff. Welsh flanker Richard Webster was at Bath then, a character if ever there was one, and a very down-to-earth bloke. This wasn't his thing at all but Clive kept on at him about it.

One day at training, Webby turned out with pristine white shorts and rugby shirt, all ironed with sharp creases, a bow-tie round his neck and his boots buffed up.

'Excuse me, Clive,' said Webster. 'Is this how Sir would like it?'

Clive took the joke gamely on the chin and we thought from that moment on that he was not such a bad bloke.

Of course, merely being a good bloke will not get you very far with England. Clive had to deliver on a lot of fronts and he went about things the right way. He knew that he didn't know everything, far from it. His experience as a coach – Henley, London Irish and Bath – was limited and not the stuff of legends, but he made no attempt to hide that.

There was a freshness and enthusiasm about him and he wasn't afraid to consult people. What's that a sign of, insecurity or self-confidence? In my opinion it's more the latter. He could see what it took to get the job done and that was all that interested him.

He sounded me out pretty early on, asking about my own future and how I saw things such as the England captaincy. He rang and asked for a meeting. That's his style, the personal contact. It didn't happen with any of the other England coaches. Different men, different ways.

We had a long chat at a café in the North Parade in Bath. I was injured at the time, having first come back from the Lions trip with a broken arm and then getting back problems.

I got one thing straight with Clive from the outset: that there are times when we discuss business seriously and there are times when we chat like two blokes, married, with kids and all that that entailed. There was Jeremy Guscott the rugby player and there was Jeremy Guscott the bloke. Clive was good in that regard. Ever since the game went professional I've made a much more clear-cut distinction between those parts of my life.

The captaincy was not an issue for me personally. I knew that and so did Clive. No, he wanted my opinions as to who would make the best job of it. I regret the fact that I never did a captain's stint at Bath because I think I had something to offer. With England it was different. I like to do my own thing in my own time. I like my own space and you have to give a lot of yourself to captain England. It wasn't for me and I wasn't going to let either myself or England down by fooling anyone that it was otherwise.

I don't think I was playing the right position to be captain for a start. I know, I know, what about Will Carling? He was in the same position and he didn't do too badly from it, nor England for that matter. Well, Will was right for his time. I think the best captains are forwards. Roger Spurrell at Bath was a classic of his kind: mean, dogged, determined, and always out there at the front. He wanted to do it and swept the rest of the team along with him. Martin Johnson is the same kind of player with England and with Leicester. He says little but does a lot. He leads by example, be it smashing forward for the Lions or playing a reserve match on a boggy, back pitch in Leicester somewhere.

Lawrence Dallaglio, on the other hand, does a lot and says a lot. There are times when you can talk too much. Will Carling said a lot without doing a great deal but achieved good results. It's just that he wasn't involved in the action as much as Johnson.

I put these views to Clive and assumed that he'd be chatting to Jason Leonard, Martin Johnson and Lawrence. Finally, Lawrence got the nod, which didn't surprise me. Johnson was the favourite because he'd done such a good job with the Lions in South Africa, but Lawrence was in tune with what Clive was about: forthright, progressive and a relatively new kid on the block. Lawrence, like Clive, is very personable, always ready for a chat. The pair of us had hit it off on the Lions tour and become good mates.

I got on well with Clive. He was a romantic in many ways, certainly at the outset. I can only imagine what the likes of Jason and Johnno thought of him when he started spouting his ideas about giving the ball some width. He wasn't too bothered about structures and lifestyle matters then: it was all about style of play and he wanted to take risks. He didn't get into personnel or anything like that, he was more concerned with the broad approach. It was exciting and uplifting, although his views were short on detail. His approach was more like two blokes getting enthused in a pub talking rugby. Clive was speaking my kind of language, but I'm not sure it was the language of the forwards.

We soon became aware that he was fighting both our corners at the RFU. I only came to appreciate later just how strong a position he was in. He'd been third or fourth choice for England coach and that actually strengthened his hand. There weren't many alternatives and Clive made maximum mileage from that and pushed them to the limit on many fronts.

After those initial chats my involvement with Clive and the England set-up cooled. The injury was a real setback. My broken arm took six weeks to mend but a back problem had flared up that was to keep me sidelined until just before Bath's Heineken Cup final in January 1998.

Woodward's England passed me by that autumn. It was a tough autumn schedule with two matches against the All Blacks, and Tests against Australia and South Africa as well. The side went through a few changes, with five news caps selected for Clive's first game against Australia. There were a couple of different combinations tried in the centre during the autumn: Will Greenwood, Phil de Glanville and Nick Greenstock were the men used as England came away with two draws from the series, 15–15 against Australia and a good effort at Twickenham when the second match against New Zealand ended 26–26.

England were based at their usual haunt at the Petersham Hotel at the top of Richmond Hill. It was a great location for all sorts of reasons, but Clive was to move us on two years later, taking the team training HQ further out of town to the Pennyhill Park Hotel in Bagshot. He wanted to change the mood after the disappointment of the 1999 World Cup so he changed the backdrop. Good idea and typical Clive: examine every angle just in case it gives you an edge.

He involved the senior players by having meetings with a regular group of us: myself, Lawrence, Jason, Johnno, Phil de Glanville and Tim Rodber. We tossed ideas around, aired a few grievances, and got things off our chest. Clive gave a bit back too. It was informal and personal, with no promises given, just a sensible exchange of views. It was a neat circle of communication and helped build trust.

John Mitchell was the other main man, the forwards' coach in essence, and all the more so once Brian Ashton was brought into the set-up in mid-1998. Mitch was a former All Black, the midweek captain on their 1993 tour and a real forward's forward.

Clive and Mitchell never seemed to be that close and by the end of Mitch's time here in spring 2000, I think that the relationship, such as it was, had cooled dramatically. Mitch had ambitions, as you can see from the way that he's going well now back in New Zealand with the Waikato Chiefs in the Super 12.

There was constant talk throughout that first couple of years of bringing in Dick Best to coach in some way or another. Dick eventually became a selector, a figure in the background keeping an eye on matters. That probably put Mitchell on edge a bit and made him feel that he was being undermined. He also was a very young, unproven coach, still player-coach at Sale when he came on board with Clive in autumn 1997, quickly switching over to more mainstream coaching.

I was back in action for the first game of the Five Nations championship, against France at the new £270 million Stade de France in the northern suburbs of Paris. A fair bit had changed since I was last with the squad. Better hotel arrangements for a start, and we also had a war room as well as a team room at hotels. The boundaries between work and play were clearly marked. The team room was just that, a place for the team to go to chill out with all the usual stuff there, pool tables and the like. The war room was where we got serious, where all the key planning was done, where the buzz words of the time were pinned to the wall. The room moved with us. Where we went, it went – or as much of it that could be shifted. It gave us continuity, a sense of purpose and a professional air to the proceedings. It didn't happen overnight, it evolved slowly. It had Clive's stamp on it and that was a good thing too.

England were based out at Versailles for the build-up, five-star splendour to the south-west of Paris. I was paired with Will Greenwood in the centre, with Paul Grayson and Kyran Bracken at half back. We were never in the game much, France winning 24–17. 'The scoreline flattered us,' as Clive Woodward put it afterwards.

That defeat hurt Clive. He's an emotional bloke, enjoying the highs and suffering the lows. Some people criticise him for it but it's just the way he is. He went through the tape of the game several times, pored over every detail of our build-up in an effort to work out why we were so off the pace. I think you can sometimes look too hard for answers. Teams simply have off-days and that was one of them. There was nothing wrong with the build-up itself. We did some good work and had some fun.

I remember that Gloucester prop Phil Vickery had been brought into the squad and was to win his first cap in the next match, which was against Wales. Phil was keen to make a good impression and worked hard during training. Like me, though, he likes a cigarette. He didn't want it to be public so, he went to his hotel room and out on to the balcony. He was looking around like a guilty schoolboy as he lit his cigarette and took a deep draw. Bliss. The only problem was that several of us, including Clive Woodward, were across the way in another part of the hotel taking it all in. Gotcha!

The Welsh game was my fiftieth cap – a great landmark, I was now officially an old man. It gave me a buzz to run out ahead of the team at Twickenham. I may not appear the most emotional bloke in the world but I do still get a kick out of certain moments in rugby. I've always enjoyed matches, pitting myself against the other man, the knocks, the runs, the crowd – it's all good stuff.

I knew that there wouldn't be too many more occasions like this. I was up against two old muckers in that match – Welsh centres Scott Gibbs and Allan Bateman. They are both class acts that I knew pretty well from Lions tours.

Scott is a good man. I respect people who go out there and give everything. He can also do things that I can't do simply because that is the way he is built, both mentally and physically. He is a hard player on the field, very direct and potentially very damaging. We worked well together on the Lions tour to South Africa in 1997, and I also liked the way too that he was able to switch off from rugby. He was one of the most driven blokes I've met on a rugby field, all blazing commitment, yet as soon as that final whistle went that was it. He'd talk about anything rather than rugby.

Allan Bateman was my rival for that Lions shirt in 1997. He is a great all-rounder with superb balance on the rugby field. It was a close thing and I was fortunate to be chosen. Allan is a fabulous defensive player. He doesn't have the bulk of Gibbs but it's every bit as painful getting hit by him. It used to be the same thing with Philippe Sella of France. Again, not that much to look at but, cripes, could he cut you in half. Good tackling is more about timing than size. Allan had a knack of getting his shoulder into the softest part of your anatomy and it really hurt. He had quick feet and a sharp eye. You could see him coming out of the corner of your eye but do nothing about it. It was like a wasp zooming in for the sting.

It's amazing that Allan is playing on still. He's even older than I am.

At least I had the satisfaction of getting one over the pair of them that day. We blitzed Wales 60–26, a record score in the history of the championship. Yet for the first half-hour Wales had really caused us problems, no one more so than Allan Bateman. He scored two tries that day and was a real nuisance all over the field. His second try, triggered from deep by Gareth Thomas, was a beauty.

We were on fire, though, fitter in body and in mind. It was the first win of Woodward's reign and a first for Lawrence as captain. I struggled to relate to him as captain for the simple reason that he was a mate first and foremost. Carling was a captain, Johnson was a captain, but Lawrence was a mate.

I thought Lawrence took too much on himself, wanted to be at the hub of everything, always talking, always on the move. He was very thorough and had a great grasp of what goes on on a rugby field. That's the way he operated at Wasps.

The England squad was still developing and there were quite a few new faces that first season. Unless your name is Austin Healey you're not going to walk in there and say: 'Hey, look at me. I'm the dog's bollocks.' It took Jonny Wilkinson a couple of years to find himself, which is not surprising. It was just the natural pace of things in terms of development.

Lawrence was a popular choice but he wasn't that influential for various reasons. Clive, quite rightly in my opinion, made a point of saying that he was going to pick the team first and then the captain. He accepted that the captain's role had a significance but did not want it to be over-emphasised. He wanted to move away from the Carling era when there was too much mystique surrounding the position. He also set up the senior players group, which meant that a lot of the important discussions were conducted there.

In former days Will was in charge along with Geoff Cooke and they drove the whole thing forward between them. I think, too, that Will had a game plan as far as the England captaincy was concerned. He saw it as a career. The game was amateur but he was aware of the commercial possibilities. Good luck to him, there was nothing wrong in that. There was a downside of course, as he and Lawrence were to discover. You are on a public stage when you become England captain and it was no good Will bleating on about the fact that he was essentially a shy person and didn't like the constant exposure. That's just naïve. I think he actually liked the attention, although it was eventually to end in tears when the publicity machine chewed him up and spat him out.

Will made a career out of being England captain. Times changed and Lawrence and Martin Johnson are professional rugby players who have had stints as England rugby captains. Matt Dawson too. He did a great job during the Tour from Hell in the summer of 1998.

Will was a key figure as captain off the field, Johnson was a leader by example whereas Lawrence was a mix of both. Johnson is the best England captain I've played under, there's no doubt about that. He commanded total respect and that was not easy to achieve. He has also adapted well, moving with the times both as a player and as a captain. His inclination is to distrust and even hate the media but he's even managed to come to terms with all that.

We were due in Edinburgh for the next match. It was a Sunday and flat as a pancake in terms of atmosphere. I would write off Sunday internationals because the buzz is an important part of the occasion. The Five Nations is more than just a series of Test matches and we've got to make sure that the whole thing works.

We won 34–20, although Scotland only got back at us on the scoreboard with two injury-time tries by Tony Stanger and Shaun Longstaff. We made four changes for the game and I was sounded out for my views on selection of a position I know so much about: number eight.

I wasn't sure why Lawrence and Clive involved me. I think they wanted to hear my view on bringing Dean Ryan back into the team. Dean, an old playing partner of Lawrence in Wasps days, was into his thirties and had done a great job at Newcastle. He'd been out of the international frame for six years, winning the last of his three caps against Canada in 1992. My view was simple: if he's the best around at the moment, then pick him. Ryan had had good notices in the media for a few weeks and Clive was influenced by that sort of thing.

The choice wasn't a great success, which was not really Ryan's fault. The pace of the game was beyond him. Tony Diprose was in the back row for the final game of the championship against Ireland, a Triple Crown match. It was our fourth Triple Crown in succession and we won 35–17 in a fitful game. When we clicked we played some decent rugby but were unable to sustain the momentum. I managed to combine with Will Greenwood to set up Matt Perry for a try after just three minutes. Fifteen minutes later that renowned try-scorer, Leicester hooker Richard Cockerill, touched down after a sharp bit of work by his Tigers' mate, Neil Back. Cockerill celebrated in typically restrained fashion.

Mike Catt put us further ahead on the stroke of half-time with a try from the wing and then it all went horribly flat. Two things stick out in my mind, although I have tried desperately hard to erase one of them. Unfortunately, every last swine under the sun, particularly those from Bath, keep bringing up the subject.

Okay, okay, it's time to come clean. So I was caught

from behind and tackled by a forward. So it was Ireland number eight Victor Costello, not particularly known as an out and out speed merchant. Yes, I did have a head-start on him but maybe I was just tired after putting in so much hard work before then. I could see him out of the corner of my eye and I tried everything to get away from him. I arched my back just to move that fraction further ahead, like Scooby Doo in the cartoons. A slight tilt of the body and the enemy goes shooting past. Except that this one didn't.

Truth to tell, I'm not the fastest bloke in a straight sprint and never have been. My pace is all right but not exceptional. Getting through a gap on a rugby field is as much to do with timing and getting the angle right as it is to do with simple speed.

The real notable moment from that game was the appearance as substitute in the seventy-eighth minute of Jonny Wilkinson. Jonny came on for Mike Catt, at eighteen years and three hundred and fourteen days the youngest England cap for seventy-one years. I think there might be a few more caps to come yet.

It hadn't been the greatest championship for us even though we ran in seventeen tries, sixteen of them in the three matches against the Celts.

Slowly Clive Woodward was evolving his strategy. He discovered things as he went along, which was fine because it meant that things never got stale. Anything to break the routine. Test matches will never be boring, there's nothing to beat the thrill of the contest. But the thrill of the training session somehow always managed to elude me and the build-up can be monotonous. For the first ten or twenty caps it's exciting because it's new and fresh. After that, it's the same old drills and routines. I always envy the forwards because their game is so technical. Scrum, lineout, maul – there's so much to work on, so much to perfect. With the backs you might have fifty flipping moves and only ever use four or five.

I'll give Clive his due, he cut down on the number of moves. We concentrated on five or six for any one game and then changed the repertoire for the next match. Clive was good on another front too. He made sure that we gave it the full metal jacket in training. For many years we'd always had fairly light training sessions with England, namby-pamby stuff where you were all frightened of getting injured so you'd ponce about for three days making sure that you didn't get any knocks. Clive changed all that. You train as you play – flat out. That was one of the reasons I enjoyed Lions tours. Training there was more intense for the simple reason that you were fighting for your Test spot. That's the attitude Clive took: if you weren't ready to really get stuck in on Tuesday training then you weren't in the right frame of mind for the Saturday match. You can't hide in a game so you can't hide in training. Sometimes you might get a knock but very rarely – no different from the match itself, in fact. I always preferred a full, hard training session to a light airy-fairy one.

There were other things Clive brought in. The half-time trot from the field was one of them. Always make a point of being really brisk down into the tunnel as if you're still full of running. You might be totally knackered, but don't let the other lot know that.

Once inside the changing-room it was down to business. It was a far cry from the five-minute half-time with a slice of orange and a few gasps. We had a routine under Clive. Nobody would say a thing for two or three minutes but there would already be a couple of bullet points on the white board, key things to do in the second half. While we got our breath, Clive would flit round the room getting a point of view from the senior players like myself, Lawrence, Jason and Johnson.

The points were put together and discussed, and then, refuelled with fluids, we would charge ourselves up again and back out on to the pitch. It was like a military campaign.

Gradually, the Twickenham changing-rooms got a makeover. They were plain breeze-block rooms until Clive gave them the *Changing Rooms* touch: in came a panelled wood finish, with 'Fortress Twickenham' written above the door. Each player had a cubicle with his name and a key slogan for the day on the wall.

I never actually used mine. I preferred to have more space so I squatted in the coaches' area. It was much bigger than my cubicle so that's where I parked my backside.

All the little touches began to add up, giving the squad a sense of a new regime and a new direction.

chapter fourteen

tour to hell

Some things, however, were not to change – my decision not to tour again being one. I'd come back from the Lions tour of South Africa in 1997 and declared that that would be my last. It almost was – I did do the World Cup build-up trip in the summer of 1999, although only under duress.

As for the 'Tour to Hell' in the summer of 1998, no chance. Four Test matches: one in Australia, two in New Zealand and, just in case the lads feel a little underused, one more on the way home in South Africa. No thanks.

Clive knew the way I felt when he took over. We spoke about it early in the New Year and I told him I wasn't going. I made all the right noises about being jaded and my injuries needing a rest but, to be honest, I was never going anywhere near the steps of that plane from Day One.

Nor, as it turned out, did many of the other lads. Lawrence, Jason, Johnson . . . the list was a long one. Clive had inherited the schedule from the old regime and couldn't get out of it. Eventually he decided that he wanted his top men fresh for the World Cup the following year. It was a good decision, even though the southern hemisphere didn't appreciate it. Tough. Some Aussie official called Dick McGruther really got stuck into us.

I didn't take a lot of notice. I felt sorry for the lads when the results filtered through. The defeat against Australia 76–0 tells its own story. Ben Clarke was on tour and he kept me informed via a few e-mails. But I wasn't that fussed about the whole thing. If I'm not involved I don't follow rugby matters too closely. I heard good things about Matt Dawson's captaincy down there and he and Ben seemed to be the only plusses from the trip.

I did hear that Clive and Mitch had a difference of opinion after that hammering by Australia. Clive had the boys booked for a beach trip the next day and he went through with it. Mitch said that if he had his way then the boys would be out getting a basting on the training field. Different men, different views.

The press claimed that there had been a huge bust-up between the two men, but I'm not sure about that. Of course, there was some friction and things did eventually go a bit sour. But there is always disagreement in the camp. You might think all is hunky-dory at the moment with England, all on the same wavelength – but it won't be.

Clive enjoys a little disagreement – it's creative and keeps everyone on their toes. It's the same in any company isn't it? Businesses have all kinds of little spats along the way. Ultimately, the boss has to take a decision but he wants input and views from all sides, not a lot of dummies coming out with the same old line.

Coach John Mitchell did a lot of good for English forward play and I think we've only really started to see the benefits in the last twelve months or so. He made the pack more dynamic and the forwards more aware of what they should be doing round the field. You see the quality of ball delivered to Matt Dawson or Kyran Bracken at scrum half these days and it's ten times better than it was.

Mitch and Clive's relationship did get prickly, but that was bound to happen. Mitch is a passionate guy and wanted to do things his way. I had it out with him one night in Couran Cove, the World Cup training camp we had in summer 1999 off the Queensland Coast. Jason and I sneaked out one night for a few beers with Mitch. We all got on well and had a few more than intended, the usual state for speaking your mind. I told Mitch that if he wasn't too happy then he ought to be man enough to front up to it. I told him that he had to choose between being one of the herd or get out there himself and be the main man.

He took it the right way – I think. He was a good bloke. Mind you, it was funny to see him coach to start with. He'd have little scraps of paper stuffed into his tracksuit pockets to remind him of the next drill. Jason and I would get the giggles every time we saw him sneaking a look. All very schoolboyish.

Gradually, Clive moved the England set-up away from the one-coach mentality. Mitch was there for the forwards, Phil Larder was brought in for defence and Brian Ashton slowly took over more responsibility for the backs. Clive made it all hang together, even if the seams did fray at the edge from time to time.

Larder's appointment was a daring one. He knew little or nothing of rugby union and we knew little or nothing of him. He had a good track record in rugby league, of course, as coach of Great Britain, but what did that mean to us? I mean, a tackle was a tackle, wasn't it? Bloke runs at you, you knock him over.

I made an instant impression on Larder when I first met him at the Runnymede Hotel in Ascot. I'd been speaking at a dinner and came out into the lobby and saw Ged Roddy, Bath's fitness advisor, talking to someone. I walked in on the conversation which was about video analysis. I was introduced to Phil and vaguely recognised his face. I just heard the tail end of the conversation. As usual I didn't let my own ignorance get in the way of giving an opinion.

I said that any coach that had to rely on video analysis must be bloody useless. There was more. All the flair was being coached out of players. There was too much science and not enough instinct in the game. We've ended up playing rugby by numbers. With that I was off to bed. Phil wasn't too chuffed, by all accounts. He let rip about me to Ged, claiming that Gary Connolly in rugby league was a far better centre. Well, there you go.

Phil and I did eventually get on the same wavelength, although I was very suspicious of him being a northerner and having such a good suntan. Everyone took time to get to grips with Phil's defensive drills and it took time for Phil to get to grips with rugby union. But it was the right way to go. You can see that from the results of the last twelve to eighteen months during which time defence has become a priority. The balance between attack and defence was sometimes lopsided in training, as I wasn't slow to point out. But our defence did change and it did bring results.

The lads on the Tour from Hell came back with some stories. Phil took them right back to basics: on their knees, toppling the other guy over with arms locked round in the tackle as they walked through the drill. Mini-rugby stuff. There was the 'quack-quack' routine, so-called because the boys had to run along with their hands in the air just waiting to get wiped out from the side by one of the boys charging in at full tilt. They were like ducks in a fairground shoot.

No one could quite see then where it was all going to end up. I remember Adedayo Adebayo having problems with Phil when he wanted to change the angle of tackling and the defensive system. Adey was one of the most fearsome tacklers I knew. But he liked to stand wide and come in and smash them down. Phil didn't like that; he wanted Adey to come in close, stay in his channel and work from there. It was different and it caused friction.

Phil realised that he wasn't getting his message across successfully, so he took himself off to Leicester to work out his drills there. It all paid off and everyone benefited in the long run.

I actually enjoyed his fresh ideas, they seemed to me to make sense. Phil compared the tackle to a golf swing and said that it all came down to technique in both games. On the eighteenth hole, one shot ahead, the only thing that kept it all together under pressure was technique. It was the same with tackling: get the basics and the system right, and they won't go past you.

We were given tackle count targets, world-class standards. My target was eight tackles a match. We had all sorts of people round the England squad compiling charts on this, graphs on that. I'm not a big one for statistics but the coaches loved all that kind of information.

I finally managed to win Phil over. That autumn series of games finished with us trying to prevent the Springboks from notching a world-record eighteen victories on the trot. We did it, winning 13–7. I got a try but it was my tackling that earned the praise that really mattered – from the suntanned northerner. Phil thought it was the best game he'd ever seen me play. I didn't let on, of course, that I valued his approval.

That match brought a strange autumn programme to a close. We played two World Cup qualifiers against Italy and the Netherlands, our penance for having lost the third-fourth play-off against France in the 1995 World Cup. The Italy match was fine in that it was competitive. In fact, they deserved to beat us, scrum half Alessandro Troncon having a perfectly good try disallowed. We scraped through 23–15, Will Greenwood rescuing us with a late try.

But what was the point in playing the Dutch? We won 110–0 and it could have been more. I got four tries but I wouldn't put any one of them down as my greatest achievement in rugby. The Dutch boys couldn't have enjoyed the experience. We certainly didn't.

The only good part of the whole experience was to get out of London. We were based in Leeds and trained at Headingley. Brian Ashton was having a hand in more and more of our sessions, but he was still far from being the main influence – that was still in the hands of Clive and Mitchell.

Brian and I go back a long way at Bath and I think we see the game in much the same way. I don't care too much if the opposition scores eight tries so long as we score twelve. That didn't cut much ice with the Phil Larders of the world and I was always fighting Brian's corner on that one. Brian is a terrific coach: very imaginative and perceptive. But he's not one of life's shouters and screamers; he won't back down on a point but he's not confrontational.

It took all of us a long time to bring the package together. I felt that we were spending too much time on defence and breaking the game down into separate aspects too much. Brian would have his twenty minutes on attack, then Phil would step in for his stint on defence before Mitch came in for his bit before he put us through the team run.

The emphasis changed from game to game. Clive would give Phil his head if the defence had been crap the match before. It was too jerky for my taste, I'd rather tackle all the problems at one time.

Brian's influence can be seen in England's play of late, although it's taken a couple of years for it all to filter through. But filter through it has. Just look at how different a player Martin Johnson is these days, how much more comfortable he is with the ball in hand. I remember Richard Cockerill being impressed with the ball-handling drills we used to do. Suddenly the forwards discovered that it was fun to run with the ball, to make decisions when there are three players on two. The donkeys were finding out how to be thoroughbreds. I'm glad the role reversal stopped there and we didn't have to get bashed about in scrums.

It all took time. At that stage in the evolution we were

giving it a good lash in games in the way that England always has. We almost put one across the Wallabies, losing out to a late John Eales penalty at Twickenham. I got our try in the 12–11 defeat and had a pretty good game all round. It was the same the following week against the Springboks. There was a fair amount of pressure going into that match. If we'd lost Clive would have had a hard time in the press. We knew that, he knew that and we let off steam as a result.

The squad didn't have as many blow-outs as it used to, but that night was an exception. We headed to Victor Ubogu's place down the King's Road – Shoeless Joe's. Legless Joe's might have been a better name, because we got hammered. We were on the tables, singing and dancing. Not a pretty sight. Darren Garforth and I took a tumble at one point. Darren, a former tubular executive from Leicester (scaffolder to you and me), is a prop by looks and by nature. Down he went with all the benches on top of him. The bouncers went to find Victor, who was on the front door, to tell him that things were getting out of hand. Victor came downstairs, took one look at us on the rampage and said to his bouncers: 'All yours.' The Leicester boys really broke the bank on champagne that night. I think they clubbed together and bought one bottle between them.

It wasn't often that we had the chance to really give it a rip. Our fitness was all-consuming. We were weighed all the time to make sure that our body fluids were up to the mark. And now that we were professional players there was a different mentality at work. It was our job and to some extent we had to be seen doing the right thing. All work and no play made us all dull boys in my opinion, but there were increasingly fewer opportunities to test out that theory.

The 1999 Five Nations was to be the last, with Italy due to make the numbers up to six the following season. We were all set to finish off in style. And then came Scott Gibbs.

Scott well and truly dented our Grand Slam plans that fateful afternoon at Wembley. I was on the sidelines by that stage and I'd also just had my problems at a traffic-light junction in Bath. It was not the most carefree few weeks of my life.

The championship had been okay up to that point. We'd not set the world alight and had been lucky to get away with a 24–21 win over Scotland in our opening match at Twickenham. Gregor Townsend, John Leslie and Alan Tait cut us to pieces two or three times. Will Greenwood and Phil de Glanville were both injured so I was teamed up with Jonny Wilkinson in the centre. All that defensive practice and we were all over the shop.

Mike Catt was at fly half. We scored two tries early on through Tim Rodber and Dan Luger but tailed off badly. We were hanging on for dear life at the end as Tait scored two tries, and then Catty coughed up the ball for Gregor to go forty metres to score.

That mistake cost Mike a place against Ireland and Paul Grayson came in at number ten. He's a good bloke is Grays but I put him in the same mould as Rob Andrew: good footballer, shrewd tactical head but where's the threat? I think we were limited in the middle of the field but it was enough to do for the Irish. The boys up front did a number on them. We drew all the fire from them, with Tim Rodber and

Martin Johnson having big games. Tim scored in injury time to give us a narrow-looking 27–15 victory, but we had always been in control. It wasn't pretty but Clive was tuning into the fact that victory was all-important. It bought you time. That's why he went for Grayson – the safer option.

The French match has thrown up any number of classic sporting occasions down the years, but this was not one of them. It was a dull game. Jonny kicked seven penalties to see us through 21–10, but France only got their one try in injury time.

Still, three games, three wins: a Grand Slam in the offing. But for me life was taking a turn for the worse. The 'road-rage' incident distracted me and then I picked up a hamstring injury. I thought it was just a slight strain at first. I'd never had any hamstring trouble before and was just running a wide arc down at the Rec in training. I felt a twinge and it didn't get better.

I thought I might just make the Welsh game but it was a few days too soon for the injury, and I ended up watching the match from the bench. After I pulled out, Barrie-Jon Mather took my place. I bet he wished he hadn't, it was his first and only cap. He took some flak. Catty was back in the frame and he tore Wales to pieces at first. We had chance after chance and scored three tries in the first half through Dan Luger, Steve Hanley and Richard Hill. It looked to be all over.

The Ginger Monster had other ideas. He kept that scoreboard ticking over as penalty after penalty went through the posts. It was 25–18 at the interval, three tries to six Neil Jenkins specials. It was to be our undoing, Gibbsy finally smashing through in the very last minute, Jenks converting and all our dreams went down the pan as we lost 32–31. Lawrence took a lot of stick for his decision not to kick for goal in the second half, opting to go for the try from a lineout. It was a gut instinct decision and it didn't come off.

The atmosphere in the dressing-room afterwards was heavy. There was also a fuss upstairs when some of the girls were not allowed into the after-match reception. When you're down, it all goes sour very quickly.

chapter fifteen

tabloid tricks

The drama of the season wasn't quite over. I was in Dubai for a week's holiday with Jayne and the kids. My brother Gary is resident in Dubai and I was doing some work for the charity SPARKS. It was a really relaxing week, just what I needed after the car incident in Bath.

We returned to England that Sunday in mid-April. Lawrence Dallaglio and his partner Alice were in Bath for a weekend break and we were due to hook up that evening for a meal. I landed at Heathrow, switched on my mobile phone and about forty messages flashed up. Oh dear. The *News of the World* had a tasty-looking bit of scandal on Lawrence on page one . . . and page two . . . and three. And so on. It was a massive story. 'England rugby captain exposed as drug dealer' ran the headline.

The front page piece pulled no punches. It alleged that Lawrence had taken Ecstasy with two other members of the British Lions squad in South Africa during the 1997 tour. The details made for terrible reading. 'We had a massive party, an all-day party,' Lawrence is alleged to have said. 'And halfway through the party one of the players in the squad came over to me with three Es and just popped one straight into my mouth. There was one for another squad member, one for myself and one for him ... We celebrated winning the series.'

And there were two silhouettes of two other players from the Lions tour in 1997. Any rugby follower would have worked out that one of the silhouettes was mine. There was also some stuff about parties and women.

It took me all day to track down Lawrence at Clive Woodward's house. He was still in a state of shock. 'Mate, what have you done?' was all I could say. I don't think he realised. The story was everywhere, leading the national news, on every TV and radio bulletin.

I felt sorry for Lawrence, but he had been naïve, there was no doubt about that. He had fallen for a sting. *News of the World* reporters, posing as advertising executives, had promised him £500,000 for a possible promotional campaign and Lawrence took the bait. He went with it, bullshitted along and thought nothing of it. We've all done it to a lesser degree perhaps. He was showing off with a few silly stories and he got burned for it. It was no big crime, although that is the way that it was portrayed.

The honey-trap ploy is disgusting. The paper wanted a story and set out to get it any way that it could. Lawrence fell for it hook, line and sinker. He had been stupid and he said so when he surfaced at a press conference two days later. God, I felt for him then. There was a lump in my throat as I watched him face the cameras as the whole sporting world looked on.

It must have been so humiliating for him. The England captaincy meant so much and here he was throwing it away in this fashion. He was entitled to be angry at the way he was set up but he knew that he played a part in his downfall. He was very, very close to breaking down in that press conference. But he's made of strong stuff and so is his family.

My silhouette implicated me in the story. I wasn't named but my blackened outline suggested that I was one of the two other drug-takers. Jayne recognised it as me straightaway, but she already knew about the partying in Johannesburg because I had told her about it at the time. We had won the series and we got drunk for thirty-six hours. It was virtually the only time on that trip that we did let our hair down. Jayne had given birth to Saskia during that tour and I was in touch a lot. For some reason she wasn't too interested in my drinking tales at the time.

I hadn't actually been with Lawrence on the night in question. He thought I had and had said so, which is presumably why the *News of the World* used my silhouette. I'd started out with him that evening but we'd gone our separate ways. We had a lot to drink in a bar called The Outback, which was opposite the team hotel in Sandton in north Johannesburg. The series was over, the lads were all splitting up and a couple were getting married into the bargain. Can you blame us for letting rip?

There had been little or no bad behaviour on tour up to that time. On the few occasions that I did venture out I'd meet Lawrence and Jason for a bite to eat, maybe arrange to see Stuart Barnes, who was there covering the tour for Sky, and share a few quiet glasses of red wine.

But those nights were few and far between. As for that last weekend, I'd gone to The Outback and then, with a couple of friends, headed off to meet Dave Powell, the solicitor from Bristol who represented a few of the England squad. We cruised through the night around an area called Rosebank and kept missing Lawrence here and there in various bars and clubs.

I actually stumbled back in the next morning to find Lawrence, good man that he is, sorting out my training kit. I'd broken my arm in a game against the Springboks and it was in plaster, so here was good old trouper Lawrence doing my packing for me.

We didn't talk about the night before. Well, not until eighteen months later when I told him what I thought. It was quite simple. He'd broken one of the golden rules by dropping a couple of us in it. I told him that I could forgive him for that but it was unlikely that he would ever captain either England or the Lions again. He was one of my best mates but that was my view then and it is now. We can occasionally joke about it these days, although it took some time before we could.

I had to give evidence at an RFU tribunal at Lincoln's Inn Fields in London, the legal heartland. I wasn't nervous and I didn't feel as if I was on trial. It was Lawrence trying to clear his name. Listening to the evidence that was on tape did provide the odd light moment at the hearing. At one point the judge read out part of the transcript that had been made: '. . . And we all left The Outback and we were mullered . . .' I could imagine Lawrence saying it in those exact words.

The judge asked me what 'mullered' meant. What sheltered lives these blokes lead. Shedded, bollixed, drunk as . . . take your pick. I told the judge that I thought Lawrence was off his face and showing off.

I gave my side of events and that was that. I didn't feel the need to have any legal representation there as I didn't feel I was threatened by the outcome.

Of course, Lawrence didn't come out of it well. But nor did the *News of the World*. I think Lawrence's case was one in a series that made people think twice about those sort of stories. We all like a bit of gossip but sometimes the methods used in obtaining it are unfair. Lawrence paid dearly for his mistake. His England captaincy was over. Little did I know then but my England career didn't have much longer to run either.

chapter sixteen

the quest for the world cup

Three World Cups, three different experiences and three failed attempts to land the big one. I'm looking forward to the 2003 World Cup in New Zealand and Australia, it will be good to see what impact a World Cup makes from the outside. As a player, you often don't appreciate the great atmosphere that builds up around a tournament, you're too busy playing it to savour it. In that regard, the Lions tours are still top of my own personal league. They really are new and exciting challenges.

Two of the World Cups were on home soil and yet it was the 1995 experience in South Africa that made the biggest impression. How could it not with all that was going on in that country at the time. And one man really made it happen: Nelson Mandela, Player of the Tournament by some distance.

* * *

1991 World Cup

It was to be the biggest month in rugby history. The first World Cup four years earlier had been a rushed affair, a good idea that happened before anyone really noticed. This one was planned in detail and the TV schedules had been cleared.

We went into it as champions of the northern hemisphere, but that didn't cut much ice south of the equator. We toured Fiji and Australia in the summer before the World Cup and it wasn't the greatest success story. We beat Fiji 28–11 at Suva, the match being notable for Rob Andrew scoring a try for England, so rare an event that he forgot to tell his biographer about it years later. The other man to make his mark was Mike Teague. 'Iron' Mike had been suffering from a nasty stomach bug but, being the Gloucester warrior that he is, he played. At half-time he looked terrible and as we gathered in the huddle he drew breath, looked up and said: 'Lads, I've given it my all. I can't go on.' It came out as a wheezing, last-gasp speech of a B-movie western hero. Poor old Teaguey. We all burst out laughing and off he went, wondering what he'd done.

Mike wasn't the only strange sight in Suza. Mad Harry's night-club had the most outrageous transvestite on the door that I'd ever seen in my life, with the biggest Adam's apple this side of the Rocky Mountains. Nice eyelashes too.

We came a real cropper against Australia at the Sydney Football Stadium, losing 40–15. It began well enough and I scored a try, the best part of which was that I managed to avoid being smashed into the back row of the stands by Willie Ofahengaue, the Tongan enforcer. Willie O got his revenge, however, when he and Tim Gavin made merry hay with our back row that afternoon.

You might think our morale would have been in pieces at the start of the World Cup after such a mauling, but it wasn't. New season, home turf – it was all in our favour. We embarked on our build-up at Tylney Hall, just outside Basingstoke.

There was a golf course nearby that we made use of. Jon Webb, full back, surgeon and man of precision, decided to do some target practice from the first tee, carving his drive off to the right through the trees. He thought nothing more of it until a man in a white van came steaming round the corner five minutes later, demanding to know who'd ploughed a ball straight through his windscreen. Webby was down the fairway by this time. Just as well. I got done as well – by a dummy ball which exploded in my face as I gave it the big swing, all caught by the TV cameras.

ITV were covering the tournament itself, the first time that rugby had been on commercial television. They gave it their best shot and came up with some lively stuff. Their main cameraman, 'OD', was a good bloke but there were times when the crew was too intrusive, on the team bus and in the changing-rooms. Sometimes the boys played to the cameras rather than getting on with the job.

It was all new and exciting. We weren't used to being together for such a long stretch in our own country. Normally, we only had the forty-eight hours before an international. The World Cup was something else entirely. We filled our bags full of new kit – how easily we were pleased in those days. We became part of the community in Basingstoke and filled the hours doing stuff in local schools. The mood was good.

It soon changed. We began the tournament by playing New Zealand in the high-profile opener, the day that the game was to be sold to the masses. It was a flop, a poor, penalty-strewn match and we were rarely in the hunt. The final scoreline was only 18–12, but the All Blacks always had the edge. Michael Jones scored their try and few non-rugby fans were converted to the cause.

The defeat was a blow. It meant that if results panned out as forecast then we would have to travel to Paris for the quarter-final to take on France. Results panned out as forecast. We beat Italy 36–6, with me scoring two of our four tries. One of them looked quite tasty as I weaved my way through the traffic, but, in truth, I should have been tackled. Our final pool match was another formality when we saw off the United States 37–9. I had a rest, letting Simon Halliday pair up with Will Carling in the centre. The old boy looked in good nick.

We were runners-up in our pool behind New Zealand, so Paris it was. Geoff Cooke had planned things well. He'd fixed up a few days break for us in Jersey, where we met up with wives and girlfriends. It was just what we needed to recharge. Or refuel. I came back into the hotel one day after a stroll with Jayne to see this bloke at the bar doing a great imitation of a collapsed tripod. He was rigid below the waist and at right angles above it. I'd never seen Peter Winterbottom in such a state. He was telling everyone that he loved them. We didn't see him the next day. Can't think why.

We got back to serious business in a good frame of mind. We knew that Serge Blanco and his mates would give us a hard time and we were bent on returning the compliment. It was a hugely enjoyable game, intense and unrelenting. The action didn't even stop at the final whistle. French coach Daniel Dubroca got his knickers in a twist – and former props tend to have outsize knickers – over the refereeing of David Bishop and made a lunge for him in the tunnel. It might have soured the day for him, for Bishop and for the World Cup officials but nothing could have soured our mood after coming away with a 19–10 victory.

Our forwards did their job well and we ran the points in. I managed to put Rory clear to the line in the early stages and Will finished them off later. The French came back at us but it was no good, the defence held firm.

And so it was back to Edinburgh for a semi-final against the auld enemy. There was not quite the same nasty feeling in the air as there had been the year before, but it was another fraught, stomach-churning occasion. And that was just the night when I had to swallow an entire dish of chilli pickles after losing the spoof game. The fixture itself was garbage, and the drama was confined to one howler by Gavin Hastings, who missed a penalty right in front of the posts. I was even chatting to Rory behind the sticks as Gav lined it up, wondering what we would do from the re-start. Oops, there it went, outside the uprights.

We'd never have forgiven ourselves if we had lost, but we offered nothing in that match. We played the percentages and the percentages almost kicked us in the teeth.

The Scots, as always, took defeat well. They turned up for our final against Wallabies the following week decked out in kilts and Aussie scarves. If it was all done for a laugh, then fine. If it was a serious show of support, and it appeared that it was, then it was pathetic. The English always get stick for being bad sports, for supposedly being aloof and arrogant. It's usually the other way around.

The build-up to the Wallabies match was frantic. We were back at our favourite old haunt, the Petersham Hotel in Richmond, where journalist Mark Ryan tried to sneak in and do the dirty on us. It was a good effort but totally wasted. There was no dirty to be had.

It was the game that the tournament needed: England against the Aussies in a World Cup final, and the Aussies didn't waste the opportunity. Or one of them didn't. David Campese lashed us for being boring. If Campo was as predictable on the field as he usually is off it then he would never have become the great winger he was. It was the usual charge: we were boring, dull and inhibited. Mind you, if anyone had just watched our game against Scotland, then they would have agreed.

It got to a few of the lads but I couldn't care less. I just wish more people had got behind us for that final. The Irish have got the right attitude. They'd been beaten in the quarter-final by Australia in a mad match won only at the death by the Wallabies. And yet Ireland were feted throughout the land as heroes.

That Campo got to us was the easy post-match assessment. I don't think he did, although one or two of the boys might subconsciously have wanted to rub his nose in it. Why then did we change our style? Why did we move away from the forward-based strategy, a style that had brought us a Grand Slam and a place in the final itself, in order to take on the Aussies at their own game?

The reasoning was not to show the Aussies that we could do it too, it was a rational assessment that we'd struggle to win lineout ball against John Eales and Rod McCall and so we'd have to find another way of putting them under pressure. So much for pre-match analysis. We won more ball than we'd had all tournament. Ackford and Dooley were magnificent.

And what did we do with it? Well, a fair bit but not enough to win. That's all it was. Their prop Tony Daly managed to get over the try line from close range, which was to help them to a 12–6 victory. However, it was one of the most exciting games I've ever played in for England. We tried everything we knew. Accuse us of being naïve, for we were in not realising that the forward game could have been more fruitful for us, but don't accuse us of not doing our absolute best. Campo was to deny us when he deliberately knocked down a try-scoring pass to Rory. He would have been at least sin-binned for such a stunt these days.

I had no regrets other than the result. That's the only way to take sport. Several of the team took it badly, forwards such as Mike Teague and Paul Ackford. I sought consolation in the traditional manner. I'd met Tim Horan at the Hong Kong Sevens and we had a few more beers that night at one of those desperate official functions. Too many people, too many hangers-on. I signed loads of autographs and one chap came up to me just as I was trying to eat. I asked him politely if he'd mind waiting until the meal was over.

'Do you know who I am?' he asked. 'I'm from the *Sun* and I'll write that it was you that lost England the World Cup.'

And off he went. And, by all accounts, he did write that. It had a terrible effect on my career: eight years later I was forced to retire.

Our first daughter Imogen was born nine months after that World Cup final. Some good came from the day.

1995 World Cup

One flipping kick. That was all we managed to do really well during the 1995 World Cup quarter-final against Australia. One flipping drop-kick. Or should I say Rob Andrew managed it. Mind you, it was some shot, one of these few moments in rugby when I lost my cool. The scores were level at 22–22 and there were only seconds to go. No one had a clue what would happen if the scores stayed that way. Extra time? Replay? Toss of a coin?

There was no time to think, only to do. Big Martin Bayfield won us a lineout, the lads gathered round, drove hard and more ground was made. The ball was flipped out to Dewi Morris, he fed Rob and old Golden let fly. I knew it was over from the second it left his boot. It was one hell of a strike. It just kept going and going. The ball soared high and the Aussies dropped to their knees. In a thousand pubs back in Britain, where the match was beamed live that Sunday lunchtime, a thousand drinks flew through the air. It was one of my best moments in an England shirt.

I had a poor World Cup. I never found form and struggled to hold my place. It was a pity because I felt in great condition coming into the tournament. I also fancied the idea of going to South Africa because I'd missed the tour the year before through injury. My colour doesn't mean much to me and I'm not big on black consciousness political stuff. But you couldn't help but be aware of the significance of colour in that country at that time. You couldn't walk down a street without a banner of Chester Williams, the coloured Springbok wing who was the symbol of the South African marketing campaign, beaming down at you.

Only in certain places does rugby make anything like the same impact as football, and South Africa was one of those places.

The squad met up in mid-May. I drove up to London with two other Bath colleagues, John Mallett and Jon Callard and checked into the Petersham. There was a sponsor's lunch to attend to thrown by Scrumpy Jack, who dredged the bottom of their own barrel to come up with the speaker: Brian Moore.

Mooro had a crack at my alleged vanity, claiming that at a moment of climax I'd been heard to cry out: 'Jerry! Jerry!' Had he been snooping?

On to the evening, another function and another tip-top speaker, Jack Rowell, witty and baffling in the same sentence. Jack had some good lines, recalling a conversation he'd had earlier that day with prop Victor Ubogu. Victor had something on his mind.

'Jack, why is it that people take an instant dislike to me?' asked Victor.

'Simple that one, Victor,' said Jack. 'It saves time.'

That gag was memorable. The other forty-five minutes of the speech were not.

We'd heard quite enough of Jack through the season. He was coach and had set out his stall for us to play expansive, fifteen-man rugby. We talked about it the whole time, the media talked about it constantly and Jack just talked. We never did get to play it.

We left for the great trek south the next morning, landed in South Africa and headed to our base in Durban. South Africa is an exotic country but the Holiday Inn hotel chain is not. In the interests of equality, every team was to stay in one of these hotels. England had stayed more luxurious places the year before. It's not that we are pampered prima donnas, just that the hotels were invariably bulging at the seams with fans, media and the general public. It was impossible to find any space or any privacy.

Durban was a good spot, however, with the Indian Ocean crashing in just across the road. The wives and girlfriends were not to be far away either, most of them turning up after the first match and staying at a nearby hotel. Jayne came out with Imogen, who was two, and Holly, who was only a few weeks old.

First, however, it was into serious training for the Big One: the Welcome Lunch in Cape Town. It was just what we needed: a 6 a.m. alarm call, a quick bite and a ninety-minute flight down to the Cape to sit in a huge, billowing marquee at the Groot Constantia Wine Estate along with four hundred other players, all looking as pissed off about the business as we were. Only the Ivory Coast lads looked happy to be there and in the World Cup. You could have put them in the middle of Johannesburg's most rundown, crime-ridden district and they'd have been happy to be there.

I chewed the fat with some old mates, notably Tim Horan, who had made an unbelievable recovery from an horrific injury twelve months earlier. They thought he might never be able to walk without a limp again, never mind play rugby. And yet here he was.

There was another familiar face floating about: a bit fat around the gills and panting as he ducked in and around the players. I had trouble placing him at first and then it clicked: Stuart Barnes, once of Bath, now of Sky. He'd already mastered the journalistic trade: pen in one hand, glass of red wine in the other.

It was time to 'hit the ground running', as Jack used to put it, but we barely got out of first gear in that opening match against Argentina. We were rusty and off-key, just managing to hold on to win 24–18. If they'd had a goal-kicker they would have buried us.

Back to the drawing board. The temperature was rising, especially in the Rowell household. Word came back from the UK of a back page piece in the *Sun* titled 'Jittery Jack'. Jack took pains to point out at the next team meeting that he'd never felt more relaxed, that he was quite at ease, and he'd never felt happier and more confident – all of which made you feel that he was jittery.

None of us had the nerve to tell Jack that the story had begun as an off-the-cuff joke remark, worked its way through Barnes and a couple of other journalists, been overheard by someone, taken as gospel and found its way to Wapping. The power of tittle-tattle. The *Sun* strikes another blow for truth.

England didn't manage to strike anything in their next match either against Italy. We won 27–20. Big deal. The southern hemisphere were not quaking in their boots when that score filtered through.

I wasn't in my boots at all for the next and final pool match against Samoa, because I'd officially been given a rest so that the others could get a run-out. Mike Catt was at fly half, with Will and Phil de Glanville in the centre. I was happy enough to enjoy a spot of R and R.

The Samoa game was much better, and England won 44–23, scoring four tries in the process. The midfield worked well. Les Cusworth had had more input to coaching for that game, perhaps that had something to do with it. Or maybe it was Catty at fly half, who provided more of a cutting edge than Rob did.

Phil de Glanville was in good form and played well in the centre. Well enough to dislodge me for the quarter-final against Australia the following weekend? That soon became a topic of media speculation.

I knew that I wasn't playing well. Form is like that sometimes, but I didn't feel that I deserved to be dropped. After all, I'd spent much of that season haring up and down the field chasing kicks. If I was going to be dropped, then I wanted it to be for a proper reason. Jack had picked me and then played a system that didn't suit my game.

Four journalists buttonholed me after the team was announced for the quarter-final.

'Are you surprised to be in the team?' I was asked.

I played the dead bat. 'Jack's made his decision and I'm playing,' I replied.

And that was that. Phil finally flipped at the end of the tournament when Jack completely bottled it and picked the supposed first team for the utterly pointless third-fourth play-off game against France. I didn't blame him. Phil had a few drinks and let Jack have both barrels.

The build-up for the game was fierce. It got to everyone and made them do strange things. Will stood up at the team meeting on the Monday and suggested a complete ban on alcohol until after the game. I blamed his outburst on the effects of altitude. Alarmingly, it seemed that most of the squad were siding with Will. Jason Leonard and Victor Ubogu made a last-ditch stand but they were defeated. We then went back to doing what we all normally did, which meant sneaking away for a few glasses from time to time.

Jack called me to his room for a chat at one stage. I was a bit wary and he could see that. 'Nothing heavy,' he said. And so we chatted. About life, the World Cup and my game. Jack was right. It wasn't anything heavy and, for once, it was good to talk.

We chilled out as well as trained hard. The usual stuff: paintballing and golf. Both activities involve spending a lot of time rooting around in bushes. Paintballing is the mock war-game thing where you fire paint balls rather than bullets at each other. Victor was caught making calls on his mobile phone in the middle of the war zone.

We flew down to Cape Town on the Friday. Jayne and the girls were still in the country and Dad had arrived by this time. It was good to meet up.

The clock was ticking. We had a sports psychologist, Austin Swain, with us on that trip. I'm not usually into all that stuff but Austin did come up with some good ideas. At the team meeting that night he gave us a sheet of paper with the numbers one to twenty-one printed down the side, signifying the team and replacements. He asked us to write something positive against every number and then the papers were mixed and cut up. That night, the re-pasted papers were delivered under our doors, each containing twenty-one positive comments about the recipient. It did the trick. We all need a bit of boosting from time to time.

There were faxes and good luck messages from home, ranging from Bill Beaumont to Gary Lineker and Damon Hill.

Will gave a final address, pointing out that we had built for this one for two years and it would be the biggest match of our lives.

He wasn't wrong there. It was hard and intense. The lead changed hands, the play ebbed and flowed. We led 13–3 at one point. I thought I was clear at one stage but the glimmer of space disappeared as quickly as it had opened up. I managed to get the ball away to Will, however, and he put it on to Tony Underwood.

We watched some video footage later which has an Australian commentary on it. You can hear this guy screaming: 'Guscott, Carling, Underwood . . . Underwood. Shut the gate! Shut the gate! Underwood has scored.'

They came back at us when Damian Smith got on the end of an up-and-under to score. Back and forth it went. It got to 22–22 and then Rob Andrew's boot swung and we were the winners.

Left: The Australians celebrate their victory over England in the thrilling 1991 World Cup final. Our much-criticised strategy of opening up the game was a deliberate ploy to keep lineout ball away from Eales (left) and McCall.

Below: We got our revenge four years later in the 1995 World Cup when we beat Australia with a late Rob Andrew drop goal.

Right: My final game for England, against Tonga in the 1999 World Cup. This sprint for the line was the final straw for my groin – it was time to retire after 65 caps and 30 tries.

Below: Making a break during the 1995 semi-final against New Zealand. Unfortunately, they had a bloke called Jonah Lomu...

ALLSPORT

RUSSELL CHEYNE/ALLSPORT

ALLSPORT

Top: No way through in the first Test against the All Blacks in 1993 – but that was the story of the game.

Above: Scoring a try on my Lions debut in the second Test against Australia in 1989. Dad celebrated our win by taking a sledge-hammer to the kitchen wall of our new house, as you do.

Above: Dropping the late goal that secured the 1997 series for the Lions in South Africa.

Opposite: Getting ready for some serious celebrations – it was a truly wonderful moment.

Below: Reminding the South Africans of the score alongside skipper Martin Johnson and goalkicking machine Neil Jenkins.

Above: Going for the smooth look.

Opposite top: People often accuse me of being laid back – I don't know why!

Opposite left: Sometimes I had to go to extraordinary lengths to get my hands on a rugby ball.

Opposite right: Relaxing on the golf course.

ENGLAND
RUGBY

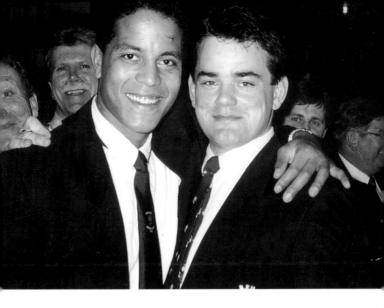

Top: With Will Carling, my centre partner for much of my England career, but because he was captain we weren't especially that close off the field.

Above: With Stuart Barnes, who I always felt should have won more caps for England than he did, because he gave any side an extra dimension.

Aussie Bob Dwyer whinged a bit in defeat afterwards, but the fact was that we'd beaten the Aussies, got a bit of revenge for the 1991 defeat and were in the semi-final against the All Blacks. The family headed back to England, and we headed to Sun City.

It had been a planned break. A few of the boys thought we ought to stay in Jo'burg but they were outvoted. Jack is a serious individual, very driven, but he knows when to switch off, one of the work hard and play hard school. So was I, it was the only educational establishment from which I graduated with honours.

We didn't fear the All Blacks. We'd beaten them two years earlier at Twickenham. The aura had faded. We hadn't seen much of them in the World Cup but the name of Jonah Lomu was on everyone's lips. I'd seen him at the Hong Kong Sevens and he looked an item then, smashing through tackles with his power. I figured that on a more crowded field he might not be as effective.

Think again. Lomu battered his way through four tacklers to score with his first touch of the ball. Mike Catt and Tony Underwood got a lot of stick after the tournament for the way that they'd been blown away. I'm not sure anyone would have got him that day.

It was to get worse when, a couple of minutes later, I lined up my opposite number Walter Little for a tackle deep in their half. There are few images that have stuck in mind from playing rugby, but that one of me sliding down Little's thigh, his shin and his rugby boots and then watching him sprint fifty metres to tee up Josh Kronfeld for their second try was one of them. It was the biggest slap in the face I've ever had on a rugby field. We were twelve points down in a

World Cup semi-final and only five minutes gone on the clock.

We were not in the contest. The All Blacks played the best forty minutes of rugby I'd seen from a side. I didn't really realise fully what was going on at the time, I was so out of breath. They'd come out of the traps as if to say, 'take this, sucker'.

Every time the ball went near Lomu a voice in my head cried 'Oh, my God.' The game was dead and buried within twenty minutes. Ever since that day people have told me that they were at wedding receptions and the like back in the UK and half an hour after kick-off they sneaked away to find a radio and get the score. The reaction was always the same: 'Bloody hell!'

We got back on the scoreboard in the second half when Will got stuck in, but it was a lost cause. Rory and Will got a couple of tries each. To cap it all Zinzan Brooke dropped a goal from forty metres – a back-row forward for goodness' sake. That was taking the piss. The All Blacks were that good that day but it was still a massive disappointment to lose. We genuinely felt that we had the beating of them. We weren't arrogant or complacent, just confident. The history books show the score as 45–29. Actually, we were blitzed.

The dressing-room afterwards was quiet. I tried the head-in-hands routine for a while and then got changed. Jack was talking to the media about 'one or two aberrations'. He was a long way wide of the mark.

There was more misery to come when we boarded the plane for the journey back to Johannesburg. The All Blacks were on the same flight. And worse still, they were at the front of the plane in business class.

We had to troop past them on the way to our economy seats.

The All Blacks didn't make it all the way, however. They in turn were wiped out a week later when South Africa came together in one joyous moment to win the World Cup.

The last few days of the tour were difficult, and no one wanted the play-off game against France. Training was actually fairly brutal and I had a dust-up with Tim Rodber, of all people. Jack kept banging on to us about how hard the All Blacks had trained, that their captain Sean Fitzpatrick had caused one of their guys to have twelve stitches. Rodber went up for a ball in one of our sessions. Unbeknown to me he'd agreed to take part even though he was nursing bruised ribs. I took him in the midriff and could hear the air screeching out of him. I could also hear the 'Guscott, you bastard'. His arms swung and I ducked. Six feet six inches and 17 stone – there's only one way to fight those types. You cling on for dear life and hope the lads will rescue you.

The match against France was one of the worst games of rugby I've ever been involved in. They won 19–9.

I didn't go to the final itself, I couldn't face the coach journey and the hassle. I've no idea how the Springboks beat the All Blacks. There were trumped-up stories later that they'd been poisoned the night before and were throwing up before kick-off. Funny how that story only came out months later – and from a Kiwi.

No, winning was meant to be for Nelson Mandela and his rainbow warriors.

1999 World Cup

The try line stretched away in the distance. Eighty metres to go, a great expanse of Twickenham turf to cover and that would be it. Game, set and match. For me it was all over about a quarter of an hour earlier when my groin had finally packed up. I'd nursed my injury through that World Cup, hoping that a miracle cure might present itself but it never did. One final twinge in that final pool match against Tonga and I knew that I would have to call it a day on my World Cup and on my international career. At least I made it to the try line for a final try.

There had been a couple of moments along the way when it didn't all go to plan. Well, not my plans anyway. World Cups last five weeks for spectators but at least five months for the players. That's the standard length of the intense build-up for most teams, a period when every thought is concentrated on the World Cup – for coaches at any rate. As for me, I'd rather take a more leisurely run-up.

Clive Woodward had booked England in for a training camp off Queensland's gold coast, at a resort on South Stradbroke Island run by the one-time great of long-distance running, Australian Ron Clarke. It sounded good value: training in a great climate, with plenty of opportunity for some R and R. So much for the soft-sell. The reality was plenty of opportunity for training and very little for fun. We were to round things off with two matches: a warm-up against Queensland at Ballymore followed by the Centenary Test against Australia.

Couran Cove was an island about twenty minutes boat ride from Surfers Paradise. Surfers is a lively place. Well, it is during the summer, but in the middle of an Australian winter, the skies may still be blue and the surf inviting but the place was shut. It was tumbleweed town, just a few out-of-season tourists, a couple of die-hard surfers and us, a few waifs in search of an occasional drink and a good time.

You couldn't fault Couran Cove from a training point of view, it was superb. The complex was spread out over 375 acres surrounded by water. It was a small community. The squad was split into groups, several of them housed in chalets on stilts in the water and we had bicycles to get from one part to another. The training pitch was about a ten-minute ride away, as was the gymnasium. And, boy, did I get to know that route well.

It was perfect if all you wanted to do in your life was train, eat and sleep. Neil Back thought he was in heaven but I had a different take on it. We trained three times a day, Lanzarote all over again but without the night-time distractions. I don't know whether a few things were weighing on my mind – a slight hamstring strain, my own court case, Lawrence Dallaglio's enforced absence because of his *News of the World* drama – or simply that Couran Cove and I were not getting on.

After a couple of days Clive called me in for a chat. I was moaning a good deal and he was concerned that I might be a disruptive influence. It wasn't quite the headmaster's study routine. I remembered that script well enough from schooldays and knew I wasn't about to get six of the best.

Clive simply wanted to clear the air. He knew that I hadn't been convinced about the need to come to Couran Cove in the first place and he was well aware of my views on touring. It wasn't that I minded training in itself, but I wanted a few bright lights too. Couran Cove had been billed as the perfect mix of work and play – someone had overlooked the play.

That breakfast meeting was a yellow card of sorts, a shot across the bows. Clive knew that I was on-side in most ways, the situation just needed a bit of smoothing out. My main beef was that Couran Cove had been sold to me as something else, not the blood and guts routine it was turning out to be.

I think I wanted the World Cup to happen there and then but it was still over four months away. I was not feeling at ease with the situation, and when that is the case everything becomes a chore. When players don't perform well in a game it's invariably because they are distracted. They might have some hassle at home, be worried about a contract or had a bust-up with someone in the squad.

It was just as well that I did manage a couple of breakouts from 'The Rock', as Couran Cove became known. Jason Leonard and I hooked up with John Mitchell one night and headed over to Surfers. Mitch was also a man who liked to put in the work during the day and then relax at night. By this stage, he and Clive were not communicating too well. I told Mitch that he had to sort himself out and decide what he wanted to do with his life. It didn't surprise me when Mitch headed back to New Zealand at the end of the next season to take up a coaching post with Waikato. Within six months he'd landed one of the prestigious

Super 12 coaching jobs with the Chiefs and was on his way.

I was on my way back to Surfers a couple of more times during that stay and once I almost didn't make it back to base. I wasn't that fussed about drinking that particular night and so offered to be the driver on the mainland for Jason and Gloucester hooker Neil McCarthy. We headed across to the mainland in a little water-taxi and off we went round a few bars in tumbleweed town. We had a good night and headed back to port for the water-taxi back to 'The Rock'.

Halfway across to the island the taxi conked out. No problem, the local Aussie seemed to know what he was doing. Or not. He fiddled and fretted while we drifted. Jason had come over all misty-eyed and was standing down one end of this piddly little boat gazing up at the stars and moonlight. McCarthy, meanwhile, was off his face, babbling on about sharks and wild currents and shipwrecks. I was stone-cold sober and getting twitchy. We were still drifting and the waves were splashing over the side of the boat. It was not a place I wanted to be.

The boatman radioed for assistance. Jason gazed at the moon, Neil droned on and I got wound-up.

'Not long now, mate,' was all the taxi driver said, as taxi drivers all around the world tend to say.

I expected another small craft – one of his mates, probably – to come alongside. Instead, about twenty minutes later, a huge boat with all lights blazing came steaming round the headland, pounding through the waves. It was at full tilt, the full sea rescue package. I don't know what it expected to find, but what it got was two drunks and one pissed-off centre. I expected them to heave a line and tow us in. Oh no. Down came a rope ladder. Another bloody training exercise.

We had three weeks on Couran Cove and at least I finished in half-decent shape. We pitched camp in Brisbane for a couple of days before we took on Queensland. They were Super 12 semi-finalists but were without eleven of their internationals, who were with the national team.

It was a useful run-out, but not one that I could get over-excited about. Leicester wing Leon Lloyd got his first start for England and got a couple of tries as we won 39–14. I got on the scoresheet too.

Then it was off to Sydney, one of my favourite places, where we were based around the headland at Manly. The weather closed in after a fine start to take the edge off the setting. The Manly Pacific used to be one of the world's great hotels, just a few yards from the beach where huge rollers come crashing in to shore. It's a surfers' Mecca, although the hotel is a faded glory these days.

The Australia Test was a full-bore Test match in billing but we all knew that our legs were elsewhere. We'd trained at Couran Cove for the World Cup, heavy-duty stuff that had taken its toll. We'd never prepare in that way prior to any normal international.

It was the Centenary Test as well, which meant that both sides wore specially commissioned shirts fashioned on the original of 100 years ago. The game was to be played at Stadium Australia, the venue for the Olympics that were taking place the following year.

We visited the Stadium on the Thursday. It was not an awe-inspiring stadium in the way that the

Millennium Stadium in Cardiff works for some people, it was too open for that. Even so, I broke away from the group to have a stroll around on my own, imagining what it would be like some fourteen months hence. It didn't disappoint when the Olympics hit town.

We didn't disappoint either. We lost yet again on Australian soil, where we had never won, but it was an encouraging show in many respects. We had a seven-point lead after half an hour but then got wiped out within eight minutes as we turned the game over to them. Matt Perry had zipped in after a great cut-out pass from Mike Catt had put him clear. But we blew it. We got turned over a couple of times, the Wallabies pounced and Ben Tune scored twice within a few minutes. We were as good as out of it.

Steve Waugh, the Australian cricket captain, had been given a tour of honour before the match in front of the 80,000 crowd for having brought home the cricket World Cup a few days earlier. The Aussies knew what it took to win.

And so did we and we returned home in good heart. We had known that we would have to struggle to last the pace for eighty minutes. Yet, compared to 1991 when we'd been really taken to the cleaners by Australia in the summer build-up to the World Cup, we'd shown that we could compete.

I was looking forward to getting home. We had a fitness test with England on July 19 – a make or break session – and I also had other things to tend to. The court case needed some attention. My lawyer David Powell was moving on from Alsters and I had to get to know his replacement, Tim Hayden.

England had a few get-togethers through the summer and there were a couple of warm-up Tests scheduled for the end of August against the United States and Canada. The tournament proper did not begin until October, but the organisers had banned any international team playing against another during September. I was eager to get on with it.

Clive arranged a four-day team-bonding exercise with the Marines at their base in Lympstone, just outside Exeter. The lads there are the real thing and the basic training they do just to get to wear the beret is incredible. I couldn't cope with it in a million years. Jason's brother is a Marine. At least one in the family turned out to be fit.

We did the standard stuff there – assault courses, trekking through the woodland, diving down into submerged helicopters. The assault course was the killer. We had to carry ammunition boxes, logs and poles across the estuary, which was basically a stinking pit of mud that came up to your knees.

The Marines were big on hammering home the value of 'dislocated expectations', emphasising the need to be able to adjust quickly when things did not work out as anticipated. One of their guys, Nathan Martin, who oversaw our visits, has now come on board full-time to work with Clive, organising all the logistical needs of the squad. It's a good appointment.

We did two stints there and I got on well with the Marines and liked them, but I'm not too sure that my feelings were reciprocated. They did individual profiles on us all, monitoring our ability to work in teams under pressure, obey orders and so on. When Clive read my report he asked for a meeting with me and laid out his concerns. The Marine assessment doubted my commitment to the cause and felt that I might be a disruptive influence and he wanted to make sure that I was full steam ahead for the tournament as well as prepared to integrate fully into the squad. We ironed out the problem between us and I explained to Clive that on the second visit to Lympstone I was already nursing my groin injury and did not want to go full blast. However, Clive knew that I was easily bored and that that could become a problem, so he made me social secretary for the tour. No more pasta meals for the boys, Chinese here we come.

I had a hard time during the build-up to the World Cup and knew deep down that I might not make it all the way through. My groin went in the game against Canada in late August. We had a ludicrously easy opener against the United States first, which we just about scraped through 106–8. I scored four tries and they were not four of the toughest I've ever run in.

Seven days later it was Canada in the dock and they gave us a more testing time. We won 36–11 but the next morning I could hardly get out of bed. It was not the result of taking my social secretary duties too seriously but the groin I'd damaged. I'd been here before, five years earlier, when a groin injury had wiped me out for an entire season.

However, this didn't feel as bad as on that occasion. I got the doc, Terry Crystal, to take a look. There was no point treating it there and then with injections as an anti-inflammatory jab is best used much nearer the time of actual competition. Clive was put in the picture and we had a decision to make. Did I play in the tournament or not?

Two days later Clive announced the World Cup party of thirty and I was in. We kept the injury quiet right through to the start of the competition and even beyond. There was no point in alerting the opposition to the problem and I was still hopeful of making a recovery. But I had to train in discomfort.

At least I was selected. One or two Bath mates were less fortunate. Ben Clarke missed out as Clive opted for Wasps young back-row forward Joe Worsley. Victor Ubogu thought he would be having a quiet October when he was left out of a training squad named eight days before the final World Cup group was announced. Game over? Not quite. Eight days later Victor was back on World Cup duty.

I was to have only a marginally more meaningful involvement in the World Cup than Victor. At least he was a good assistant social secretary – the Buddah Bar in Paris was one of his better recommendations.

I sat out the ad-hoc warm-up matches against select XVs drawn from the Premiership and was once more on the bench for the start of the first match proper, against Italy. After the game we came clean and Clive made the announcement that I'd been labouring with the injury for over a month.

'It's frustrating,' I said later at the press conference. 'I feel generally as fit as I ever have done. The real downside is not being able to compete properly for the place. It would be unfair on all those who have put the work in over the last month if I were to come straight back into contention.'

I also stated that there was no long-term problem and that I was on my way back. It wasn't one of the most truthful statements I've ever made to the press, but it was important to maintain the front that all was going well with England's preparation.

I actually got on in the Italy match far earlier than expected when Will Greenwood went off with a hamstring strain after thirty-five minutes. However, I was at half-cock and I didn't enjoy it particularly, even though we ran out comfortable winners 67–7.

Still, I was in the frame for the Big One, the game that had loomed over us ever since the tournament schedule had been revealed. It was not that we feared the Kiwis but that the loser would be faced with an uphill struggle. It was odds-on that both ourselves and New Zealand would qualify from the group. However, the runner-up would have to contend with a midweek play-off to see who went through to the quarter-final proper four days later. That extra game would take its toll.

But first the All Blacks. I got the nod. Will Greenwood made it as far as the bench so I teamed up with Phil de Glanville in the centre. The All Blacks had picked a novice centre against me – a bloke by the name of Christian Cullen. Just when you thought it might be getting a touch easier the opposition experiment by putting one of the most potent finishers the game has ever seen up against you.

They also had a chap called Lomu on their teamsheet. My memory is going a bit but I think he played against us in the 1995 World Cup too.

'If you can't get excited by the thought of playing this lot, then you shouldn't be in the game,' I said at the time. 'It's like a massive game of chess out there, each trying to second-guess the other. Hungry for it? You bet.'

And ready. Sort of. I'd had an anti-inflammatory injection administered at a hospital in High Wycombe under local anaesthetic on the Monday. It kicked in as it should have done about twenty-four hours later and the pain eased.

I wanted a fairy-tale ending, to go out helping England win the World Cup and score the clinching try. Doesn't everyone? All the sacrifices had been made but it was not going according to plan.

Nor did the match itself. We were on an equal footing but Lomu, as ever, was on another planet. All the Kiwis needed was a glimpse, a half-chance to set him free and we would be in trouble.

That's all he got and he took it with both hands. And both huge thighs and pounding legs. We'd clawed our way back to 16–16 midway through the second half after falling behind to a Jeff Wilson try early on. I chipped to help tee up Phil de Glanville's try and he had the presence of mind to dot the ball against the base of one of the posts. Jonny Wilkinson's conversion got us back on level terms.

There was nothing between us until Lomu got the ball. We were turned over in midfield, they flashed the ball wide and the big man was on the wide outside. I went for him first, dived and got a fingernail on him. Somehow it was not enough and on he went. I looked up to see him ploughing along the west touchline, through Austin Healey, Matt Dawson and Dan Luger.

Matt Perry has managed to bring Lomu down before. He does it by sticking his head in between the giant's knees and pulling him down on top of him. By the time Matt got to him all Jonah had to do was to stretch out and plant the ball over the line. The timing of the tackle is everything with Lomu. Even the textbook can't help you much unless you were to flatten him with it in the tunnel. You can go for the classic round-the-thighs approach but his legs are so big that it's impossible sometimes to get a full grasp. Mehrten's conversion made it 23–16 and New Zealand had struck with a vengeance. They got another one before full-time, a dodgy effort when they nicked a ball in an offside position, scrum half Byron Kelleher rounding it off.

We'd had a lot of possession but we hadn't done enough with it. Did we take too many easy decisions along the way rather than opting for the tough one that might have reaped a reward? I know that I chipped for the corner early on when I might have been better backing myself to make some yardage with ball in hand. What might have been.

We still had one pool match to go, against Tonga. Understandably, my name wasn't on the team list. I wasn't even named to be on the bench. However, twenty-four hours later I was back in the side. Phil de Glanville had bruised ribs and there I was, back in my familiar spot for the sixty-fifth time.

It was the last hurrah. I was desperate to make an impression because I knew the sands of time were running out – too desperate. At one point I was following up a kick through and noticed Mike Catt coming up on my shoulder. I nudged him out of the way to try and be sure of the touchdown. As it was, neither of us got pressure on the ball and I did the next best thing by appealing for the try anyway. It wasn't given.

A quarter of an hour before the end my groin injury

got even worse. We were coasting by that stage. I got a try and then, with the last action of the game, got the ball with a clear field ahead. I made it – just – and flopped over the line. God did have a bit of a conscience then, letting me finish with a flourish. Paul Grayson's conversion took us past the century and 101–10 was the final score. The Twickenham crowd gave me a standing ovation. They must have sensed something was afoot.

I called Clive over to my cubicle in the changing-room and told him that it was all over.

'Oh, Jesus, that's all we need,' said Clive, knowing what lay ahead in the next few days.

The news was passed to the medical boys, Terry Crystal, Kevin 'Smurf' Murphy and Nigel Henderson. They took my opinion as read.

And that was that. It was a real downer. The news was officially announced two days later after the boys had seen off Fiji 45–24, in the quarter-final play-off. My Bath team-mate, Mike Tindall was brought in as a replacement. And I contacted Victor to see what the plans were for Paris. The social committee was still on the case.

I decided to stick with the squad. Clive gave me the option stay or leave, although he mentioned that he valued having me around. Paris it was then. There were some compensations to be had. Victor, under-used to the point of exclusion in the World Cup, gave me a good send-off. I didn't fancy going home if only to avoid having to think about the court case, although I was fairly philosophical about the whole thing in context. I believe in destiny and just getting on with things.

I did some summarising for ITV on the quarter-final against the Springboks, which didn't tax my range of vocabulary too much. Drop goal, drop goal, drop goal. What the bloody hell was that? Another drop goal.

I felt for England. They'd been done for by a freakish sequence of kicks from Jannie de Beer. There's so little you can do to defend against the drop-kick and it's a depressing way to lose a game. England were already at a disadvantage before the game even started because the Springboks had been in Paris for a week and were fresh whereas England arrived Thursday evening after playing Fiji the day before.

And that was it. We all trooped back on the Eurostar that Monday morning, fed up to the back teeth. I was at Twickenham the following weekend to watch the French do what only the French can do in beating the All Blacks. I was in Cardiff on corporate hospitality duty on the day of the final. I didn't make it to the stadium and I didn't miss much. The Australians had come to do a job and they did it.

the british lions

The call came on a Monday morning in 1989. I was living at my parents' house and was sleeping off the weekend celebrations following Bath's Cup final win over Leicester. I was not in the mood to take a phone call. Bath second row John Morrison did a passable imitation of several voices and had caught me out before. This one purported to be Clive Rowlands, manager of the British Lions party that was leaving very shortly to tour Australia. Good effort, John. A very plausible Welsh accent and it sounded sincere too. I knew, of course, that the squad had been picked a few weeks before, but Will Carling was pulling out though with a shin injury, said the voice. Not a bad line. Decent wind-up this. I let him drone on for a bit. And for a bit longer. Just as well really – I would never have found out which plane we were catching otherwise.

And so began the first of my three tours with the British and Irish Lions. They were, without question, the highlights of my rugby career. Maybe if England had won a World Cup and I'd been swept along with all that that entailed then I might push World Cups up the rankings. As it is, the podium goes one, two, three to the Lions.

A place in the Lions is like the chief executive's job in a company, the editor's job on a newspaper, the politician who makes it to Number Ten. For a rugby player, there's no better feeling, no greater status to be had than to be selected for the Lions. It took a while for it to really sink in. At that time in my young life I was more bowled over by all the free kit handed out than the historical significance of the Lions. It felt good but I didn't appreciate what it really meant. I was intent just on doing it rather than analysing it. I'd gone from Bath and England to Lions within the space of a weekend. If you'd pinched me, I wouldn't have woken up. It felt too good.

It still felt good eight years later when I managed to swing my right boot at just the right time to send the ball between the sticks to help win the series in South Africa. The more I had to do with the Lions the more I got swept up by all that it entailed: the historic battles, the glorious victories, the valiant defeats.

Think of the great names of British and Irish rugby, names such as Gareth Edwards, Willie John McBride, Ollie Campbell, Gavin Hastings, Tony O'Reilly, Barry John, and you immediately think of them in a Lions context.

There was talk in the mid-nineties, with the onset of professionalism, that the Lions would fade away, there would not be enough time to fit them into the new professional order. It was merely a media talking point. The Lions are bigger than they have ever been, more popular both home and abroad then ever. Twenty thousand people have just followed the Lions to Australia for the 2001 tour, which is a higher figure of overseas supporters than went to the Sydney Olympics.

The southern hemisphere countries would never give up on the concept either because a Lions tour is such a big earner and rooted in their own history as well. In South Africa and New Zealand we'd pitch up at a new place and the local papers would be full of cuttings from papers back down the years of previous Lions visits to those parts. It was fascinating to read the fading old cuttings. That just doesn't happen when you tour with England. I think the southern hemisphere players are envious too. The Lions is different, a new challenge, a chance to test yourself in a unique way. And the players all start from the same base, you are all equal when you first meet no matter what you may or may not have achieved up to that point.

1989 Lions to Australia

Once I'd established that I had bigger thighs than Finlay Calder I settled into the tour. They roomed me with the Lions captain as soon as we got to Australia. It was a nice gesture, but I wasn't going to play the shy, innocent, unsure new boy role. I was too shy, innocent and unsure of myself for that. So I pointed out to Finlay that his thighs were disappointingly thin for an international back-row forward. We hunted round for a piece of string and measured up. I won.

I didn't win on the discussion about who I thought

should be the openside flanker for the first Test. Andy Robinson, Bath colleague, was my choice.

'Not me, then?' said Finlay. 'Lions captain?'

'No,' I replied.

I lost that one. Finlay played in all three Tests and I came to appreciate him as a full-blooded captain. Robbo might well have been playing better in the early stages of the tour, but Finlay really came through in the third and decisive Test. I wouldn't have fancied playing against Finlay, he was one of those players who was driven by adrenaline. But he was a born leader, with a knack of saying the right thing. I was motivated by what he said – and that hasn't happened too often.

I had no designs on a Test place when we landed in Perth, Western Australia. Well, not until the end of the first day at any rate. There's something about the Lions that brings you together yet makes you competitive. There were three other centres in my sights: John Devereux, Brendan Mullin and Scott Hastings. For the record, a Welshman, an Irishman and a Scot, although on Lions tours the nationality disappears from day one. Everyone's a mate, everyone's a rival.

I didn't expect to make the Test team because I was still the new boy, the young bloke who was still happiest meeting up with Chalkie and Pete on Sunday mornings in the Pulteney Arms in Bath to piece together what had happened the night before.

I stuck close to Gareth Chilcott. I knew that everyone got on with Coochie and I figured that some of it might rub off on me. However, there was no need to worry, because the 1989 Lions were a good bunch. Clive Rowlands was manager, the archetypal Welshman, and a great bloke. He was so passionate, so caring about the Lions, that you couldn't help but feel the same way. He was often in tears in the dressing-room when we'd won. He was on the one occasion when we lost too. And he'd often grab the badge on his Lions blazer and tell you: 'The Lion is getting bigger.'

Ian McGeechan was coach and it was my first contact with him. He made an impression from the start, a nice bloke who talked my language. It amazed me that he could get through to props as well as to wingers. He had an idea, a thought and a tip for everyone. What struck me was how small he looked, how much like a back he was in stature. It was great: all backs and forwards together, all nationalities together. And you were running at each other in training, none of this half-cock, unopposed stuff. This was competitive, fresh and it was exciting.

Geech encouraged me from the start. During training he'd slip past and say: 'Well done. Keep it going.'

I kept it going on all fronts. We were based at the Burswood Resort Hotel in Perth. It was huge and it had a casino. That took care of any worry as to how I might use up that generous tour allowance.

I first officially wore the red shirt of the British Lions on a wretched night on a crappy pitch in Melbourne against Australia B. I didn't notice the surroundings, I was only interested in the shirt. Several of the forwards, such as John Jeffrey and Mike Griffiths, did the climbing-walls routine in the warm-up. I joined in for all of a half a second and then had to try hard not to giggle. I barely touched the ball all evening, but I was now a Lion and the tour was under way.

I only had half an eye on the Test team. I was a dirt-tracker, a member of the mid-week side. Perhaps

I ought to have had a full eye on the Test team, and then I might not have gone out and got wasted the night before I was picked for the shadow Test team against New South Wales at the North Sydney Oval. I was selected initially for the bench so I went out with my dirt-tracker mates for just a couple of beers on the Friday night. My maths never has been much good. A couple suddenly became a shedful. We reeled from one bar to another and then into a dingy night-club.

A little voice at the back of my head did nag away to ease up just in case. I finally listened to it a few hours before dawn and poured coffee down my throat, which meant that my hangover hit before I even managed to get to sleep back at the hotel. The early-morning pounding on my door finally got through to me and I opened it and peered out. Through my slit eyes I could see Geech, who was telling me that Mullin had pulled out and that I was in the starting line-up.

Ah. Right. Just coming. Kevin Murphy, the physio-therapist, bailed me out. Smurf had also had a bit of a night and knew a sad case when he saw one. He worked his magic on my body and the opposition didn't get too near me that afternoon. Can't blame them, I smelt like a brewery. Craig Chalmers dropped a late goal to win us the match.

My late-night escapade did not seem to be counting against me. A few nights later, in Sydney, as we prepared for the first Test, Roger Uttley came calling.

'Make sure you get an early night,' he said, fresh from a lengthy selection meeting.

He told me to keep the news to myself. What news? Was I in the Test team or not? I was dying to tell Robert Jones my room-mate and it was just as well I didn't.

Roger contacted me again very early the next morning. He'd got his wires crossed: Devereux and Hastings were unfit but the selectors had gone for Mullin and Mike Hall. Big Rog apologised profusely. And I took it on the chin.

Roger was assistant coach on that tour and he had a hard time of it. As I've said before, I came to appreciate Roger the more I found out about him, that he too had been a Lion, a hard, unselfish player in his day.

There was friction with the Scottish contingent from the outset. Finlay and the likes of John Jeffrey did not want to go down the route of England's mauling style of play. Roger was frozen out and I'm not sure quite how much time England lads such as Dean Richards and Brian Moore had for him either. That relationship blew hot and cold.

Later in the series the forwards took control themselves, with the English boys reverting to what they knew best. Finlay simply didn't get on with Roger, known as 'Claypot' after the ugly clay doll that we carted round with us for some reason. Calder made no mention of Roger whatsoever when he submitted his official end of tour captain's report.

Rog would set himself up sometimes. Wade Dooley had worked his way into the Test team, replacing Bob Norster, and Roger was delivering a training talk:

'Dai Young, you're in the Test team because you're raw and aggressive. Mooro, you're there because you get stuck in at all times. David Sole, you're there because you're mobile, Ackers because of your lineout presence, Teague because you're on fire round the field and Dooley, you've won promotion because, because . . . you're big.'

I got on with everyone. Well, almost everyone. Wasps winger Chris Oti got up my nose. In an early match on the tour against Queensland Country in Cairns, Chris messed up a pre-planned move by coming in when he shouldn't have done, and I gave him a mild, very mild bollocking.

After the game, Roger took me to one side and asked me what had happened between myself and Chris Oti. He said that Chris wasn't very happy with my comments. I couldn't believe that an on-field remark, quite right in its context, had been turned against me by Oti.

He was injured shortly afterwards and went home.

I got stuck into everything: training, drinking, the whole works. It was the trip of a lifetime. I did my stint in the dirt-trackers, 'Donal's Donuts' as they became known after the midweek captain Donal Lenihan, the Irish lock who has just been manager to the 2001 Lions. If he brought any of the spirit he conjured up in 1989 to the most recent trip then it will have been a great tour.

I played hard after working hard. Everything was a step up. Training was murderous but fun and I remember one session in Melbourne, in the mud, when we did shuttle run after shuttle run. Then star jumps. Then burpees. I was dying and it was only when I looked across and saw Andy Robinson literally on his knees crawling forward that I realised everyone else was dying too.

It was first Test time. And we lost, convincingly, 30–12. We were outplayed up front and never got a look-in behind. Four days later we were in Canberra playing Australian Capital Territories, not at that time the slick Super 12 outfit they are these days. We were losing 17–0 and that was the moment that the tour could have come off the rails. That was the moment when I realised just what Lions tours are all about. You don't get second chances, there is no breathing space. The tour ends and everyone goes their own way for four more years or, maybe, forever. You either make it happen then or you never will.

We made it happen. We came back to beat Australian Capital Territories 41–25 and the next day I was named in the side to face Australia in the second Test at Ballymore in Brisbane. It was the day before my twenty-fourth birthday. Scott Hastings was alongside me in the centre, and Rob Andrew, a late arrival for the injured Paul Dean, was also on board as was big Wade Dooley, as big Rog Uttley would say.

No late nights for me. I wasn't going to let anything spoil this party. Unless you count my comment to a radio reporter, followed up by every single newspaper on the planet, that Australian referees are 'all one-eyed and crap'. Clive Rowlands had a word to say about that. Or three.

It was the only minor blot on a great build-up. The squad had really pulled together and I looked around at the calibre of player taking the field: Gavin Hastings, Ieuan Evans, Rory, Robert Jones, Ackers, Deano. We were not going to lose this one.

We were losing 12–9 as the game wore on in the second half. It was tense and it was close. We sneaked in front when Scott threw a long, bouncing pass to brother Gav, who touched down. They came back at us.

And then I had one of those wonderful moments.

I don't know precisely why I did what I did. I had actually tried a similar little stunt in the ACT game but it hadn't come off and no one had noticed. It looked like a doomed ploy – and that, apparently, was what went through Finlay's mind as he looked up from yet another bruising maul, having secured hard-won possession for us, to see me shape to kick. What the hell was he doing now?

I was on cruise-control. Nothing could touch me. The Australian back line closed on me. Closer. Closer. There it went, a little, stabbing kick behind them, a dab on the accelerator, a whiz past them, the ball bounced up, thank you very much, a try under the posts.

Did it feel good? It felt like hundreds of moments all rolled into one. Bath mini-rugby with my dad at the age of seven, Walcot Old Boys, my best mates Pete and Chalkie, old rugby figures such as Robbie Lye, George Norman, working my way through the Spartans into Bath first team – it was all there in the blink of an eye. I rarely show emotion on a rugby field but I showed it that day all right. I could have kept on running and running. It was a mega moment.

Behind the bench on the touchline someone bellowed behind Kevin Murphy: 'He'll never have to lay another flippin' brick in his life.' They weren't wrong there.

Back home in Bath, the party was just beginning. We'd won 19–12, the series was tied 1–1 and I was the hero of the hour. Dad did what proud dads always do at six o'clock in the morning. He walked out his house in St Saviour's Terrace, carrying a sledgehammer. He headed to the small terraced house in Larkhall that

Jayne and I had just bought, let himself in and demolished the wall that we had earmarked for removal in order to extend the kitchen. It was the perfect release of tension for him.

Twelve thousand miles away we found other more traditional ways of letting off steam. I think we'd earned our drink. The job was only half done, of course. The third Test in Sydney now assumed colossal proportions.

We headed up to Surfers Paradise for a break. There was no mid-week match – and no surfers either, it was mid-winter and the place was closed. All our best-laid plans for a spot of R and R went out the window, but all Geech's best-laid plans for finishing off the Wallabies now came into play.

The Aussies were hurt and it showed. They whinged and criticised us for our supposed brutality. There had been several skirmishes during the match, including one catchweight contest between the scrum halves, Robert Jones and Nick Farr-Jones. If that was laughable then Dai Young's kick on the head of Aussie lock Steve Cutler was not.

The Aussie press accused us of premeditated violence, and of orchestrating the whole thing in much the same way that Willie John's '99' call in reference to the Boer War had so upset the Springboks in 1974. We listened and we lapped it up. They were squealing.

There had been no deliberate plot to beat them up. It was a ferocious Test but that was just the way it was. They were seeking to destabilise us through the media and it led to some of the most savage and disgraceful editorials I've ever seen.

It was laughable and it had the opposite of the

desired effect. We now knew that they respected us and even feared us a little – just what we wanted.

Geech drove us on. I had got on famously with him throughout the tour and was to do so for the next two. It was not so much what he told me as what he didn't tell me that made such an impression. He didn't preach and he didn't lay down plans in stone. He's like Brian Ashton in that regard, there is no black and white in his world, only possibilities. He did some basic stuff – such as getting me to pass a bit longer – but his great strength was to make you believe in yourself and in those around you.

I think he might have got more out of the back line in 1989 and he felt that too. But he knew where the route to success was: up front with the forwards. That's where he was going to take the Aussies. And he did.

Finlay came into his own in the few days and the few hours before the Test. Even I started to get all emotional and hyped. However, I refrained from head-butting walls – plasterboard has never been on my diet.

It was a mighty match. The sporting wheel threatened to spin full circle for me in that game: from the high of scoring in Brisbane to the shame of letting Michael Lynagh hoodwink me in midfield and go steaming through to set up Ian Williams for a try. I was horror-struck.

There was no time to dwell on it, thank goodness. It was a furious match and it turned on one of the biggest mistakes of Test rugby when David Campese tried to run the ball out from near his own line, misjudged it, got closed down and threw a loose ball in the vague direction of his full back, Greg Martin. He was not ready for it, Ieuan Evans pounced and we scored.

From hero to zero: Campo got the full treatment afterwards as we hung on to win 19–18. He trudged out early from the post-match dinner and the Aussie press gave him both barrels. Praise him one minute for his genius; slaughter him the next. The press can have it both ways, a player can't.

I was too busy celebrating to worry about Campo's plight at the time. There was still another week of the tour to go although there were no Test matches. Geech came up to me and said: 'You've done enough.' I had the week off. I think you can guess how I spent it. I'd loved the Lions and I wanted more.

The Lions 1993

'You go first.' 'No, you go.' 'Come on, one of us has to go first or we'll be up here all afternoon.'

Lions tours are serious affairs, the pinnacle of a player's career, the point he's been striving towards for four years. He wants nothing to jeopardise his chance of making the trip, of . . .

'Bunnggeeeee!'

As I launched myself into the north London air I did wonder for a split second just what the hell I was doing. The ground rushed up towards me and I could see some faces down there, several of which were laughing. Two, those of my mother and father, had a more concerned look on them. Thank God Ian McGeechan wasn't there, it might have been a hefty tour fine before the tour had even started.

The Lions had already gathered for the 1993 tour to

New Zealand. We assembled at the Oatlands Hotel in Weybridge but took a break for the final league matches of the season. As always, good fixture planning – the Lions had only been on the schedule for about ten years. Still, it was an important league game for Bath. We had to beat Saracens to win the Courage title again. We did – just. It was time to celebrate and someone mentioned the bungee jump that was taking place at the back of the clubhouse.

Next thing I knew, myself, Ben Clarke and Stuart Barnes were being hoisted skywards, Lions all three. Good effort. Lions stick together. Or perhaps it was the champagne we'd glugged in the dressing-room. We all landed safely and pretended that it had been a doddle. No one noticed the bicycle clips at the bottom of the tracksuit trousers.

We were off and away to rugby country. I loved New Zealand and it didn't bother me that the place was supposed to be slow and behind the times. Those tired old gags just didn't feature for me, although Invercargill may not be top of my holiday destinations. The 1993 trip was socially the best trip I went on, a gas from first to last mainly because of the company I kept, often with the Welsh boys: Richard Webster, Robert Jones, Ieuan Evans and Scott Gibbs. Barnesie was there, and so was Ben Clarke. Coochie managed to get himself into the country too, but this time as a tour leader for a travel company.

I loved the fact that people cared about their rugby in New Zealand. The woman in the post office, the lady who cleans your room, the guy at the petrol station – they all knew more about technicalities of rucking and mauling than do most backs. The taxi-drivers in particular were clued up as to what was going on. They knew everything and everybody, which is why I had to pay a bill of $400 after one evening when we'd returned late and I'd somehow managed to put my foot on a taxi-driver's dashboard. Lions manager Geoff Cooke summoned me the next morning. There had been several of us in the taxi.

'You were the only one he recognised,' said Cooke. I wonder why that was.

The first task as always with a Lions tour is to make the cut. All the confidence built up over several months disappears on the weekend of selection. Particularly if you've been smashed at Lansdowne Road by the Irish. That result led to a very twitchy thirty-six hours.

In Bath, in Wales, in the Scottish Borders, in corners of the four countries that make up the Lions, little gaggles of players worried and fretted during those last few hours. In London, Peter Winterbottom, Jason Leonard and Brian Moore could contain themselves no longer. They rang Dick Best, their club coach at Harlequins and assistant coach to Ian McGeechan on the Lions tour.

Bestie told them that he was sworn to secrecy so the boys rang off and had another pint. Another phone call followed. By the end of the fifth pint and fourth rebuttal, even Dick had had enough.

'You're in. Now leave me alone,' shouted Bestie down the phone.

Peter Jackson of the *Daily Mail* has been known to use similar tactics.

The rest of us heard of our selection at various stages through the Monday. Gavin Hastings was to be captain. There had been long-running speculation as to who would be selected between him and Will Carling. Will had won back-to-back Grand Slams with England and Gavin had far less to his name as a captain. And yet there was never any doubt in my mind that he would be a good leader. He had a presence about him. I don't know when the actual decision was made. There was talk that Will withdrew himself from consideration before the final selection meetings. Geoff Cooke was manager and Geech coach, so they would each have had their thoughts close to home.

Will and Gavin did not get on too well in later years. I've never sat down with either of them to find out why because it didn't bother me then and it doesn't bother me now. For that trip Gavin was captain and that was fine by me.

There were seventeen Englishmen in the final party of thirty. Jon Webb and Jeff Probyn were the only regulars to miss out. Jon was up against a host of top contenders, including Gavin himself and Tony Clement of Wales. Jeff was a casualty of politics and England's dodgy day in Dublin, when we were swept away by an emerald tide in the final match of the Five Nations championship. Two Scots, Paul Burnell and Peter Wright, were chosen, which was a decision that didn't look too bright at the time and was to look stranger as the tour progressed.

The great debate passed me by. I was in and that's all I was really bothered about. That and who the tour judge and prosecutors were. Irish prop Nick Popplewell was elected judge, and Barnesie was prosecutor. The court is an old tradition. Many things in rugby have moved with the times but the court has not. It is hidebound by convention. In the old days it was an excuse for a huge piss-up. In the modern era it is an excuse for a huge piss-up.

The mood was set at Weybridge as the squad got to know each other and Geech set out his tactics; the slow, rumbling play of the northern hemisphere would not be good enough to take on the All Blacks in their own backyard. We had to go at them with a direct, hard-running game. It sounded good to me.

For once, I was interested in more than a lot of direct, hard running. I was also interested in defence – my defence. I'd built up something of a reputation as an attacker but I knew that wouldn't cut much ice down in the land of the Kiwi. They would test me out in the tackle and would want to know if I could hack it when their big men were running at me. They would be keen to know if I was more than a pretty boy. So was I.

I really fancied the challenge. The 1989 tour had all been a blur, a fast-moving experience with everything whizzing by but this time I had an idea of what I would be getting into.

From Auckland we headed up to the Bay of Islands on the north-east coast for our build-up to the first game. We landed at Kerikeri, a one tarmac strip, one hut, one taxi sort of place. It felt like New Zealand. It felt like the beginning of a Lions tour where you were far away from home with no one but yourself to rely on. That's where you had to find out pretty quickly who was up to it or not.

The tour routine settled pretty quickly into the usual mix: a slog through training, dragging your body off some muddy field while back home they get on with their summer; a wonderful series of distractions, from white-water rafting, golf and fishing to clay-pigeon shooting; and a stint at the bar of the Irish pub that is to be found in even the most desolate parts of the planet. Even Invercargill has one.

Clay-pigeon shooting almost reduced the thirty-man party by one when Richard Webster took a gun to his contender for the openside flanker position. It was an extreme way of trying to edge out a rival, but Webby is a very competitive man. His excuse that the gun had gone off by accident, churning a great lump of turf about six inches from Winters' right foot, didn't fool any of us. Webby was to prove one of the great characters of that tour, one of those blokes who works hard and plays even harder. I was delighted when he joined Bath a few seasons later.

But before the play there was lots of work – too much of it at times. We trained endlessly. And then talked endlessly about training. There was an awful lot of technical analysis and numerous people standing up at team meetings having their two-pennyworth. That was the only part of my tour allowance that came back in credit. I didn't spend my two-pennyworth.

It's always a relief to get the tour under way. Barnes was to be captain for our first match, against North Auckland at Whangarei. I was paired with Scott Hastings in the centre. Will and Scott Gibbs were the other contenders for the centre Test spot. I didn't have the greatest of beginnings and nor did the team as we laboured to a 30–17 victory. My legs felt heavy – I knew training was bad for you. So was tackling, as Ian Hunter found out when he dislocated his shoulder and was on his way home before he'd even grown tired of eating pumpkin soup with every meal.

The weather in the sub-tropical Bay of Islands had been terrific and the temperature on the pitch itself also began to rise. You know that you are always going to get some stick on a Lions tour from the locals, it goes with the territory. In New Zealand it began in the second match.

Four years earlier the Australians had whinged when we took them on at their own physical game. The Kiwis got sour when we took them on at their rucking game. We took it as a compliment. The second match was against North Harbour. We won 29–13, but the big talking point was the rucking incident that involved Dean Richards and Frank Bunce. Deano caught the head of Bunce at the back of a ruck. Foul or fair? For me, Dean is the type of forward who will stand there toe to toe to protect his patch or his mates. He's a forward's forward, a hard, no-nonsense type, but he would never deliver an intentional cheap shot.

New Zealanders worship the ruck. If a bloke lies over the ball you get him out of there with the boot. I've never had a problem with that. I would always give Dean the benefit of the doubt. Except when Bath are playing Leicester.

That incident was a perfect pulling-together moment and we needed all the team spirit we could summon in the next game against the New Zealand Maoris. We were 20–0 down at one point but somehow clawed our way back to scrape home by four points, 24–20. A brilliant effort from Ieuan Evans, who scored a typical solo try, and a superb try-saving tackle by Ben Clarke rescued the day for us.

That win was notable for another milestone: the

Wellington Three were formed. We went out to celebrate that win in a typical, down to earth Kiwi watering-hole: an Irish pub. Dean, Jason and myself were the last three to return and came into the hotel in the early hours with all the subtlety of an All Black pack crashing into a ruck. To our ears we were tip-toeing across stage as if we were the Bolshoi Ballet.

Next morning at the team meeting, Dick Best finished the business by asking if the 'Wellington Three' could stay behind. We'd been rumbled. Then my eyes roamed round the room. Ten other shifty, guilty, bloodshot, narrow slits were doing the same. That confirmed it. Safe. We had not been the only ones out on the lash. Wade Dooley, Mike Teague and Dewi Morris had been doing the same.

The fourth match was against Canterbury. We won 28–10, I scored and the team went well, although I did knock on a simple try-scoring run-in from Stuart Barnes, who came on late in the match. I don't think Barnes was best pleased.

His mood was to deteriorate further over the next week as it became clear that Rob Andrew was the favoured choice for the Test spot. My views on Stuart have never changed: he's a mate who is also a bloody fine player. However, the tide was turning against him and the Lions. We were swept away by Otago 37–24 in our fifth match, a result that had a profound effect on our style of play. From that day on we moved away from the open game and reverted to type, drawing in towards the forwards and becoming more pragmatic. Once again the ball became a distant object, buried in the midst of sixteen grappling blokes.

Stuart suffered on two fronts: from that switch of style and from a stray Kiwi boot in the next game against Southland. I came into the dressing-room afterwards to see his ear dangling down like that of a basset hound. His skin was like a hanging curtain; you could lift it up and see the skull beneath. It was also the final curtain on his Test chances.

We swung into Christchurch for the first Test. Gavin had been fairly quiet in the early stages of the tour but by now he was in passionate mode, winding us up for the big one. Will and I were chosen as centres, which was a hard call on Scott Gibbs, who had been playing fantastic rugby.

We were up against Frank Bunce and Walter Little, a formidable pair. Ieuan Evans had an even more daunting prospect in Inga Tuigamala. We knew that we would all have to close his space down. No problem. Inga was so big there was never that much space in his part of the pitch.

Inga didn't see much of the ball and neither did I. I'm not sure referee Brian Kinsey saw too much of what was happening either. It was a poor game all round. Both sides were nervous and both made mistakes. The ref caught the mood. Grant Fox put up a high kick towards our try line early in the match and Bunce and Ieuan jumped for it. Although Bunce did appear to come down on the ball, Ieuan seemed to have a hand on it too. Kinsey didn't hesitate. Try to the All Blacks.

We scrapped our way back into contention and led 18–17 with a minute to go, Gavin having kicked all our points. The All Blacks came again, driving hard in midfield. Bunce smashed forward only to find Deano, who wrapped him in one of those smothering tackles. They came to ground with Bunce facing our way. The forwards drove in and the whistle went. Scrum to the Lions? Penalty to the Lions? No, penalty to the All Blacks, even though the body language of every player around the breakdown told you that the advantage should have been ours. The ball had been on our side but he penalised Dean. It was nonsense.

Grant Fox still had forty-five metres to go but he doesn't miss those. He didn't.

We were devastated. We knew we couldn't bang on about the ref too much in public because it would not only appear to be sour grapes, it would also seem a sign of weakness. We had to sort this out ourselves. We knew we had to improve.

The focus turned to the Saturday side. Perhaps that's why the tour went downhill a bit. In 1989 Donal Lenihan did a great job of giving the midweek boys a sense of identity and purpose. Here, there was no similar rallying point. Some of the boys went off-tour long before it was all over and the Scottish contingent among the forwards got the work hard, play hard equation out of balance. In fact, they were mathematically dyslexic. The descent began in Napier when the forwards threw in the towel and allowed Hawke's Bay to run all over us to win 29–17.

Barnes was leading the side and still pushing for a Test spot. He was not at all happy and let the side know it. He flipped in the post-match debrief, accusing the front five in particular of shirking their responsibilities. Geech backed him.

The rest of us made up for it on the work front. We were murdered in training leading up to the second

Test as we covered every blade of grass at Wellington. By then the die had already been cast. Scott Gibbs was in the frame for the centre shirt and Will was out in the cold. It made sense in that Scott had been playing well.

We planned endlessly as to how we could level the series and there was too much talk for my taste. We went through every conceivable scenario in training until even Geech realised that he was laying it on too thick. He apologised for the length of the session.

He should have apologised about the dithering over Gavin's selection. He'd come off against Auckland the week before with a hamstring problem. By Thursday he didn't know if he'd be fit. By Friday he still didn't know and the uncertainty was getting to all of us. Geech would get us to go up and whisper to Gav that he had to play because we needed him. It was hardly morale-boosting stuff.

Gav played and we won. Did Gavin make a difference? If you'd asked me after twelve minutes I might have given you a different answer to the one I give now: of course he did. His leadership, his motivation, his kicking all made up for the bloomer in the opening phases when he fluffed a high kick to let in Eroni Clarke for a try.

The Kiwis all went mad, the wind howled even louder and the stands started swaying. What the hell was going on here? It was balls out or die – and so out they came. We tackled and chased, chased and tackled. I spent the afternoon screaming at Ieuan to close Tuigamala down. He spent the afternoon screaming at me to close Bunce and Little down. We finished hoarse but happy.

The pack put in a monstrous performance, first holding and then nudging the All Blacks back on our own line. On such small margins were many tales told at bars later in the night. On the hour we got the decisive, match-winning break when Sean Fitzpatrick spilled a ball, Dewi swooped on it and put me away. I made yardage into their territory with Rory outside me and All Black wing John Kirwan between us and the line. I wanted him to come to me so that I could put Rory away. Come on John. Just six inches further. A bit more. A bit more. Slowly does it. Kirwan in, ball out, Rory away.

It would be nice to record that movement as one of the perfect sequences. And so it was until Rory's belly-flop over the line. *Nul points* for style, *dix points* for substance.

The final tally was 20–7, our highest score and biggest winning margin in Tests against the All Blacks. A record number of pints were sunk in Wellington that night just to round off the occasion. The first sightings of the Barmy Army came that day when thousands of British flags began to wave at the final whistle. Deano went back out to join in a sing-song on the terraces. Up until then the Lions had been in perfect harmony.

The tour had been salvaged and I'd come through my own personal test by showing the Kiwis that I could defend as well as attack.

It's just a pity that, having risen from the grave, we went back into the hole over the next week. The midweek side rolled up the white flag in Hamilton when they caved in utterly, losing 38–10. It was a wretched performance. Peter 'Teapot' Wright had by now earned his nickname with his hands on hips stance at the side of rucks. There were others too who were not putting it in much to the disgust of the likes of Barnes and Webster, who were.

There was a lot of hype around the third and decisive Test. A lot of hype and not much else. We were well beaten 30–13. The All Blacks got their lineout functioning after we'd built an early 10–0 lead with a penalty by Gavin and a try by Scott Gibbs. But their forwards were really wound-up and, much as we hammered away, we were always on the back foot.

They'd worked us out. Martin Bayfield, who'd had a stormer in the second Test, was squeezed in the lineout here. Modern rugby is unforgiving. You have to keep on the move and try new things because the opposition spends as much time studying you as they do working on their own game.

It was something of an anti-climax to lose in such fashion at Eden Park. We'd forsaken our open game in the early stages of the tour because we didn't have the nerve to take it to the Kiwis. I think we played into their hands. Our final record, of seven wins from thirteen matches, is a poor return in the history books but it doesn't show how close we came in that first Test. History books never do and that's why they are required reading. People remember the winners, not the good losers, as we were to find out four years later.

The 1997 Lions to South Africa

Just three minutes to go. Time to break out. Keith Wood belted it downfield. Good boy. Percy Montgomery fumbled it. Excellent. Lineout. Gibbsy took it up. Crunch. Recycle. Back to Gregor. He had a dart. Checked. Recycled. Daws got his hands on the ball. Back to me. Honiball and Teichmann tried to close me down. Too late, boys. It was on its way. Drop goal.

The sight of the ball sailing between the King's Park posts was something special. The thought of it a few years later is still as fresh and warm. What else could I do? The scores were tied, the series was on the line and Austin Healey was outside me. I certainly wasn't going to pass on the glory to him.

As soon as I hit it I knew that it was through. Somehow we'd got our noses in front and were ahead 18–15. They might have outscored us on the try front three to nil but just take a peek at the record books. We'd taken a 2–0 lead in the series and there was no way back for the Springboks.

I knew what was in the offing at half-time and when I got into the changing-room I spoke my mind. I normally keep quiet, the big speech is not for me, but this time I told the lads how it was and how it was going to be. We were leading 6–5 at the time.

'Lads,' I said in my best Churchillian tones. 'We can win this one. We've been working on defence all this trip. Now it's time to cut loose and play some rugby.'

South Africa scored two tries within thirteen minutes of the re-start. I think I'll leave the speech-making to others.

Our eventual victory was extraordinary. We had outboxed the 'Boks. We were hard in mind and body, something they'd prided themselves on for years and years. They missed five kicks at goal, we landed five and then I knocked over a drop goal. I couldn't believe how naïve they had been in giving Neil Jenkins so much room. We had Jenks at full back for one reason and one reason only: to kick goals. He would never win a beauty contest or a 100-metre race, but he will win you matches. The worry at the time had been that he might lose us a Test match too, a novice full back, vulnerable under the high ball. That theory was never tested. Jenks was left alone and he kicked us to victory. He's the Tiger Woods of rugby. Give him a pressure eight-footer to bring home the goods and he'll get it.

The victory changed the whole complexion of the tour and turned it into the experience of a lifetime. But if we'd lost then I think it might all have seemed a bit heavy-going. The tour had been intense and unrelenting, with none of the social looseness of the previous two. Maybe it was because it was the first professional Lions tour, or perhaps we were all a bit older if not wiser. However, there were times when we broke out. John Bentley was entertainments officer and a good job he did too. Once we'd worked out what he was saying he had a lot to offer. Bentos had been hell-bent on making the Test side but didn't make it. He has a video recording of him opening the letter which told the lads about selection.

'And here's the letter coming under the bedroom door. And here's me opening it. And, shit, here's me not in the Test team.'

Bentos had come from rugby league, as had Alan 'Pidge' Tait, Scott Gibbs, Allan Bateman and Scott Quinnell – all lads with union roots but with hefty league experience. It was done deliberately to get us into a professional mind-set. Rugby league players are used to clocking on and clocking off, to treating the job seriously from the first hooter. Tour manager Fran Cotton had a big hand in bringing in so many ex-rugby league guys. He soon became known as the 'Pink Salmon' because of the colour his face turned in the South African sun.

I wasn't sure how I'd get on with Fran because he had been involved in a couple of media spats in the months leading up to the tour. One was with Will Carling, who apparently announced that he'd withdrawn himself from captaincy consideration. Fran replied that he'd never been asked. It all got messy. As ever, it passed me by.

The second incident did not. Phil de Glanville was not one of the initial sixty or so names released early in spring. Contracts had to be presented to the players and approved in broad terms by their agents, which is why such a large provisional group was named. It was surprising that Phil, who was England captain at that time, was not among them. Fran could have taken the diplomatic route when asked why Phil had been omitted. Instead he was blunt and harsh on Phil, which seemed unnecessary. My relationship with Fran was fine in the end. The same couldn't be said about his suntan.

At the time I thought if Phil didn't make it, then what chance for me? I'd not been a regular starter for England that season. I had, though, bumped into Geech during the season and he'd intimated that I should be involved. More or less certain. The 'less' rather than the 'more' grew bigger in my mind the nearer we got to the final party being named.

I was in Manchester with Bath when the squad

was announced on Sky TV one Wednesday in April. We were due to play a league game that evening against Sale. I don't think my mind was fully focused on what Heywood Road had in store for me. Not until the thirty-five names were read out that is. Mine was there: the only one from Bath. Ireland and Bath wing Simon Geoghegan had been in the squad until Monday evening, when a foot injury got the better of him.

However, Mike Catt and Ollie Redman were to increase the Bath contingent before the tour was over. When the Lions beckoned, club loyalties and country allegiances go out of the window. There was the tour contract to be dealt with first and then other paperwork. I've never been much bothered with forms and legal documents and, besides, I'd play for the Lions for the two free pairs of socks. But it had to be done.

Contracts tend to raise matters that you'd never have thought of: newspaper columns, marketing rights, curbs on books and other publications. At least we got to draw up our own code of conduct, the twenty Lions Laws that we were to abide by. There was no mention of a ban on alcohol. It was a grown-up view that if people were used to a glass or two on a Friday evening then that was their affair. As it turned out no one tended to drink after the Wednesday. Barnesie would never have made it in the professional era.

There was to be a Lions video. Former Wales and Lions flanker John Taylor and his mates had funded the production, taking a gamble that the Lions would be successful. Their faith paid off and the video was a hit, showing life with the Lions in the raw.

Gareth Edwards was telling me recently that he

thought the video had taken away some of the mystique of the Lions, that it had revealed too many inner secrets. It's a point of view and there have been times when I've found TV cameras intrusive. However, this story, warts and all, brought rugby to a wider audience. It had soap opera appeal.

There was not the same leisurely build-up to this tour. The domestic season was ever longer and there was no time for a laid-back handing out of kit, a bit of chit-chat and a couple of beers to get to know the boys. We met at our usual haunt, the Oatlands Hotel in Weybridge. Ian McGeechan and Jim Telfer were to be coaches, Fran Cotton manager, James Robson doctor, Dave McLean fitness advisor and Andy Keast video analyst.

It was an impressive cast. There were other faces at the hotel, a corporate motivational company by the name of Impact. They were going to bring us together and make us bond. I fancied that a few pints down the pub would have the same effect and be a touch less expensive. On the first lunchtime at Weybridge I sat alongside my old mate Scott Gibbs.

'What have these wankers from Impact got in store for us this afternoon, then, Gibbsy?' I asked. 'You'd better ask them yourself, Jerry,' came the reply. 'One of them is sitting next to you.'

Impact finally did come round to my way of thinking. The best session of the week was in the local boozer on the last day. Still, their methods did get us on the move in a round of bridge erecting, raft building, catapult flinging and wet sponge throwing. Five thousand miles away the Springboks were taking no notice whatsoever.

Their complacency was to cost them dear. There was a patronising tone in the air from the minute we first arrived in South Africa. 'Pussycats in town,' read the poster in Port Elizabeth. The official welcome wasn't much better when Louis Luyt, the president of the union, gave us the usual spiel and then hoped we'd go back home after a 3–0 whopping.

I only noticed the eye patch as Luyt left the room. Why are people so one-eyed? It's fair enough backing your men all the way, but you should at least respect the opposition. I don't think the South Africans did on that tour until it was too late. The Lions were only ever seen as a warm-up act for the tri-nations and such arrogance was to be the undoing of them.

The Springboks didn't greatly impress me. Sure, they'd won the World Cup two years earlier, but that was a book of life job, written on high that they were going to win. They had God looking after them and Nelson Mandela on the blindside.

Two years later, though, I couldn't see how they had moved on. Percy Montgomery had come through at full back and was an exciting prospect; Andre Snyman, a centre or wing, was devastating, although he was to be hampered by injury; and van der Westhuizen was his usual handful. But it was not a team to make you tremble. The pack was full of classic Springbok workhorses such as Os du Randt, Mark Andrews and Andre Venter. Decent players but not world-beaters.

I looked at them and I looked at us and I knew that we were in with a good chance. We had a lot of classy players on our books, which meant that I'd have to battle to nail down the Test spot. Gibbsy was there and in good shape, while Allan Bateman was a class act. Allan is one of my favourite players: technically very sound with a low centre of gravity to give him fabulous balance. The league boys would ensure that we had a hard edge. Alan Tait was another who'd won caps for Scotland before switching codes and he was now back in union at Newcastle, a good operator. There was talk that we'd fallen out after the tour but I certainly don't remember it that way. I roomed with Pidge at the start of the trip and he supposedly took offence at me asking him if I snored! It was built up into a tabloid episode when he wrote his own book. I've appeared many times on television with Alan since and we're good mates.

Will Greenwood was also on the trip as a centre, although he'd yet to be capped by England. Will repaid the faith in him by having a terrific tour until he got an horrific head injury against the Free State, when he was unconscious for several minutes and had stopped breathing. Will got an early reminder of how tough it might be when Gibbsy smashed him for six in the first training session of the tour at Weybridge. That's the way Lions tours are. Training sessions are for making your mark with the selectors as much as they are for working with team-mates.

Gregor Townsend was to play a significant part. I like Gregor but I struggle to relate to him at times. I once accused him in print of having the attention span of a gnat, which is perhaps too harsh. I respect him as a player for the very obvious reason that he has done magical things with a rugby ball that no one else has done. I'd rather play with him than not have him there, but there were times when he was away with the fairies. Perhaps that's how people see me at times, but I do think others can work off me, link with me on the field and anticipate where the play is going. With Gregor, I didn't have a bloody clue where he was going.

We flew south, from Heathrow to Johannesburg and no sooner had we landed and the roar of the engines died down than the whine started all over again. Louis Luyt was in full presidential address mode. We listened, shrugged and moved back on to the plane for the short hop down to the coast and steamy Durban.

The temperature was in the eighties and all would have been bliss except for the little matter of training. Once again, it was hard. By the end of the eight weeks I made a pledge never to tour again. There is only so much training you can do in one lifetime.

Lions sessions are always longer than those of other teams. The coaches are starting from scratch and want to make sure that every base is covered. We did a lot of eight on eight in that first week as we built to the first game against Eastern Province. Eight of the boys would be in full protective clothing while the other eight would go at them full tilt. Then we'd swap roles. Then we'd change again.

There was only one consolation in all this: I wasn't born a forward. For every bucket of sweat that we filled, they filled two. As the backs trooped off towards the bus, all I could hear behind were grunts and this Scottish voice giving it large doses. The boys must have put in forty-five minutes more than we did on every routine.

But it paid off. I liked Telfer, 'Creamy' as he was called. He was known as a hard bastard and he lived up to his reputation. I didn't have a huge amount to do with him but I did see his softer side, the humorous touch. He took a dirt-trackers session before the second game against Border in East London and I was drafted in for a tackling drill. I thought I'd try to get one over on Creamy and I kept shouting that the lads were cutting corners, that they weren't hitting all the bags in the grid while Jim's back was turned. He twigged straight away that I was having him on and said nothing. But who was it that ended up having to tackle twice as many bags as anyone else? He took me to the knacker's yard. He was viciously competitive but enjoyed the banter.

Not that the forwards ever had any breath left to give him any stick back. They were beasted. One session on the back pitch at Loftus Versfeld in Pretoria is the stuff of legends. Scrum after scrum after scrum, all the time with Telfer's voice screaming at them.

Sleep was all we were interested in that first week. Training was tough in those conditions with the sun beating down. However, it did make all the difference. Who would have picked the Lions pack that took the field for the first Test at the start of tour? I certainly wouldn't. Props Tom Smith and Wallace came through, and so did Irish lock Jeremy Davidson. Eric Miller also made a run for the side but had to pull out with illness. Paul Wallace was a good tourist and one of the few who was happy to ship a few beers. He still managed to train as if he'd had fifteen hours sleep.

Finally, we headed down to Port Elizabeth for the opening game against a Presidential XV at the Boet Erasmus Stadium. Martin Johnson was tour captain – or Ryder Cup captain, as I called him for the first couple of weeks, non-playing as he nursed a dodgy shoulder. Johnno and nursing is not a great mix and in the end he preferred the pain of playing to the pain of me taking the mickey.

Our style was set from the outset: we were to play with ball in hand. That suited me, although I'd heard these sort of ideas floated before at the start of a tour. This time, though, we stuck to it. We didn't go into our shells in the Test matches. We were just forced on to the back foot.

Geech laid down the defensive strategy, which was to be aggressive defence. The whole system hinged on putting the squeeze on the likely Springbok fly half Henry Honiball. Geech had done his homework and watched the entire series between South Africa and New Zealand the year before. He figured that the 'Boks were not too flexible by nature and would not be able to adapt on the hoof. He wasn't wrong there. He knew, too, that the scrum is the raison d'etre of the Springbok pack. It's macho land and if they don't give you a hard time of it in the scrum it's been a bad day at the office.

The boys worked the scrum and we worked on Honiball. It didn't matter who lined up against us in those warm-up games, to us he was Honiball. One player would come one side of him, one the other and we'd close him down. He was forced to drop further and further into the pocket to operate and was in the first row of the stands by the end of the second Test. He was out of sorts and, before long, out of the team. The subtlety of all this passed the South Africans by. They'd written us off and had even pulled all the Test players out of the provincial matches so as to rest them for the bigger battles ahead.

We slipped into gear straightaway, beating the Invitational XV 39–11. I got two tries, partnering Will Greenwood in the centre. Geech told us that he was going to mix and match for the early matches and he did. Too much so for my liking – I was either playing or on the bench.

The bench at the Basil Kenyon stadium in East London was not one of the world's great landmarks. It was surrounded by a sea of mud and the boys really had to battle to stay afloat. They scraped home 18–14, and out came the Springbok stick. That's where I first heard the 'Pussycat' jibe. The label stuck.

The circus, with its mix of big cats and so-called pussycats swung along the coast to Cape Town, my favourite part of South Africa. We were lined up for the kill against Western Province, yet it was the locals who were licking wounds as we came away with a 38–21 victory and played well into the bargain. Ieuan Evans got a good try, with Bentos weighing in with two. There was friction between him and Springbok wing James Small in that match. They refused to shake hands at the end of the game and Small laid into Bentos in print afterwards. It was a promising sign.

We cared less and less about what was going on in the outside world and more and more on what we were doing in our own. The sessions were still hard and we were monitored constantly by our fitness advisor Dave McLean. He weighed us night, noon and morning to make sure the body fluids were up to par. Mine were. Not sure they were always the right fluids though.

We were up-country in Witbank, an old mining town, to take on Mpumalanga for our next game. It was classic Afrikaner country: stark and harsh, with clear blue winter skies and hard ground. The result was never in doubt as we romped home 64–14, Rob Scottish flanker Wainwright getting a hat-trick. All his Scottish mate, lock Doddie Weir, got was a kicking. Doddie was stretchered out of the tour by a stamp by Mpumalanga second row Marius Bosman. Doddie, who was pushing hard for a Test place, was cleaning out Bosman at the lineout. At one ruck, Doddie had his leg pinned by a pile of bodies and Bosman gave it the full treatment. Doddie's cruciate ligament was in bits.

He headed for the airport a few days later. Fly half Paul Grayson was already back home. We'd given him his farewell drinks in Oscar's, a neon-lit bar near our Holiday Inn Crown Plaza base in Pretoria. Now it was Doddie's turn. Down to Oscar's again.

By this time the Lions phone was red-hot to Argentina to summon replacements. England were touring there under Jack Rowell. Mike Catt was the first request, which didn't go down too well with Jack. Then came the call for Nigel Redman, another Bath colleague. Jack summoned 'Ollie' to his room.

'The Lions have selected you to go to South Africa,' said Jack.

'I can't believe it,' said an overwhelmed Ollie.

'Neither can I,' said an underwhelmed Jack.

It was good to get the Bath boys on board. It was good, too, to get my performance against Northern Transvaal under my belt. We lost 35–30, our first defeat, but I scored a couple of tries and went well. It's not like me to concentrate on my own game and to hell with the result. This was one of the few exceptions when I didn't feel too bad about losing. The first Test was only a fortnight away and now was the time to make my mark.

It was during that game that I learned a new word: sledging. Bentos was outside me, shouting: 'Jerry, Jerry. Look at my fucking winger.'

What for? Just get on with the game.

'Jerry, Jerry,' screamed Bentos once more. 'Look at my fucking winger.'

Eventually I gave in before my eardrums did.

'What is it?'

'Look at him! Look at him! I'm going to fucking walk all over him!'

Welcome to the art of sledging. Bentos might have been better off picking on a guy whose first language was English. Bentos's northern insults lost a bit in the translation to Afrikaans.

Bentos at least excelled himself in the next game, when he scored the try of the tour against Gauteng Lions in Ellis Park. Or at least he told us that it was the try of the tour. He did beat half a dozen blokes on his way to the line. Two of them were on his side but that's a minor detail. It was a fantastic effort and laid down a marker for the selectors. I played again, for the second time in four days as we came through 20–14. That was it for me. There were ten days to go to the Cape Town Test and I'd done my stint. I knocked on one simple pass from Catty in that match, a schoolboy howler, but I didn't figure it would count against me. The Gauteng victory put us back on track. Ellis Park is an intimidating place but we went out there and battled.

I sat out the next couple of games, against Natal in Durban and the Emerging Springboks in Wellington in wine country along the Cape. Scrum half Rob Howley dislocated his shoulder against Natal and was forced to fly home the next day. It's the way it is with Lions tours: relish it while it's there because it can be snatched away from you in a second. Rob was trussed up in his sling as he gave a final press conference at the hotel in Umhlanga Rocks just outside Durban. It was an idyllic backdrop, with the Indian Ocean crashing in just below the pool deck where Rob was sitting but I don't think he paid it the slightest bit of attention.

I knew that I had a couple of days in which to relax so I enjoyed a couple of sessions at TJ's bar and Cottonfields, a small bistro nearby, in the company of Andy Keast, our video analyst. Keasty had done his stuff well. We knew all there was to know about the Springboks. Pity for them that they skimped on their homework.

I was in the Test team alongside Scott Gibbs with Ieuan Evans and Alan Tait on the wings. Gregor and Matt Dawson were at half back. It was a disappointment for Allan Bateman. As for Bentos, well, his form had been up and down. The selectors went for Tait's consistency, which at least saved my ears from a bashing.

Newlands is one of my favourite stadiums in the world. It doesn't look like a stadium from the outside, more like an ordinary building, and yet there's a real sense of history about the place. The cricket ground is next door, through the railway sidings and past the brewery. And the backdrop is stunning, with the Table Mountain range running across the skyline.

Our hotel, once more a Holiday Inn, was only a

few hundred metres away. The coach trip was only minutes from the ground, which meant that there was not too much time for the Springbok supporters to give us the finger and their best wishes. Actually, the Cape Town crowd is more sophisticated than that. It's Danie Craven country, the great old doyen of South African rugby who'd set up his famous academy at Stellenbosch University. There was more respect for us by this stage too because we'd only dropped one game, against Northern Transvaal, and showed that we could play rugby.

The preparation had been excellent that week. Geech revved us up and Telfer was in normal form with the forwards: four expletives to every actual word spoken. And yet we weren't tense. The Tests were scheduled for 5 p.m. kick-offs so there was a lot of the day to get through. It's a difficult time and you can get wound up far too early. I walked down the corridor of the hotel just before midday and could hear this heavy rock music pounding out. Inside all the boys were just lying about with the jukebox at full blast, a few of the squad were playing pool. It was like a lads' day out. Just my scene.

We'd done the serious stuff the night before when we'd had a video session, first watching clips from the 1974 Lions series against South Africa when Willie John's boys had wiped the floor with them. It was weird watching the footage because it looked so slow by comparison. Gareth and JPR and Phil Bennett were the greats of the game and great they remain. Faster does not mean better. And the lineouts were just one big scrap with fists flying everywhere. The forwards got turned on by that bit. You noticed the differences in size too. Morne du Plessis, the Springbok number eight and manager to the World Cup winning side in 1995, was considered a giant of his day. He would not looked have looked out of place alongside me.

History, history. Time to get up to date and hit the fast-forward button. There was a compilation of our stuff on this tour so far, the best bits from everyone: the tries, the big hits, the huge scrums. All thirty-five players got air time.

The next day Geech made a speech, the Pink Salmon made a speech, shirts were presented and the temperature began to rise. We were shown a newspaper flyer: 'The Lions are in town – the "Pansies" have arrived,' it read. Subtle as ever. Still no respect. That was Geech's message.

By the time the kick-off came round I was in a rare old state, which is unusual for me. I thought in fact that I was in normal mode, relaxed and cool, but when I saw the tape later I look as if I'm just about to have a nervous breakdown. I'm fidgeting, kicking my feet and looking pale, almost white. That takes some doing.

I wasn't the only one. Neil Jenkins is a quiet bloke by nature, or he is until he starts retching before kick-off. You're trying to concentrate and then this barking noise fills your ears. Keith Wood goes into mental mode and a highly articulate sound it is: 'Fuck, fuck, fuck,' shouts Woody at no one in particular.

It was a relief to get started. And it was a relief to get finished. We'd done them. We may have been on the back foot for spells, we may not have played the wide-ranging rugby we'd produced early in the tour, but we'd beaten them 25–16. The Pussycats had turned nasty, the pansies had stood tall. The Springboks looked shattered at the final whistle. We scored two tries in the last seven minutes just to rub it home.

Matt Dawson's try was a classic and I can still see it now as Teichmann, Joubert, van der Westhuizen and about half of Newlands bought his dummy as he broke blind and headed to the try line. The Springboks are probably still waiting for his pass inside. On the whistle Gibbsy drove hard, won some yards, the ball went left and Rodber threw a long pass for Alan Tait to score in the corner. It was all over.

Woody was in tears in the changing-room and the Pink Salmon looked choked. None of us could quite believe it. It was one of those famous backs to the wall victories, a gang of blokes in a big country, up against it, who came through.

Jason, Lawrence and myself had a meal out with Barnesie near Newlands at the Cantina Tequila and then met up with the lads at the Café Verdi before heading off to Sirens night-club for a few Jack Daniels. There had not been too many nights out and I think this one was merited.

However, there was still a feeling that we had unfinished business. We'd won a Test – but we wanted the series.

We flew to Durban the next day, where for the only time in the tour the party split up, the midweek side heading to Bloemfontein where they had a game against the Northern Free State. Geech reckoned that a switch to altitude and back within a few days was not the best preparation for us. The South Africans probably figured the same thing, which is why the fixtures might have fallen that way in the first place.

Ollie Redman was named as captain and it was fantastic to see him lead the Lions out. I know it meant a lot to him – and what a game to captain us in. We played our best rugby of the trip and Free State, who were rated, were defeated 52–30. Will Greenwood suffered a bad head injury and was unconscious for several minutes – a nasty moment.

Bentos got a hat-trick, an effort which was rewarded when Ieuan pulled out because of injury and Bentos was in for the second Test. More tension. More speeches. The light relief came from Fran, who was winding us up for the big one with a tub thumper of a talk. He moved to a conclusion:

'There will be defining moments,' said Fran. 'Moments when the game will be won and lost. Moments when, as the great French leader Napoleon put it in words that we are all familiar with, er, words, that er . . .'

He reached into his pocket for the piece of paper that bore the words that we were all familiar with.

Geech also did his bit. His theme was simple: 'This is a wounded Springbok. It will now be fighting for its life. Finish it off.'

There were loads of messages of support and, better still, Mom arrived in town. It was great to see her – and not only because she had the first pictures of Saskia, who had been born on the 14th.

King's Park has its own special atmosphere. It's not as intimate as Newlands but there's a feel-good air about it because it has so much space where the fans light up their braais (barbecues) and have a party. There were also several thousands of British supporters in the stands.

It was like a coliseum into which we were about to

be thrown. As we huddled, waiting for kick-off, Scott Gibbs came into his own. He gave us the jabbing finger – I'll take it from him.

'Enjoy the contact,' shouted Gibbsy. 'Enjoy the contact.'

And he did. I can't say the same for Os du Randt when Gibbsy put the big Springbok prop on his arse. As Napoleon would say, in words that are familiar to all of us . . .

There were several other defining moments. How the Springboks lost that game I'll never understand. They scored three tries. Van der Westhuizen went over from short range in the first half, Montgomery was over the line after Pidge Tait made a bit of a cock-up, and Bentos was handed off by Joubert about ten minutes later and we were in danger of being swamped.

But they couldn't hit a cow's backside with a banjo as far as kicking went. They missed five, Jenks hit five, I hit one and we were home and hosed.

At the final whistle chaos erupted. I was leaping in the air and whooping with delight. The changing-room was packed with people wanting to congratulate us. There was a very disturbing incident which, thankfully, we managed to keep out of the papers, as Fran went round kissing everyone in sight. Mom came to give me a hug and I phoned home. Pete and Chalkie were having a bit of a party and they were very complimentary. 'You jammy bastard!'

I had a massive, massive smile fixed on my face for hours. The party went on until dawn. I'm not sure which dawn.

We were well rewarded for our efforts by being

despatched to the ugliest part of the planet in the Vaal, at Vanderbiljpark. It was Surfers all over again but without the surf, dead and dull. The management probably had had no confidence in us months before when they planned the schedule. They thought that we might have been preparing for the decisive Test, with the series tied at 1–1, and we'd need somewhere away from temptation. They weren't wrong there, the devil himself couldn't have sinned in that place.

Geech tried to keep our minds on the job. However, it was hard, especially when you are being addressed by a Mohican. Geech had foolishly pledged that he would have a number one haircut if we won the second Test. He was true to his word. 'Whitewash week' was how he described the final few days of the tour. 'Slaphead' was how he was described.

We travelled by coach for the two-hour trip to Welkom to cheer on the midweek lads against Northern Free State in the final game for many of them. It was a good send-off, Tony Underwood getting a hat-trick as they won 67–39.

I never thought I'd be relieved to see Johannesburg again. It was paradise by comparison. For all Geech's efforts to wind us up for the third Test it was impossible to shake off the feeling that the war was won. There were several changes because of injury and Keith Wood, Alan Tait, Gregor and Tim Rodber didn't make it. Tony Underwood, Catty, Rob Wainwright and Mark Regan got the call-up, as did Neil Back, who came in for Richard Hill.

It didn't happen for us. We were within reach at 23–16 with a quarter of an hour to go, but the Springboks desperately wanted victory and they got it, 35–16, scoring four tries. I only made it to half-time. I broke a bone in my left arm just above the wrist after smacking it against Percy Montgomery's head. I watched the second half on TV from hospital, where I'd gone for an X-ray.

There was only one consolation. It wasn't my drinking arm. Johannesburg got the full treatment that weekend. It was the end of an era for me. No more Lions. I'll miss them.

chapter eighteen

what now for england?

No more protein shakes, no more massive fluid intakes, no more carbo-loading and no more bananas by the barrow-full. Do I miss international rugby? No I don't. Huge sacrifices are necessary in order to play at that level. The rewards are great, but at a cost.

I would not trade any of my caps with anyone and the matches themselves all gave me a huge lift in one way or another. True, the ball didn't always find its way to me but that was never as big a deal as the media made out. Winning is the important thing – and England won three Grand Slams in the nineties and scored some pretty good tries along the way. Not many people remember the tries, but they do remember the successes.

Clive Woodward's England are playing great rugby at the moment. They are fast and dynamic and there's lots of movement and ambition in their game. But that doesn't mean I'm desperate to be out there. You have your time and you move on. However, it was eerie watching the Lions in Australia recently because they have been such a big part of my life.

This could be a great England side but it's not yet. It may have broken records by the hatful and taken teams to pieces time and again, but it hasn't yet won anything of lasting significance and etched itself into history as an all-conquering side. The potential is fantastic but Clive Woodward hasn't yet got two Grand Slams and a World Cup final to his name as has Geoff Cooke. Jack Rowell also managed a Grand Slam and a World Cup semi-final. That's the target for Clive and the team, and that's how they will see it. Marks for style quickly fade but records and trophies last in the mind forever.

Clive has without question done an excellent job for English rugby. He realised what it would take to make a success of the professional era and went out there to get it. He also brought in all the coaches and back-up staff to make it happen. He's not a great technical coach. He realised that and found a way round it. The senior player meetings were good in that regard: you just had to plant the idea of what was needed and he would make it happen.

I remember when Matt Dawson, Lawrence Dallaglio and myself headed round to Clive's house near Maidenhead to bring up the question of coaching. The boys were unsettled and we needed to move it on. I knew that Brian Ashton was already in Clive's mind, so rather than confront Clive and tell him how dodgy things were we went for another tack and praised Brian's credentials. It was the positive spin and everyone was happy.

The team knows that Clive can throw wobblies and that he can be a bit nutty. But they can also see the fantastic things he has done for England. The twenty-four-hour players' strike in November 2000 did cause scars that will take time to heal, because Clive did get stuck into them. It's known as 'Wacky Wednesday', the day that Clive really went over the top with them, threatening that they would never play for England again. He left several angry messages on their mobiles. It was emotional stuff.

I was long gone from the scene by that time but heard all about it from several of the team. They know that Clive wears his heart on his sleeve, but he went too far in that situation. Of course, he was angry at having his build-up to a Test match ruined, but he knew that the lads had been backed into a corner. There are a few who won't easily forget the way that Clive lost it for that twenty-four hours. The younger ones saw another side to him and it will stay in their minds.

But they also know how supportive he can be. Look at the way he backed Lawrence all the way during his troubles with the *News of the World*. It took courage to do that. Clive could have been more neutral, played for time until all the facts were known, but he didn't. He put his own career on the line.

But that's the way he is. He goes with his gut instinct. He does talk too much for his own good at times and gets himself into impossibly tight corners because he's said something, only to change his mind later. There was the occasion when he said that Martin Johnson, a player of real stature, would have to play himself back in after injury, that he was just another player. It's stuff for public consumption but the players also read it and think it's tosh.

Clive sometimes tends to shoot from the hip and it can occasionally get him into trouble. But change that and you might change the character of the man who has achieved success on all the other fronts. He had a vision of where he wanted England to go and persuaded the likes of Francis Baron at the RFU to give him the finance to bring it about. It's not come cheaply but it's been worth it.

The biggest change in my time has been in fitness. Even my body shape has changed. I may always have looked a skinny sod but I've lost a whole heap of body fat, coming down from a rating of high thirties to low twenties. It's far more than just a question of diet, it's lifestyle, it's the whole thing.

You have to eat stuff you don't really enjoy. Each day you might have to take five protein or carbo-hydrate shakes, a drink composed of water and rice. It's unpleasant but you get used to it. Eating has always been one of life's pleasures for me but with Clive's England I was seeing food as just fuel, a way of making me able to do more work, and I didn't take to that. We would stay in the best hotels round the world and they all offered wonderful food. Clive brought in nutritionists to liaise with the hotel chefs and there went one of the most enjoyable perks of my early career.

It's all very well but we weren't robots. One of the traditions of an international week was that we would go out on the Wednesday for a squad meal. Pretty soon the nutritionist was dictating the restaurant and it was pasta every time. On one occasion I'd had enough and marched us off back to the Chinese in Richmond, telling the lads to say diddly-squat to the nutritionist.

It was our little protest, our way of staying sane.

Of course, you could see the benefits, but rugby is about the head as well as the body and there has to be a balance. Clive was right to go looking for the small percentages: that's where he thought you could find the edge, any edge. I'm not sure it's that simple, however. I may have had a great week's build-up, slept like a log, been in terrific shape and felt good and still played like a drain. On other occasions I've had only a few hours' kip after a drinking session and yet played out of my skin on the Saturday. Logic doesn't always deliver in my book.

Clive left nothing to chance and the fitness work we did was extraordinary. Dave 'Otis' Reddin was the main fitness man. He's a top operator who trained under Rex Hazeldine from Loughborough University who looked after our fitness through the nineties. Dave, who'd played a good standard of semi-pro football, took fitness on to the next level when he came on the scene in 1998.

He'd got hold of the fitness programmes that the southern hemisphere boys were operating to and set us targets. We took one look and thought 'No way. They're taking the piss.' But we got there. We were continually monitored and it took us the best part of eighteen months to get anywhere near the levels needed. We were set world-class performance standards in every category: sprint, endurance, weights, the whole lot. You may not have had to hit the 10/10 mark in every category but you had to get pretty close.

The progress sheets were always there at England sessions, a constant reminder of where you were and where the opposition were. Slowly, we closed the gap.

From being a million miles away, suddenly we were knocking on the door, opening it and walking in. In the end even an old cynic like me bought into it because I could see the benefits. Fitness is not the only thing that matters but it does enable you to express your talent. The big thing for me was to overcome the boredom factor but I got there in the end.

In the old days under Geoff Cooke, the squad were all given an ergometer, a rowing machine. I was buggered if I was going to have that in the house. I was an amateur and didn't want a constant reminder of all that hard work. But in a professional era, time is the most valuable currency and if you have your own makeshift gym at home, then it saves time and puts you ahead in the race.

The foundations are there for England to go on and be successful. The top tier is in place and in good working order and the next level is being prepared at the moment. Ellery Hanley has come into the frame and he'll be ready to step in if Phil Larder should move aside. It's a good coaching set-up that is extending down to the under-nineteen and under-twenty-one level. Clive is good at selling the whole deal, calling it the best coaching system in the world. It's a good pitch and if you keep repeating it, then soon everybody accepts it as fact. It's marketing and Clive is good at that.

But he's certainly right in one regard: England have got the best resources in terms of numbers playing the game. The potential is huge and England could be truly formidable in a few years' time.

I don't know how Geoff Cooke or Jack Rowell would have got on in the modern game. Pretty well, I'd have thought. As long as Jack gave up the day job, which was the reason that he didn't achieve with England what he might have done. He didn't have the time to do himself or the job justice. It was not a failing as such, just that he happened to be around as the game moved from one era to another, from being an amateur part-time activity to a full-time professional one.

Geoff Cooke and Clive are different characters but both very focused on what they want to achieve. Geoff was the great planner and organiser and he was running a pretty good operation back then, sorting out English rugby after so many years of under-achievement. I don't doubt that he too would have managed to make it happen.

You need to have people with rugby instincts involved. I don't go for the view that because rugby is now a professional game that you need businessmen to run it. Some commercial understanding is needed, but the key thing is to know your rugby. It can't be mere coincidence that Leicester have made the best fist of professional rugby on the club scene. That is because they have retained their rugby roots while at the same time gearing up their commercial operation.

Clive's biggest asset is that he understands rugby and rugby people. And it's paying off. England is on the verge of great things.

And the game itself? Well, it will survive and eventually thrive. The club game has changed a great deal and so have my views on it. At one point I was squarely behind the clubs and all that they were doing. I even went on record as saying that if the players were to sign for the RFU alone it would be like turkeys voting for Christmas. Now, I'm not so sure. I think central contracts are the way forward. They are working in cricket, despite the results of summer 2001, and I can see that they could be successful in rugby. It shouldn't be a take-over, however, more a responsible sharing of power.

There's only so much money in the game and it could be better controlled. Just consider how Leicester's wage bill could be lightened if the RFU looked after the salaries of Martin Johnson, Neil Back and all the rest. That would enable the Tigers, or whoever, to use their resources to develop young players, set up academies, develop the stadiums, market the game and work on a much sounder footing. Everyone would benefit.

It's important that the clubs be given proper status and recognition. In cricket, the counties have little say as to when their Test players appear. In rugby, I was pleased that the total number of club and inter-national games anyone could play in a season was set at thirty-two.

The international game is the shop window of rugby and Clive has done a brilliant job in projecting the England brand. You can see that from the way support for the game has grown, particularly with the young. Leicester did a terrific job in winning the Heineken Cup but how much real passion was aroused outside Leicester. England reaches a bigger audience, it's as simple as that. The system should be geared to that, and that way Bath, Rosslyn Park and Walcot Old Boys all benefit.

The club game is very different to when I first started out. No surprise there, I suppose, going from amateur to professional was a big step. As I've said before, once the game became professional in 1995 I changed my own outlook. The Rec became a place of work, the Saturday afternoon match the real focus of my job. We had always been serious about our rugby before that, but the mood of the club changed. There were still some good nights there and a few drinks taken, but there was certainly never much chance of a party in the clubhouse if we'd lost. The supporters would never have stood for that.

There is also more of a division now in the club between members, corporate clients and players. It's certainly not player-driven. They have a job to do, part of which involves visiting the corporate boxes after the game to meet sponsors and guests. I don't think the supporters are too fussed. The price of tickets has gone up a lot and, quite rightly, they want value for money, which means they want to see the team win. They want a professional performance on the field and they're not that bothered about the performance in the bar. However, Mom and Dad are still regulars and they are more than capable of looking after the Guscott presence in the clubhouse.

As for the Guscott presence on the Recreation Ground itself, that will be no more. I didn't want a thunderbolt announcement, I was quite happy to fade into the background. I'd come to an arrangement with Andrew Brownsword and director of rugby Jon Callard at the start of the 2000–01 season that I would be available as often as suited us both. It was a loose sort of deal because I knew that I had other interests to look after, from my testimonial to TV and radio work.

I also knew that Mike Tindall and Kevin Maggs were doing a good job in the Bath midfield and that I was only around as back-up. As it turned out I didn't feature quite as often as I thought I might, mainly because I injured my knee in November and was out of action for eight weeks. During that time I really got stuck into work with the BBC so that by the time the knee was okay I had other things on which to focus.

I knew that the time was right to retire. I'd made a couple of appearances from the bench early in the season and had one full run-out against Sale. I was first choice again against Rotherham the following week, November 26. The moment my boot hit the turf I realised that my time was up. For the first time in my career neither my heart nor my head was in the game and I just wondered what I was doing out there. There had been other times in my career when things weren't as they should have been, such as when I returned from the Lions tour in 1989. I also had that mid-career crisis talk with Jack Rowell in the mid-nineties. If that hadn't panned out as it did with Jack convincing me that I had a role to play with England then I could easily have thrown in the towel.

But this was different. It wasn't a shaft of light from up above, more a mood. I can look lethargic at the best of times but I knew that this was the real thing. I played for an hour, was replaced by Sam Cox, walked to the touchline and realised that I'd probably never wear the blue and black of Bath again. I didn't tell anyone. I just let it pass and let life move on.

There was to be one final hurrah – and what a great crack it was. The Barbarians had an end of season tour round the UK, playing Wales, Scotland and, finally, England. They wanted me to take part in all three games but I knew that I wasn't up to it. You can't flit in and out in rugby these days. It's serious stuff, even with the Baa-Baas.

I fitted in some training around my other commitments. It was good fun meeting up with the boys, just like an old-fashioned tour where the social side is as important as the playing side. The southern hemisphere lads, such as Josh Kronfeld, Jonah Lomu, Joost van der Westhuizen, Ian Jones and many others, hold the Barbarians in huge regard. It was fascinating. They were as chuffed about meeting up with us as we Brits were with them. They knew how to divide their time too, how to switch on and switch off. They were here to have a good time but they were here to play good rugby too.

I think they find that division of focus easier than we do in the northern hemisphere. Perhaps it's their climate that makes them so laid-back once they've clocked off from their sporting duties. I think that we've closed the gap a lot and we're still behind the eight ball when it comes to mental preparation and technical ability. We have some great players coming through. Take Josh Kronfeld. I've always said that Jon Hall was the best rugby player I've ever seen. Well, Josh is right up there with him. He's got unbelievable ability and a fantastic work rate. He'll be a huge hit in the Premiership with Leicester.

During the tour we stayed at Gleneagles in Scotland, which is in quite the best setting I've ever seen. The hotel staff were fantastic. I mentioned to a couple of the boys that if Clive Woodward ever got to hear about this place then he'd be there like a shot. He likes to make sure that the England boys get the best treatment. And why not? I'm with him all the way on that one. However, All Black prop Craig Dowd saw it differently. He reckoned that as long as the backdrop was comfortable then that was enough. Training and playing were the thing and the rest could look after itself.

I wish the Baa-Baas had had these sort of tours before. I know it would have been nigh on impossible because of the way the game was structured and because the boys had day jobs, but it was one hell of an experience, one hell of a way to finish off.

I actually got on at Twickenham, in the final match of the tour, earlier than I thought I would, replacing Jason Little, who got belted in the face. He got eight stitches. And me? Almost immediately I got a perfect chip kick from Pat Howard to score in the corner. Mom thinks that was all part of the script, a deliberate curtain call for her son. I tried to explain that it was a full-on match, that tackles were flying in everywhere, that I wasn't meant to be on the field, that we'd not had time to rehearse anything and that I'd just called the chip from Pat and he landed it perfectly. But Mom was having none of it.

She and Dad had taken me to the Rec as a seven-year-old with a smile on his face. I went down the Twickenham tunnel at the end of the Barbarians game with an older face but with the same smile.

england by foot

'Yeah, no problem. I'll do it with you.'

'800 miles you know.'

'Yeah, fine. I mean it's not as if we'll have to walk all the way. You'll do a few interviews, quick photo call, stride off over the horizon, knock out a few miles then into the back-up bus to be taken for a pub lunch, dropped off again for the final bit, smile nicely to the TV cameras, job done. That's how it is isn't it?'

'No, Chalky, it's 800 miles. Every single step out on the road. This is for real.'

Was I mad? What was a man whose first instinct was to take the car to the corner shop doing on an 800-mile, 29-day, 60-town walk round England? I did ask myself that a few times in those early days of the walk. My great mate Chalky Wardle was with me on the trek. We shared a room. On the fourth night we just happened to roll over in our beds and catch each other's eye. We were moaning like fools from the pain and effort of just turning over.

'What the hell are we doing this for?' we said at the

same time, laughed, groaned and went straight back to sleep.

If it wasn't clear then quite why we were putting ourselves through all that, then it was by the time we finished. The walk, which began on 10 October 2001 and finished at Twickenham where England were playing Australia on 10 November, raised £230,000 for leukaemia research. That was a great effort from all those that gave of their time and money. But more than just that were the people with their stories – of young children diagnosed with leukaemia, of parents who had lost their loved ones, all really moving tales. One guy joined us one day and told me that he'd been out in Australia for the Lions tour and was having a great time. Then, on the morning of the third Test in Sydney, he got a call to tell him that his 21-year-old son, who was studying for a degree at Newcastle University, had just been diagnosed. It put the sport into perspective all right.

The tales were all moving but the amazing thing was how positive people were. It certainly hit home with me, an old cynic on many fronts. But not on this one. Dad came up to me at the end of the walk and told me that for all the things that I'd achieved in rugby he'd never been prouder of me than at that moment. I nearly cried.

So, why did I do it? Well, I'd had a call about 12 months earlier asking if I'd take on the Ian Botham role. Both's body had had enough. He'd done eight years, raised £8 million along the way and just couldn't get the old legs out there any more. I quickly agreed to do it without thinking about it too much. I knew that there were good people involved: Tim Buttimore's people at SCG who managed the event for Carlsberg

Tetley and provided so many of the back-up staff. Without them I would not have been able to get out of bed in the morning, let alone slog my way round the English countryside.

Ruth Cross – what a star, top physio. She listened to the moans and somehow got the body to stir into life. She did 120 massages in all and used up two litres of surgical spirit for the cuts and blisters. Poor old Chalky got through 480 specialist anti-blister plasters on the last week alone. God knows how many he'd have got through if they hadn't been specialist.

There were two great blokes, Frazer Grant and Gary Smith – the Big G – along with us as support walkers. They're committed men, these guys, having walked with Both many times.

Sally Prudhoe from SCG was the manager of the operation on the ground with Richard Delderfield, making sure that we didn't get knocked over at traffic lights and road junctions. Traffic lights and road junctions – I've had enough trouble with them before. I paid attention to what Richard said.

SCG helped put the whole thing together. I just forgot about it for 12 months. I was pleased that Tetley's were involved because it gave the event a rugby feel. They planned the route to call in at as many rugby grounds as possible.

I hadn't done much during the previous months. My rugby had finished and I was enjoying some R & R for the first time in years. I was busy on a few things: from commercial work with Zurich to more involvement with the BBC. There was a lot of rugby broadcasting to get on with but also a few tasters in other sports. I did a day at the Open working on the highlights show and also did a Master Class at the Benson & Hedges with Padraig Harrington.

A couple of months before the trek was due to begin Chalky let on that he'd just started going to the gym to try and get in shape. Not for me. I wanted to only suffer once. It seemed like my tactics were paying off. Chalky was already moaning about his feet and he'd only been on the treadmill. I knew the training would be boring. I didn't fancy it. I'd face the demons on the walk. No point giving yourself grief twice over.

A few days before the off I did go out with Chalky for about half an hour just to get the pace. We were aiming for between 4 and 5mph. It doesn't sound like much but it felt it.

Before I knew it there was everybody down at the Rec waving us off. The folks, the kids, a few Bath boys and away we went. Like madmen. We went far too quickly, around 6mph. The adrenalin was pumping through us. We tore into it.

Bristol was the first destination. Jack Rowell was due to drop in. He was only scheduled to do a few miles. I was doing a TV interview when he joined us. The camera had stopped rolling but I carried on talking.

'Yes, Jack Rowell's coming with us all the way to the finish,' I said. 'I know he's getting on a bit but he reckons he's up to it.'

As intended, Jack overheard what I was saying. He thought it was going out to the nation. Would he let himself give in? Would he heck. Even though we upped the pace and he dropped back he still made it to the finish. Top effort, although I'd never tell him that.

*   *   *

People along the way were brilliant. That first day was a beautiful sunny day. Lots of people dug deep and one primary school turned out to give me a cheque for £100. We finished in Thornbury that first day.

We soon slipped into a routine. Back to the hotel. Cold bath – yes, *cold* bath – and then an hour-long massage. Food and then a bit of a laugh in the lobby with the kangaroo court fining people for whinging, cutting corners, talking too much – the usual daft stuff. I got done once for tap-dancing during the walk. The usual fine was 20p but as I had no change I got done for £10. Bed by 9.30 p.m. Boring or what? We only came off the wagon about five times during the trip. Once after England blew the Grand Slam big time in Dublin and another when Ben Clarke turned up. For the most part we were good boys. No booze and plenty of sleep – not a lifestyle I'd advocate.

We were knackered boys as well. I woke up after that first day feeling ten times worse than I ever did after a pre-season training session. It was a shock to the system. I felt like a million dollars on the top half and like a 90-year-old on the bottom half. Day Two saw us do 25 miles from Thornbury to Gloucester, aiming to arrive at the finish at Kingsholm at half-time in the match against Harlequins. I've had some tasty receptions at Kingsholm down the years. You know the scene – nothing too friendly for a Bath boy. This time they were magnificent. Fair dos.

It was the first time I'd ever been cheered on to the ground by the cherry and whites – and been pleased to see them!

The rest of that week was a real chore. I seriously doubted that I was going to make it. I had really bad tendonitis in my ankle. I could deal with blisters, stiffness, all the usual aches. But this was something else. Somehow I stuck it out until we found a fantastic consultant in Manchester, Steve McGloughlin, who prescribed these powerful anti-inflammatories. I was cart-wheeling after that. What a difference. The other lads wanted some but I guarded my stash.

The days passed – somehow we pushed ourselves through it. The celebs that joined in pushed themselves through it as well – Steve Redgrave, Tim Henman, so many rugby mates including Phil Vickery and Martin Johnson, and Steve Rider from the BBC, too.

Steve fancied that he would be good at this sort of stuff as he'd done a couple of London Marathons. He joined us on Day Six, Shrewsbury to Whitchurch, a 21-mile stretch. He breezed in, smart and laid-back as you like. By the end he was a wreck. He had a shoe full of blood and was dizzy and disorientated. He had to be wrapped in a space blanket to get his circulation on the move. Back at the hotel he had a bath and got ready to come down for some dinner with us. Three hours later he woke up in his bedroom with his trousers half-on. He'd literally fallen asleep on his feet.

Chalky wasn't much better. He was looked after by the nurses at Whitchurch Community Hospital. He needed emergency treatment for some horrible blisters on his feet. The staff in the Minor Injuries Department were fantastic.

The end of the first week was tough. The novelty had worn off and the weather had turned. Manchester to Burnley and then on to Threshfield the day after. We got a right soaking. A few rugby league lads helped us out – Denis Betts (Wigan and ex-Great Britain) and

Andy Johnson (Castleford) walked with me for the first hour or so, and young lads from Bury Rugby Football Club joined us to collect donations as we walked into the town. It rained, and it rained, and it rained. And the Yorkshire Dales went up and down, up and down, up and down. We were absolutely shattered when we finished.

The support we got from all sorts of rugby clubs along the way was brilliant. One morning early in the second week, for example, I received £200 from seven-year-old Liam Murray, on behalf of Wensleydale RFC, and later in the day I was presented with a plaque from Richmondshire RUFC. Those days were hard yakka. The long mileage and hills took their toll. I was already into my second pair of trainers and would soon be on my third. The scenery, though, was absolutely stunning. Next time I'll take a proper look.

Arriving at Newcastle on Day Thirteen was a turning point. It was the fifth Premiership rugby ground we'd visited so far and the most northern so it was downhill from there on. I could barely believe my eyes the next morning when I saw a road sign for 'The South'. We'd reached halfway!

There were so many touching little things that happened. No big deal in the great scheme of things, perhaps, but very meaningful to those of us involved. Ferryhill Town Council asked me to bury a time capsule next to a sundial unveiled by Prime Minister Tony Blair the year before as part of the town's celebration of the new millennium. The sundial sits in the garden in front of the town hall and was unveiled by the Prime Minister as the town falls within his constituency of Sedgefield. The capsule contained items reflecting various aspects of life in the town, such as videos of local events and CDs of local bands, as well as information about the Tetley's Trek. It was a real honour to be asked to bury the capsule and to meet Catherine Readshaw, the eight-year-old grandaughter of the Mayor of Ferryhill, Councillor Cath Conroy. Catherine is putting up such a brave fight against the leukaemia she was diagnosed with in January.

There were many memorable days. The stint through Leeds was uplifting. Former Ryder Cup captain, Mark James, a former cancer sufferer joined us, as did the entire Leeds Tykes squad. Terry Crystal, the long-standing England doctor, took us out for a few beers and a curry. That passes for sophistication in Terry's world. We spoofed for the bill. Terry lost. Nothing changes.

The Carlsberg-Tetley brewery was in Leeds and Simon Cox, brewery director, presented me with a £10,000 cheque for the charity to really boost the running total.

The days passed by in a blur. The routine helped. I used to find the first half of the day OK but the last three hours were always murder. Somehow the final days arrived. It was weird. We had come so far since setting off from Bath a month ago. Despite being out injured for months, Lawrence Dallaglio managed to walk the last eight miles from London Wasps. It was a great effort – he had only been given the all-clear that morning to do it. Some of the players from Harlequins joined us in Richmond to escort us for the last few miles to the ground where the club presented us with over £1,000. I can't tell you how fantastic it felt to cross the finish line for the very last time. What a mixture of emotions – relief and elation tinged with a bit of sadness. It had been such an experience.

The final day was just a formality – a short stroll to Twickenham. The reception we got as we walked through the crowds was fantastic. The atmosphere was electric – so many people came up to me to offer their congratulations and donations. Our moment came at half-time when myself, Chalky, Gary and Frazer walked through the players' tunnel and on to the pitch to present a cheque for £150,000 to Douglas Osborne, chief executive of the Leukaemia Research Fund. I had run out of the tunnel scores of times before, but I think that time meant more to me than any other.

The final total raised was £230,000 – unbelievable. I lost just over three-quarters of a stone on the trek. There wasn't that much to lose on my frame in the first place. My feet weren't too bad although people did say I looked haggard and ropey when I appeared on Sunday Grandstand the day after the finish. That was nothing to do with the walk and everything to do with the celebrations we'd had the night before.

It took me several months before I got my weight back and my body started to behave itself again. If I'd been really on the case then I should have trained myself down again to re-acclimatise myself. But I didn't.

Will I do it again ? I don't know. It would be hard to find the time if nothing else. Thirty days is good chuck out of anyone's working schedule. The BBC were great last time in giving me time off when I should have been in the studio for the various internationals. Those BBC commitments look like they might increase. Rugby Special is back on air and I do some stuff there. I'm also keen to branch out into other sports and there are possibilities there that might come to fruition in the next few months.

I have no burning ambitions at the moment to go back into rugby as a director of rugby. However, I wouldn't rule out some sort of involvement at some stage. It would be more managerial than anything. I know I can be a bit sharp-tongued at times but I also feel I know my way around the rugby scene and am down-to-earth enough to get on with most people.

My domestic life has settled. I see more of the kids now that I'm separated than I did before.

Life is ticking over nicely. Even my blisters have almost healed.

index